ALTERNATIVES TO HITLER

HANS MOMMSEN

ALTERNATIVES TO HITLER

GERMAN RESISTANCE UNDER THE THIRD REICH

Translated and annotated by
Angus McGeoch

With an introduction by
Jeremy Noakes

Princeton University Press
Princeton and Oxford

Published in the United States, Canada and the Philippine Islands by
Princeton University Press, 41 William Street, Princeton, New Jersey 08540

First published by I.B.Tauris & Co Ltd in the United Kingdom

Originally published in 2000 as *Alternative zu Hitler – Studien zur Geschichte des deutschen Widerstandes.*

The translation of this work has been supported by Inter Nationes, Bonn.

ISBN 0-691-11693-8

Library of Congress Control Number 2003102879

www.pupress.princeton.edu

This book has been composed in Adobe Garamond
and Raleigh DmBd BT by Steve Tribe, Andover
Printed and bound in Great Britain by MPG Books Ltd, Bodmin

10 9 8 7 6 5 4 3 2 1

Contents

Introduction

Between 1933 and 1945 tens of thousands of Germans were
actively involved in various forms of resistance to the Nazi regime
and many thousands suffered death or long periods of incarceration
in prison or concentration camp as a result. Among these actions
were a series of concerted efforts to overthrow the regime between
1938 and 1944. They were undertaken by a number of partially
inter-linked circles, consisting mainly of army officers, senior civil
servants, clergy and individuals formerly associated with the labour
movement. Their actions culminated in the unsuccessful attempt
to assassinate Hitler by planting a bomb in his military
headquarters in East Prussia on 20 July 1944. Though the bomb
went off, Hitler survived. It is these efforts and the people
associated with them that have been the main focus of interest,
both for historians and the wider public, because they represented
the form of resistance most likely to succeed in destroying Nazism;
these men had thought longest and hardest about the alternatives
to Hitler and it is they who form the subject of this book. However,
we should not forget that there were many other resisters,
unconnected with these conspiracies, such as the simple
Württemberg carpenter, Georg Elser, who very nearly killed Hitler
with a bomb in a Munich beer hall in November 1939. They
showed equal courage and commitment in their resistance.

Ever since the defeat of Germany in 1945, the question of resistance by Germans to the Nazi regime has provoked controversy

both within Germany itself and in the rest of the world. Outside Germany the Resistance has, on the whole, not had a very good press. 'Too little, too late and for the wrong reasons' might be a fair summary of how it has generally been viewed. Yet such a perception, although not without an element of truth, both seriously underestimates the difficulties facing any resistance to the Third Reich from within and grossly oversimplifies and misconceives the complex and varied motives of those who became involved.

Within Germany politicians in both the successor states of the Third Reich, the Federal Republic in the West and the German Democratic Republic in the East, tried to exploit aspects of the Resistance to legitimise their respective regimes and, in the process, the history of the resistance became caught up in the Cold War. The East argued with some justification that the Communists had been the earliest, most consistent and most persecuted of the resisters, glossing over the party's ambiguous behaviour during the period of the Nazi-Soviet pact in 1939–1941. They also pointed out the extent to which many of the 'bourgeois' resisters had occupied various positions within the regime and had come to resist only rather late in the day. By contrast, some in West Germany tried to denigrate the Communist resisters by arguing that, since they were seeking to establish a totalitarian dictatorship in Germany, there was little to distinguish them from the Nazis, and hence their resistance was politically and morally flawed. Moreover, in response to foreign accusations of the collective guilt of the Germans, the Federal Republic claimed that it was the true heir of that 'other Germany' which in the dark days of the Third Reich had sustained Germany's true humane values. However, for most Germans of that generation, who had succumbed in various ways and in varying degrees to the temptations of Nazism, the heritage of the resistance remained deeply problematic. It gave rise to a general unease and even outright hostility among some who regarded the resisters as traitors for plotting against their nation's rulers in time of war. It is only comparatively recently, aided by the ending of the Cold War and above all by the change of generations, that Germans have been able to achieve a balanced perspective on the resistance through a deeper understanding of its flaws, certainly, but above all of the daunting personal challenges faced by those who took part in it. In this process of a nation's coming to terms with the resistance German historians have played a key role and none more so than Professor Hans Mommsen.

Behind this book is almost 40 years' research into the history of the German resistance. Professor Mommsen's major contribution has been his thorough and sensitive elucidation of the ideas and plans for a post-Nazi Germany, elaborated by the various individuals and groups within the resistance. Mommsen was criticised in some quarters for demonstrating that these ideas and plans had little in common with the notions of Western liberal democracy that came to be accepted, first in the Bonn republic and then, following the fall of the Berlin Wall, in the whole of reunited Germany. Yet he was right to point out the need to understand the ideas and actions of the resisters within the historical context in which they were operating. It was a situation in which liberal democracy, whose roots in Germany were shallow at best, appeared to have been comprehensively discredited, not just in Germany – through the failure of the Weimar Republic – but in much of the rest of Europe as well.

In this situation the resisters sought alternatives to Nazism within existing German political and cultural traditions. Their diagnosis of the problem focussed on the alleged 'massification' (*Vermassung*), atomisation and alienation produced by an industrialised and urbanised society operating under unbridled capitalism and fragmented by a political system (parliamentary democracy) driven by divisive and selfishly motivated political parties. They saw this as a systemic crisis that required a fundamental transformation of German politics, society and culture. They sought a 'third (German) way' between western liberal democracy and eastern 'Bolshevism'. Some of them had initially welcomed the Nazi takeover in 1933 with its rhetoric of a 'national revival' and its promise to reunite Germany in a 'national community', as offering precisely the kind of fundamental social and cultural transformation required to produce a German revival. And the following years saw them forced to undergo a painful learning process through which they came to view Nazism no longer as the solution but as part of the problem. For some it required an agonising reappraisal, since they had succumbed to the temptations of Nazism and in fact shared some of its core beliefs and values – its nationalism, its hostility to western liberal democracy, its anti-Communism, even to a degree its anti-Semitism.

Depending on the individuals concerned, this learning process was initiated either by professional disappointment, or by particularly shocking actions on the part of the regime (notably the Röhm purge of 1934 and the *Reichskristallnacht* pogrom in November 1938), or, in the case of many military and diplomatic personnel, by the fear of war and defeat by the West in 1938 and 1939. It was then reinforced by the day-to-day experience of the lawlessness, corruption and fundamental mendacity of the regime. In this situation resisters took their stand on the need to reassert humane values, drawing in particular on their religious beliefs. Even those who had hitherto not been active churchgoers, when confronted with the diabolical nature of Nazism and in the personal crisis provoked by the mortal danger involved in resisting a totalitarian regime, found comfort in religion.

These impulses also informed their plans for an alternative order to that of the Third Reich. Distrusting mass and party democracy, which had apparently been incapable of providing stable government and had proved vulnerable to plebiscitary dictatorship, they turned to the German traditions of corporatism and federalism, local and regional self-government, hoping to overcome the 'massification' of the modern world by reviving a sense of responsible citizenship rooted in local communities and building up the polity from below with a stress on the importance of subsidiarity. In many respects an elitist and utopian vision, it nevertheless marked a fundamental repudiation of Nazi political theory and practice.

In the case of the more conservative resisters the nation state remained the central political category and German leadership in Europe was assumed, albeit distinguished from Nazi notions of German hegemony by a respect for the interests and cultures of other nations. However, the group which came to be known as the Kreisau Circle envisaged the replacement of the nation states by a federation of sub-national European regions. In fact what emerges very clearly from Professor Mommsen's work is the variety and complexity of the views of the various individuals and groups who composed the resistance and how they reflect the different generations and the social and occupational backgrounds of those involved. Even within the group of left-wing conspirators, as his chapters on Julius Leber and Wilhelm Leuschner demonstrate, there were marked differences of emphasis, for example on the nature and role of trade unions within a post-Nazi Germany. It has sometimes been argued that the resisters spent too much time and energy discussing and planning the future state and not enough on getting rid of the existing one. Again, while there is an element of truth in this, given the experience of the revolution of 1918, it was understandable that they should have wished to establish sound foundations for a state capable of filling the enormous vacuum that would have been left by the fall of the Third Reich.

Responsibility for overthrowing the regime had to be in the hands of those with access to the instruments of power – the Army. In fact, the military is considered the most controversial group among the resisters. Only a tiny fraction of the German officer corps took part in the resistance. By 1933 its proud traditions had been largely eroded in the process of its becoming merely a functional elite. Moreover, this had been accelerated by its rapid expansion following the introduction of conscription in March 1935. This had led to a dilution through the large influx of young officers who had been through the Hitler Youth. The military resisters have been accused of trying to overthrow the regime only when it appeared that Germany might be defeated in war, first in 1938 over the Czech crisis and then when the tide of war itself began to turn against them in 1942. There is some truth in this accusation but, as Professor Mommsen points out, it applies to some officers more than others (mostly the senior generals) and for a certain number it does not apply at all. Colonel Hans Oster of the military intelligence department (*Abwehr*) is perhaps the most striking example of an officer who, from 1938 onwards, systematically resisted the regime. He uncompromisingly confronted the dilemma that faced the German people at this time, as the pastor and theologian, Dietrich Bonhoeffer, put it: 'either to hope for the defeat of their nation in order that Christian civilization might survive, or to hope for victory entailing the destruction of our civilization'. This was a particularly acute dilemma for the military whose whole professional *raison d'être* was to try to win any war in which they were engaged. However, by informing the Dutch military attaché of the German invasion plans, Oster, who was steeped in the traditions of pre-First World War Germany, showed that it was still possible for a German officer to rise above his purely functional role and affirm his wider responsibilities, both to his country and as a human being, thereby acting as a true patriot.

However, in his chapter on the military opposition to Hitler, Mommsen has drawn attention to a second criticism of the officer corps which has emerged from recent research on the Wehrmacht and, in particular, on its role in the Soviet Union. For it has been shown that a number of key figures in the military resistance, including Tresckow, Gersdorff, Stülpnagel and Wagner, were involved either, as in the case of Quartermaster General Wagner, in the planning of the war of extermination in the East, or, as many others did, participated in its execution, at least to the extent of condoning brutal actions against partisans and Jews, although they evidently became increasingly unhappy about such actions.

This raises the sensitive issue of the attitude of the resisters towards the Jews, covered in the final chapter. Professor Mommsen shows that almost all the resisters shared the basic prejudices against the Jews that were common among those from their backgrounds at the time. In the case of the Jews in the Soviet Union they were influenced by the association of the Jews with Bolshevism that had been widely prevalent among the European upper and middle classes since 1917. Some of the resisters sympathised with the Nazis' initial policy of segregating the Jews from German society to the extent of treating them legally as aliens, thereby reversing the emancipation measures of the nineteenth century. However, where they parted company from the Nazis was in their rejection of the savage methods with which the Jews were treated and which led ultimately to the programme of extermination. Indeed, in the case of individual resisters these measures prompted them to embark on resistance to the regime in the first place; in the case of all of them the actions against the Jews provided an additional motive for their resistance.

Following the successful Allied landings in Normandy in June 1944, Colonel Claus von Stauffenberg, leader of the 20th July plot to kill Hitler, posed the question to his colleague Henning von Tresckow, as to whether it was worth carrying out the assassination plan since it would no longer serve any practical purpose. Tresckow's reply was uncompromising:

> The assassination attempt must take place at whatever cost. Even if it does not succeed we must still act. For it is no longer a question of whether it has a practical purpose; what counts is the fact that in the eyes of the world and of history the German Resistance dared to act. Compared with that nothing else is important.

It is at this point that the moral principles which lay at the core of the German resistance were clearly revealed and it acquired a heroic dimension. For these men were fully aware of how isolated they were among their own people, a fact demonstrated only too clearly by the subsequent strongly negative response by the German public to the assassination attempt. On the day following the failure of the coup Tresckow told a fellow-conspirator:

> The whole world will vilify us now. But I am still firmly convinced that we did the right thing. I consider Hitler to be the arch-enemy not only of Germany but of the world. When, in a few hours, I appear before the judgement-seat of God, in order to give an account of what I have done and left undone, I believe I can with a good conscience justify what I did in the fight against Hitler. If God promised Abraham that he would not destroy Sodom if only ten righteous men could be found there, then I hope that for our sakes God will not destroy Germany. None of us can complain about our own deaths. Everyone who joined our circle put on the 'Robe of Nessus'. A person's moral integrity only begins at the point where he is prepared to die for his convictions.

In his first chapter Professor Mommsen draws attention to Germany's flawed tradition of the right of resistance, the result of a philosophical and legal tradition which saw the state as an expression of moral as well as political values and conceived of the law primarily in formal terms as the expression of the sovereign will of the state. As he makes clear, arguably the most valuable contribution of the German resistance was to demonstrate the importance of refusing to treat the state and the nation as absolutes. Through their actions they were urging that citizens should give their primary allegiance to a set of values that transcends state and nation and affirms mankind's humanity. It is a lesson whose relevance is not confined to Germany and one that needs constantly to be reaffirmed.

Jeremy Noakes
Professor of History, University of Exeter

CHAPTER

1

Carl von Ossietzky
and the concept of a right to resist
in Germany

Carl von Ossietzky (1889–1938) was the pacifist editor of a small weekly paper, Die Weltbühne, *('The World Stage'), in which he exposed the secret rearmament of Weimar Germany under General von Seeckt. The Reichswehr (the regular army of the Weimar Republic) called for Ossietzky's prosecution and he was jailed briefly in 1932. When the Reichstag was burnt down in 1933 he was suspected by the Nazis of involvement and sent to Oranienburg concentration camp. During his imprisonment he was awarded the Nobel Peace Prize. He died of tuberculosis in Oranienburg in 1938. [Tr.]*

On the morning before the Reichstag Fire, on 27 February 1933, Carl von Ossietzky was urged by friends to go abroad and escape imminent arrest by the political police. He felt that such a move was premature, but probably also hesitated because of his wife Maud's poor health. However, the crucial consideration was that by leaving Germany he would be abandoning his life's work as a political activist and pamphleteer. It was the very thing for which, years before, he had reproached Erich Maria Remarque.[1]

Ossietzky had already been faced with the question of whether to go into exile after his conviction in the *Weltbühne* trial. Before beginning his prison sentence he published an editorial about the trial in the *Weltbühne* of 10 May 1932. In it he wrote:

When someone who opposes the government leaves his country,

his words soon sound hollow to those who remain. To be more precise, in the long run the pamphleteer cannot survive if dissociated from everything he is fighting against, or fighting for; he will simply lapse into hysteria and distortion. To be really effective in combating the contamination of a country's spirit, one must share its entire destiny.

Ossietzky sacrificed his life for this conviction.

The 'contamination' to which Ossietzky was referring arose from the rampant authoritarianism which he, as a dedicated pacifist, pointed to in the historically inappropriate glorification of the military. Indeed, the enforced demilitarization of the German Reich under the Treaty of Versailles brought about an all-embracing *militarization* of civil society, which, from the start, Ossietzky consistently fought against, especially in the pages of the *Weltbühne*. Ossietzky possessed an astonishing knowledge of the internal political imbroglios which led to the build-up of the 'Black Reichswehr' and later the preparations for the creation of an army of 21 divisions. Thus Ossietzky's clash with the authorities was in a way pre-ordained. In November 1931 proceedings were opened in the Fourth Criminal Chamber of the Reich High Court against Ossietzky as publisher of the *Weltbühne*, on a charge of treason. The so-called '*Weltbühne* Trial' was one of the most spectacular political court cases under the Weimar Republic, and it attracted great international attention. The fact that more than a year and a half had elapsed between the publication of the incriminating article and the laying of charges strongly suggests that the Reich Defence Ministry under Wilhelm Groener, operating in the background, intended to make an example of Ossietzky to the pacifist movement, and to the parties of the left, whose criticism of the illegal rearmament was increasing in vehemence.

In Ossietzky they were targeting one of the most consistent opponents of the creeping militarization of the Weimar political system – a system which with good reason he mercilessly attacked as 'the military state in intellectual form'. He repeatedly and sarcastically pointed out that the 'enthusiasm for arms' promoted chiefly by Groener and his successor, Kurt von Schleicher, had replaced the civilian virtues of the Republic. The essential falseness of the Republic lay not least in the fact that in 1919 it had not conclusively called the representatives of the imperial army to account. It was these men who posed a threat to the stability of the democratic system well beyond the early days of the Republic. True, Gustav Stresemann[2] had, despite holding on to the notion of a powerful Germany, put up some modest opposition to the ambitions of the military under von Seeckt. But on 2 June 1932 Chancellor Papen's cabinet decided to dissolve the Reichstag; in the new phase of rule by presidential decree, as Ossietzky stressed, there was a fundamental change. Government thinking and rearmament were now indissolubly linked.

It was symptomatic that not only the noisy nationalist right but also the 'bourgeois' centre parties were unwilling to take pacifist positions seriously, let alone tolerate them. The sentence to 18 months' imprisonment, for the publication of facts that had long been known to the initiated, was blatantly unjust. Yet it was happily accepted by his opponents, as were subsequent similar verdicts. Resistance to the power of the state in this area was considered intolerable. Very few voices were raised in protest; but one was the liberal *Frankfurter Zeitung*, which wrote ironically:

> It is true that we live in a democracy, but anyone who applies its principles, particularly against military authorities, or those which would like to be seen as such, is punished with imprisonment and – what is worse – with the odium of being branded a traitor.

The paper was alluding to the fact that, unlike normal press trials, Ossietzky was accused of acting not out of conviction, but from dubious motives. It was a charge which, despite being inured to ignominious accusations, he had difficulty in disproving.

It was precisely this evidence which the Nazi arrest warrant on 28 February 1933 made specific reference to. It described Ossietzky as a 'malicious agitator' who had not hesitated 'to betray the vital interests of the Reich'. This continuity from the latter days of the Weimar Republic reveals the murkiness of the allegedly constitutional nature of the presidential regime, even though it adhered nominally to due processes of the law. In many respects Ossietzky's battle against the militarization of Weimar anticipated the later resistance to the Nazi regime. Ossietzky challenged the way in which the nationalist loyalty of the ordinary citizen was being perverted for the purpose of establishing absolute military power.

In the 'final report' written by Ossietzky before he went to prison in Berlin, he committed himself to maintaining the *Weltbühne* as a voice of opposition:

> Even in this country trembling under the elephantine tread of fascism, it will keep the courage of its convictions. Whenever a nation sinks to the murkiest moral depths, anyone who dares to take an opposing line is always accused of having violated national sentiment.

Very similar words were spoken by Henning von Tresckow[3] in the weeks before the attempted coup of 20 July 1944, when he referred to the 'Robe of Nessus' that the conspirators had donned, in the full knowledge that the patriotism which had prompted them to act would never be apparent to the mass of the people.

Ultimately Ossietzky was fighting against Germany's persistent belief in the supremacy of the state, against an idealized concept of the state which lay at the heart of German governmental tradition, and which made it impossible set the interests of the individual citizen against a state seen as standing above party politics. As Ossietzky repeatedly observed, the authoritarian attitudes of broad sections of the population had by no means been removed with the collapse of the Kaiser's empire. The problem was not simply that the overt or covert opponents of the parliamentary system were in the majority and were forcing the democratic parties into ever greater concessions. It was rather that the leftwing liberals, among whom Ossietzky counted himself, had since the beginnings of the Weimar Republic found themselves in a dwindling minority.[4] Ossietzky wanted a different, genuinely liberal republic, based on broad civic participation, and it is clear that he assumed too much political insight on the part of the majority of citizens, in whose name he expressed unconditional opposition to the encroachment of the state apparatus.

It is a fact that, precisely because his views were ethically based,

Ossietzky belonged to the minority of political activists under Weimar, who shared a western understanding of politics that viewed the state as essentially an instrument for the service of the citizen. In his book *The German Idea of Freedom,*[5] Leonard Krieger, the most important American historian writing on Germany in the early post-war years, was one of the first to point out the fact that German liberalism, unlike its counterpart in western Europe, ultimately claimed that state and society were identical. This can largely be traced back to the impact of Kantian philosophy, which conceived of the state primarily as a moral structure and assumed the virtual identity of the citizens' interests with those of the state, whether this took the form of a monarchical regime or a constitutional system.

This can be demonstrated by the role of the right to resist, which Adolf Arndt, the social-democrat constitutionalist, once called an inalienable human right. It is significant that this right does not get a mention in the philosophy of Immanuel Kant and is only developed in a rudimentary form in Hegel's philosophy of government. Similarly, Friedrich Christoph Dahlmann[6] and Karl Rotteck,[7] the two principal advocates of liberal constitutional theory in Germany, rejected this legal concept. They saw the state as a moral entity and invested it with a purpose that was independent of the individual citizen. Hence they did not relegate the state to being a guarantor of civil liberty, with the added task of providing the greatest possible happiness to its members, as conceived by western pragmatism.

This loading of ethical content into the concept of state was most pronounced in Protestant church circles and found theoretical expression in the philosophy of identity developed by Kant. The notion that there could be justified civil protest against arbitrary acts by the state, as in the case of the Göttingen Seven in 1833,[8] and later with the revision of the constitution of the Saxon monarchy in 1851, may still have been alive in the first half of the nineteenth century. But in the wake of the newly acquired national confidence of the German Empire it became completely obsolete. This is perfectly demonstrated by the views of the historian Heinrich von Treitschke, which were representative of German public opinion in general. Treitschke saw 'the right to resist' as a contradiction in terms.

In contrast to the western constitutional tradition, which – as in the Declaration of Human Rights of 1793 – granted a central place to the right to resist, the German constitutional tradition remained wedded to the fundamental assumptions of the philosophy of identity, and negated any claims of natural law. This position was reinforced under the dominance of legal positivism in the late nineteenth century, which used the principle of a state founded on the rule of law to exclude any legally based protest by the citizen. Even Max Weber, the sociologist of law, takes no account of the older doctrine of tyranny and despotism and ignores the problem of the abuse of any political dominance that has a formal legitimacy.

The notion that a modern constitutional state cannot, by its nature, be an unlawful state, explains why even the Weimar constitution, which adopted the basic rights of the Paulskirche Constitution,[9] stopped short of including a right of resistance. During the 1920s, when largely unfounded criticism of the 'party-political state' became widespread, the illusion grew that conflicting social and political interests could be overarched by adhering to the formal principle of legality. That is why the senior officers of the Reichswehr, who shared many of Adolf Hitler's anti-constitutional aims, nonetheless sought to bind him to the 'pillar of legality' and restrain him from revolutionary action. In doing so they, like the rightwing political parties, prepared the way for Hitler's pseudo-legal acquisition of power. Similarly, the centrist democratic parties bowed to blackmail and the threat of civil war by the NSDAP and the SA and, on 23 March 1933, approved the Enabling Law in order to avert a breach of ostensible legality.

Even the political left, by adhering to the principle of legality, missed their last chance of opposing the steps that led relentlessly to their dissolution. As late as 30 January 1933 the Social Democratic Party and the Free Labour Unions adopted a stance 'with both feet on the ground of legality'. They failed to see that this 'legality' had long ago become a tool in Hitler's hand, even though Benito Mussolini had already demonstrated how, without a formal breach of the prevailing constitution, it was possible to take the road to dictatorship.

As the *Weltbühne* trial showed, the cult of formal legality had already been exploited to criminalize minority positions and eliminate them by quasi-judicial means. What had begun under Weimar, continued on a greater scale after the Nazi *Gleichschaltung*, or 'co-ordination', of the judicial system. Until the collapse of the Third Reich, the judiciary functioned as a loyal instrument of the regime. The Special Courts, established in 1944 under the Gauleiters and Reich Defence Commissioners and staffed by the regular judiciary, proved themselves willing enforcers of the brutal orders issued by the foundering regime, right up until April 1945.

The fixation with the principle of formal legality went so far that, when the leading figures of the SA were murdered on and after 30 June 1934, the German public did not regard this as a breach of legal order but as a move to restore it. The securing of the formal rule of law, which at the time was promoted by Carl Schmitt,[10] was undertaken in the legislation to justify the national state of emergency of 1 July 1933. However, the formal rule of law collapsed with the dismantling of the state. In a similar process the administrative civil service of the Reich placed itself at the disposal of the Nazi leadership, in order to preserve the principle of legality and to avoid losing the initiative to the Party. The price paid for this was a massive infringement of rights, which finally led to the complete abolition of the stricken *Rechtsstaat*. In order to retain 'control in the Jewish question' – as the Reich Minister of the Interior, Wilhelm Frick, put it – the senior ranks of the civil service were prepared to give way in this matter and to accept the progressive marginalizing and impoverishment of the Jewish citizens of Germany.

The complete usurping of the administration of justice by the Nazi system was only possible against the background of an overvaluation of formal legality, which caused many to close their eyes to the fact that the regime did not hesitate to break the law consistently and gave itself ever greater scope for action that was immune to the normal processes of law. This reached from the Party's own internal courts, through the increasing judicial prerogatives of the Gestapo, down to the denial of access to proper justice for Poles, Jews and other 'alien races'.

The adherence to the legality-principle imposed a lasting handicap on middle-class conservative resistance, which was only sluggishly taking shape. This resistance did not emerge until the resistance-groups formed in connection with the Weimar associations and parties had been largely wiped out by the Gestapo, or, like the communists, had to limit their activities to re-establishing the cadres that were constantly being broken up. The oath of allegiance to the Führer, which the conspirators elevated to a near-religious problem, and the aversion to tyrannicide, were significant inhibiting factors.

The obsession with legality doubly handicapped the German political elite in making a decisive move against Hitler, quite apart from the fact that there were considerable affinities between the attitudes of the middle-class elite and those of the National Socialists, specifically in foreign and military policy. On one hand the idolizing of Hitler as head of state led to his being dissociated from the crimes of the regime. With the oft-repeated formula 'If the Führer only knew about this', he was presented as the victim of deceiving advisers. On the other hand the elite was prevented from acting by an exaggerated fear of a 'revolution from below', which represented an indirect reaction to Germany's traditional lack of a right of resistance.

This applied, first and foremost, to the Protestant camp, which showed a high degree of affinity with the Nazi regime, both ideologically and through the German Christian movement and Reich Bishop Müller's ambitions for a nationalist Church. Leading Protestant theologians made it emphatically clear that a Christian had no right to oppose the established authority. As Paul Althaus put it

> Every power that maintains order is there by God's grace, has authority and a claim to our obedience, even if it is a foreign power; as long as it maintains order, it is better than chaos or an impotent national government.[11]

Even the anti-Nazi Dietrich Bonhoeffer hastened to concede to the state the right to take action, including the use of force, against the Jewish section of the population, and that this had to be accepted by the Church.

Greater flexibility was shown by the Catholic Church, which could draw on a long tradition of resistance going back to Thomas Aquinas, in which tyrannicide was not automatically rejected but was subject to certain conditions. Among these were that all means to a peaceful resolution of the conflict must have been exhausted, that there were good grounds for believing an improvement to the existing situation would result and that the violence used would be limited and would not be allowed to descend into a bloody civil war. These provisos, which were adopted by Protestant theologians after 1945, admittedly proved to have little practicality under the conditions of Nazi dictatorship. Nonetheless, Helmuth James von Moltke[12] was anxious to obtain from Hans von Dohnanyi[13] theological credentials for the right of resistance, in order to push the hesitant generals into action.

The younger members of the 20th July movement, especially Claus Schenk von Stauffenberg, Henning von Tresckow and the Kreisau group, tended to put aside legalistic concerns of this kind. By contrast, Carl Goerdeler[14] and his supporters, who belonged predominantly to the older generation, wanted at all costs to avoid an assassination and advocated having Hitler arrested. They were convinced that, in all circumstances, violent resistance should be considered only after all available legal remedies had been exhausted. Early in the summer of 1944 the Prussian Minister of Finance, Johannes Popitz,[15] declared: 'Every effort has been made to get rid of the regime legally. Now only a dead Hitler can save us.' For only Hitler's death would free soldiers and civil servants from their oath. Nonetheless, even the planning of 'Operation Valkyrie' gave a nod to the fiction of legality.[16] In the circular, which von Witzleben sent to his army subordinates on 20 July, there was mention of 'an unscrupulous clique of battle-shy Party leaders' having staged a coup, which had been met by the imposition of a military state of emergency.[17]

After the German surrender on 8 May 1945, interest in the German resistance movement was slight and only revived when the appeal to 'the other Germany' offered a chance to counter the notions of collective guilt that had occasionally arisen on the Allied side. However, it cannot be said that the German opposition to Nazism was rated highly either by the occupying authorities or by the German public. Rather, the relationship with the resistance remained largely severed, and this situation became more acute following the rearmament of Germany from 1954 onward, even though the Department of 'Moral Leadership' (*Innere Führung*, dealing with the political re-education of officers) was anxious to encompass the memory of the military resistance in the Bundeswehr's cultivation of tradition.

The debate about the justification of resistance was renewed from the mid-1950s onward, and it is no surprise that attention was focussed on the question of the right to resist. In 1960 the second edition of a semi-official publication, *Die Vollmacht des Gewissens* ('The Prerogative of Conscience'), was published. This carefully restricted the right to resist to those people who distinguished themselves through social status and moral insight, who carried 'positive responsibility in the state structure' and who 'risked the decision to resist' on the basis of knowledge of 'a positively better way for the state to fulfil its function of maintaining order'. The 'interim status', since it lacked any legal safeguards, must be reduced to a minimum and not be allowed to become 'turbulent and anarchic', in the jargon of traditional German thinking on law and order.

Views of this kind found their way into the highest echelons of the judiciary of the Federal Republic. They limited the right of resistance to the ruling elite, to resistance 'from the command level', as otherwise the criterion of 'expert insight' could not be fulfilled. In 1962 the General State Prosecutor, Fritz Bauer, protested in vain against this restriction of the right of resistance to an elite minority and the exclusion of the ordinary citizen, as well as of resistance by socialists and communists.

A further criterion stressed by the leading writers on the subject was the serious examination of one's conscience, which had to precede the decision to engage in active resistance. This doctrine, essentially influenced by Protestant theology, arose from the longstanding tendency among historians to declare the decision to resist to be exclusively a matter of conscience and to regard the political motives of the conspirators as secondary. At the same time, this denial that the anti-Nazi resistance had any political substance was motivated by the desire to conceal the close affinity between the aims of some of the conspirators with those of the Nazi regime.

The debate over the right to resist was first seriously launched in 1963 with Eberhard Zeller's influential book *Geist der Freiheit* ('Spirit of Freedom'), in which the coup of 20 July 1944 was described as 'a responsibly managed revolution using the existing command structure of the reserve army, which avoided chaos and civil war' and as 'a controlled transition to a new, albeit provisional, order'. It was only in the 1960s that the historians' restricted view of resistance was challenged and its characterization as 'apolitical' was increasingly questioned. Even so, the most recent study of the 20th July Plot, by Joachim Fest, slips back into the old tendency to make moral heroes of the conservative-nationalist resisters. In public discussion any mention of the political objectives and motives of the resistance-fighters is still seen as an attempt to disparage them.

Judicial rulings in the early days of the Federal Republic adopted the narrow view, a fact which prompted Adolf Arndt to issue his now famous 1962 polemic, *Agraphoi Nomoi* ('Unwritten Laws'). Behind the judgements of the Federal Supreme Court, he wrote, there lurked 'the notion of an order whose supremacy is self-justifying'. Arndt warned against endowing the Nazi regime with the character of statehood in a legal sense. 'No state exists that can survive at the cost of justice.'

It was precisely on this point that, in the early Federal Republic, there was a relapse into political habits of thought, which maintained a more or less clear-cut separation from western constitutional tradition. True, after 1945 a certain recognition of the right to resist gradually took root, and the Evangelical camp, under the pressure of Nazi crimes, retreated from older notions of unquestioning acceptance of the state, no matter how unjust it might be. Nevertheless, when Hans Nawiaski formulated his view of the right to resist – 'If basic rights are encroached upon by official violence which is itself unconstitutional, then resistance is everyone's right and duty' – he received no support from the Parliamentary Council.[18]

The majority, even including Carlo Schmid,[19] considered it inappropriate to give positive constitutional validation to the right of resistance. For this reason, a version modelled on the United Nations Charter, as proposed by Ludwig Bergsträsser,[20] was rejected. It is clear that two contrary currents came together here. Those who affirmed the right to resist on principle, but refused on juridical grounds to include it in the list of basic rights, met those who clung to the notion that the power of the state stands above party interests and is an end in itself.

In fact, nearly two decades later, the German Bundestag did eventually incorporate the right to resist in Article 20 Section 4 of the *Grundgesetz* (Basic Law, Germany's federal constitution). This arose from a compromise with the labour unions, which wanted to be assured that in the event of a coup d'état the right to stage a political strike would be preserved. The wording takes account of the preservation of constitutional order and restricts legitimate resistance, assuming all political and judicial remedies have been exhausted, to ensuring the 'survival of the fundamental order of a free democracy' – to quote Ernst Böckenförde. As Jürgen Habermas[21] has pointed out, this provision is principally directed against groups considered 'disloyal' and which are accused of being outside the framework of a constitution capable of defending itself. In this way, as the nonconformist exponent of public law, Ulrich K. Preuss, argues, the constitution can be used as 'a tool of political and moral disenfranchisement'.

In fact, the drafting of Article 20 Section 4 of the Basic Law achieves just the opposite of the desired relativizing of state action and disregards the fundamental lesson of totalitarian regimes. This is that those in power do not attack the prevailing legal order frontally, but deliberately evade it and thus throw the odium of the breach of legality onto their opponents. In such circumstances the traditional criteria for the right to resist are no longer effective. Individuals and entire institutions are thrown back on 'petty resistance' and civil disobedience, which renounces the use of violence to confront violence.

The difficulty the Federal Republic had in ridding itself of the authoritarian mindset was shown by the '*Spiegel* Affair' in 1962–3,[22] which showed clear parallels with Ossietzky's clash with the Reichswehr, even including the fictive formula of 'betrayal of secrets'. Today the military question in the Federal Republic has been settled in all essentials, and the idea of the 'citizen in uniform' has largely become a reality. Incidents involving rightwing extremists in sections of the Bundeswehr have done nothing to alter this. At the same time the marriage of militant nationalism with militaristic pomp has given way to a widespread absence of nationalist fervour and a relatively indifferent and sceptical attitude towards the military *apparat*.

In this way Germany has removed the overheated combination of elements which, even before the First World War, prompted Carl von Ossietzky to raise his voice in protest. However, residual features of traditional state omnipotence still remain, for example in the area of citizenship law and the rights of foreign residents. Even though Germany has become accustomed to a functioning democracy, underpinned by the law, it is not immune to a relapse into authoritarian attitudes, which take the form of intolerance toward marginal groups, foreigners and radical critics.

Adolf Arndt had hoped that the right to resist, which he conceived as a human right, though not one that can be given positive expression, could be bound into the complex of fundamental rights and their impact on third parties. However, there is the contrary tendency which holds that fundamental rights are not so much established to counteract encroachment by the state, but rather are used, under the label of the 'liberal and democratic order', to stigmatize dissenting political opinions as aiming to achieve a different republic and to avoid engaging in any dialogue with them.

It is widely thought acceptable to express intolerance towards outsiders and to criminalize attitudes that are critical of the system. Similarly, racial prejudices have by no means lost their virulence and voices are heard on all sides calling on the state to remove allegedly troublesome foreigners. Nonetheless, the internal democratization of German society is on the right path, though it needs constant attention to prevent a creeping recidivism. In the spirit of Carl von Ossietzky it is necessary to stand up for frankness and tolerance in the political forum, not to restrict the right of minorities of whatever kind to exist, but to insist tirelessly on the realisation of this right – just as the *Weltbühne* did by opposing every attempt of state authority to harass or manipulate the ordinary citizen.

2

German society
and resistance to Hitler

It is nearly 60 years since the 20th July Plot of 1944 failed to bring an end to the destructive frenzy of the Nazi reign of terror. Today there are at least two reasons why it is necessary to reassess it. First, it has to be situated in the history of German resistance to Hitler in the light of new research and of the paradigm shift in our overall picture of the Nazi era. Second, as an essential element of German and European history, it presents a challenge to present-day politics. The historic and political contexts in which German opposition to Nazism once took centre-stage in twentieth-century history, has faded. That context was the rejection of Allied charges of collective guilt and the need to throw a bridge of historical continuity across what was seen as a 12-year abyss – the fateful irruption of the demonically destructive energies of Nazi rule.

Equally, there is no longer any need to invoke the resistance in order to create an additional historical and political legitimacy for the new democratic order of the Federal Republic. Given its thoroughly respectable success at home and abroad, the search for historical affirmation seems superfluous. This is in marked contrast to the (former) German Democratic Republic, which saw its identification with the 'anti-fascist struggle' as an indispensable feature of its 'national' self-image.

Does this mean that politicians have ceased to appropriate the anti-Hitler resistance for their own ends, and that it has retreated into the 'neutrality' of past history? Has it become the subject of a natural consensus, from which a self-regenerating image of the nation's history emerges? Many general surveys only give the resistance a marginal mention.[1] In research into recent history it has lost its former importance, if one disregards latecomers who have dealt with leftwing and emigré resistance. On the other hand the history of German opposition to Nazism has been introduced into the syllabuses of German history teaching, and the President's Prize – conferred by the President of the Federal Republic – has intensified interest in resistance specifically at a local level. History workshops on the left have made an effort, in the same rather starry-eyed way as in the resistance literature of the early post-war years, to reinstate the memory of resistance by the workers, though without finding much of an echo in official historical research. The Year of Remembrance gave the media an excuse to use the resistance to boost their circulation, and recently both the CDU/ CSU[2] and, more cautiously, the SPD[3] have been seeking to present the resistance as their political legacy.

There is general agreement that the resistance cannot be measured by the criteria of its outward success. Rather, our own experience of dictatorships, as well as the more detailed knowledge we now have of the conditions under which the plotters were trying to operate, teaches us that their chances of bringing down the regime from within were virtually non-existent. On the other hand, our consideration of the resistance should not be limited to isolating its moral dimension. The phrase 'rebellion of the conscience' rightly reminds us that deliberately taking action that bordered on high treason required deeper ethical commitments, beside which political interests and social motives were secondary. Indeed, a proper understanding and assessment of the resistance are only possible if the political motives and objectives of the plotters are placed in the dangerously unstable context of Nazism and against an intellectual background of social and historical thinking that reached back to the Weimar era.

Making heroes of the men and women of the anti-Nazi opposition is thus no more appropriate than is an outward identification with the forces of the 'other Germany', which all too easily ends in our ignoring fact that Nazi rule had its roots in German society as a whole. Similarly there is a tendency in today's Germany to remain silent about the role of communists in the resistance. It is unjust to dismiss communist resistance on the grounds that they were fighting for a 'totalitarian' system analogous to Nazism. They were fighting the Nazi evil, and sacrificing themselves for their cause, with just as much courage as other German resistance movements. We should regard the various forms and directions taken by the resistance in their totality as a mirror of existing political alternatives to National Socialism in German society.

For a long time there has been an inclination to interpret the history of the resistance in a dualistic sense and to posit the existence of the 'other Germany' in opposition to the reality of Nazism. However, this conflicts with actual facts; for not only were the boundaries between non-cooperation and resistance fluid, but so also were those between strategies that remained within the bounds of the existing system and those aimed at overthrowing and destroying the regime. Even then, the decision to commit high treason could be compatible with loyal collaboration in other political fields. At the same time, active resistance was not simply the result of a once-and-for-all decision made on ethical grounds, but depended rather on changing expectations, dispositions and opportunities for action, as well as on internal and external changes in the regime itself. It is precisely this conflict of loyalties which can give younger generations an insight into the actual conditions under which resisters operated in Nazi Germany.

Even someone who fundamentally rejected Nazism, regardless of his or her individual willingness to take risks, required a political perspective from which to take the step into resistance. There is no disputing the fact that, even outside the communist and socialist camps, which from the outset were irreconcilably opposed to the Nazism, there were numerous people who opposed Hitler from the earliest days: the old-guard conservative Ewald von Kleist-Schmenzin is a vivid example.[4] But opposition did not yet mean the same thing as resistance. In the early years of the regime, at least, middle-class and conservative circles still cherished the illusion that by taming the radical forces within the Nazi Party – among which they significantly did *not* include Hitler himself –

some political moderation could be achieved. It took bitter experience to recognize that it would never be enough just to make corrections to the course, for instance by removing Himmler and Goebbels, forcing the SS into retreat or eliminating the extremist SA leadership, as Hitler himself did on 30 June 1934.

Some of the conservative-nationalist resistance held unequivocally National-Socialist views and most occupied significant public posts within the regime, or else were members of the officer corps. Until the outbreak of war, at least, the majority of them continued to hope that they could circumvent the more extreme tendencies of the regime – which seemed to jeopardise the international status of the Reich – without introducing any significant changes to the internal structure of the regime itself. The contingency decision to arrest Hitler if necessary, which was taken when the Czechoslovakian crisis was boiling up, was certainly not aimed at overthrowing the existing regime, and even in the 'X Report', sent by Beck and Hassell to Britain via the Vatican, we find the proposal to appoint Hermann Göring as Reich Chancellor.[5]

For the German Communist Party (KPD), which had already fought uncompromisingly against the Weimar system, the Nazi seizure of power in 1933 led to bloody street brawls in which many lives were lost. They then decided to adopt different campaigning methods, in the widespread expectation that Hitler would soon run out of steam. Significantly, the Social Democrats, some of whom sought to adapt to the regime, held on to the notion that it would be possible, by keeping a low profile, to bring the party organization safely through the phase of openly Fascist dictatorship – this despite warnings from within their own ranks, from people such as Rudolf Breitscheid. Only determined groups like *Neubeginnen* ('New Beginning')[6] and *Roter Stosstrupp* ('Red Assault Force')[7] saw the necessity for underground resistance, which however went against the traditional self-image of socialism in Germany. In the confessional field, especially the Catholic youth movement, reliance was placed on self-advertisement. In general people succumbed to the illusion that they were in a political situation that was susceptible to change.

What is true for the formative stage of the resistance, also applies to its development during the Second World War. Hitler's gain in popularity as a result of the rapid defeat of France made his removal appear a virtually hopeless undertaking. The entire war in the west and the consequent continuous changes in the military and diplomatic situation confronted the conservative-nationalist opposition with a novel situation, as indeed did the opening of the eastern front with the invasion of Russia in 1941. The policy of preventing war changed to one of stemming its spread or ending it altogether. Senior military officers, who as late as 1939 had sympathized with the opposition group around Beck, Hassell, Popitz and Goerdeler, now withdrew from any active collaboration. Under the banner of an anti-Bolshevik crusade Hitler gained support among the army commanders, many later prominent members the military opposition, who now became implicated in issuing or following criminal orders. The Allied demand for unconditional surrender narrowed the psychological scope of the opposition, no matter how much most of them cherished the hope of evading such an outcome. After all it was doubtful whether, once the Allies had landed in Normandy, an attempt by the military to stabilize the situation would have had any chance of success.

On the domestic front as well, the new conditions changed opposition activities fundamentally. Traditional ministerial responsibilities were progressively undermined, the exercise of power was split between mutually antagonistic *apparats* reporting directly to Hitler; he in turn deliberately sought to destroy the homogeneity of the officer corps and curb the autonomy of the Wehrmacht commanders. All this made it impossible to achieve the hoped-for internal transfer of power merely by reshuffling the government and sidelining certain Nazi power-centres such as the SS and the Reich Ministry of Propaganda. Thanks to the Hitler-myth so assiduously built up by Goebbels, there was no institution, other than the dictator himself, which could be called upon to provide legitimacy for a post-coup government, as the monarchy had done after Mussolini's overthrow in Italy.[8] Stauffenberg's brilliant attempt, through 'Operation Valkyrie',[9] to make the army the stabilizing factor in a new order failed, not least because the

internal homogeneity of the Prussian-based officer corps had long
been lost due to rearmament and war policy.

What was required, therefore, was a fundamental rethinking,
as well as insight into the essentially criminal and inhumane nature
of the Nazi regime. In view of the 'legitimacy' which it had
arrogated to itself, nothing less than an act of revolution, going
beyond removal of the criminal elements of the Nazi elite, could
lead to the root-and-branch changes they aspired to. In the given
circumstances this would involve killing the dictator. Regardless
of the problem of the oath of allegiance – which in retrospect has
been overstated – the unifying force of the Hitler myth could not
be extinguished in any other way. Goerdeler hoped that, by
exposing the crimes and irresponsibility of the Führer, they could
bring the masses over to their side. But he overlooked the fact
that the irrational public need for national identity took the form
of a loyalty to Hitler, which did not break down until the final
months of the war, accompanied by widespread criticism of the
Party, the SS, their representatives and all their works.

When Henning von Tresckow spoke memorably of the 'Robe of
Nessus' which the plotters had to wear, he was expressing the fact
that any attempt to destroy the deep-seated bond of loyalty between
Hitler and the German people would inevitably result in their being
considered traitors to the nation. Therein lies one explanation of
why the active resistance-groups were so extremely isolated. Not
only was Gestapo surveillance pretty effective and the population
cowed by Nazi terror-tactics, but there was also a psychological
barrier to breaking away from the national fraternity so tangibly
symbolized by Hitler. It is thus clear that the step from partial
criticism of the National Socialist system to out-and-out resistance
could only be taken by people who, like the communists and leftwing
socialists, were able to resist the pressure of the Hitler-myth, from
strong ideological and political convictions; and by others who, due
to their social background and position, and also to a deep-rooted
national consciousness or an alternative utopian vision, were able
in varying degrees to shake off this psychological compulsion.

This is reflected also in the social composition of those opponents of the regime who opted for active resistance. Hans Rotfels,

in his book *Die Deutsche Opposition,* articulates a widespread view that the men and women of the 20th July resistance group were drawn from all levels of the population and thus mirrored German society as a whole. Helmuth James von Moltke[10] was anxious to avoid any appearance of social exclusivity and to bring members of the working class into the activities of the Kreisau Circle, and much the same was true of Goerdeler. But the recruitment pool of the conservative-nationalist opposition was limited to the upper-middle and upper classes and this necessarily made it appear to be made up of 'the great and the good'. The great majority of members of the civilian opposition groups were senior civil servants, some of whom worked in the Ministry of the Interior and the judiciary, others in the diplomatic service. Labour union leaders like Wilhelm Leuschner and Jakob Kaiser and white-collar representatives like Max Habermann and Hermann Maass found themselves in a situation comparable to that of people such as Beck, Goerdeler and von Hassell, who had resigned from public service. Self-employed lawyers such as Josef Wirmer or parliamentarians, as in a qualified sense Julius Leber was, were the exception; the groups were also joined by intellectuals who were of indeterminate class, like Carlo Mierendorff, Theodor Haubach, Adolf Reichwein and, in a certain sense, Father Alfred Delp.[11]

The prominent role of members of the aristocracy, specifically in the military opposition, is a further indication of the fact that the conservative-nationalist resistance was drawn primarily from social strata which resisted wholesale Nazification and provided channels of communication, as it were, outside the political sphere. Professional motives played an important role in recruitment; this was true both for the diplomats and the military, and in this connection it is worth recalling that the 9th Infantry Regiment was the recruitment source of choice. Social and family contacts were used widely as a substitute for a clandestine organization, of the kind developed by the outlawed German Communist Party (KPD),[12] through the formation of cells and the use of codenames. Paradoxically it was these circumstances, as well as the widespread criticism of the regime among the upper class, which explain why the Gestapo did not intervene until a comparatively late date in the case of the Solf Circle[13] and the Abwehr.[14] Not until some weeks after the attempted coup did the authorities realize the extent of the conspiracy.

Judged from a sociological standpoint, the conservative-nationalist conspiracy represents above all a revolt by servants of the state. Their unquestioning identification with the idea of the German state explains why the conservative-nationalist opposition took a long time to act in the name of the nation, without taking on board the desirability of democratic legitimation. Thus the plans for a new order, developed by the groups around Moltke and Goerdeler, exuded a spirit of 'revolution from the top down', even though by invoking the idea of subsidiarity of 'small communities' (*kleine Gemeinschaften*) and of the principle of self-government, they were targeting the centralized, authoritarian state. The early plans for a new order, especially those developed within the Abwehr and by the von Hassell and Popitz groups, started from the assumption that the political slate had been wiped clean. This was the apparent result of the Nazi policy of *Gleichschaltung* ('co-ordination') and the general depoliticising of the population through Nazi propaganda. No one entertained the possibility of a multi-party system and a return to parliamentary democracy.

Indeed, a glance at the map of continental Europe left the impression that the parliamentary principle was outmoded. This coincided with the fact that the political personalities of the Weimar republic – though not those of the presidential cabinets of its final period – were largely absent from the conservative-nationalist resistance. The Social-Democrat and Christian labour leaders thought predominantly in corporatist terms, and in this they followed the lead of the united labour union executive formed in April 1933. Even the socialists in the Kreisau Circle joined the general effort to prevent or at least restrict as far as possible the re-emergence of centralized party structures and a multi-party system.

We have already seen how the conservative-nationalist resistance only proceeded tentatively from corrections to the system and alternative strategies, to the idea of a coup d'état and the introduction of a fundamentally new order. In this the role of intellectual advance guard fell to the Kreisau Circle. The early plans to overthrow Hitler were largely a continuation of the failed authoritarian schemes during the Papen and Schleicher chancellorships, and were inspired by the gruesome events of June 1934.[15] (We should not overlook the fact that senior military officers like Beck gave credence to the false information from Göring and Himmler and saw an SA-led revolution as a real possibility, leading to a declaration of martial law). It was not until the social basis of the resistance had broadened somewhat that proposals emerged which allowed for greater political participation by the public; even so, the example of Horthy's Hungary and monarchist considerations continued to exert a decisive influence.

The later plans for a new political order drew to a large extent on the neo-conservative and corporatist ideas of the Weimar era, and especially on Oswald Spengler's model of 'Prussian socialism'. For quite a number of the plotters, including Fritz-Dietlof von der Schulenburg, the Prussian tradition represented a key motive for resistance. However, this did not go unchallenged and was questioned mainly by Yorck[16] and Moltke, who rejected any form of 'deification of the state' (*Staatsvergottung*) and saw clearly that the 'lie of the authoritarian state', in Gustav Radbruch's phrase, was one of the roots of the National Socialist *Führer*-state.

The plans of the conservative-nationalist resistance for a new political order represented an attempt to reactivate the alternatives to parliamentary democracy, including the principles of government by professional institutions (*Berufsstände*) and of local autonomy. There can be no doubt that there were similar aspirations among those National Socialists who retained an attachment to governmental institutions and were opposed to the progressive entropy of the political system. With particular regard to the plans for restructuring and reforming the administration, there was no lack of agreement between the conservative-nationalist resisters and the isolated champions of institutional reform in the higher echelons of the Nazi Party. Originally the resisters were willing to allow the continued existence of specifically Nazi organisations, including the German Labour Front, and only intended to revise the Nuremberg Laws where they were discriminatory, while welcoming racial segregation, especially applied to Jews from Eastern Europe who had migrated to Germany since 1918 (see Chapter 12).

However, a significant feature of the socio-political thinking of the resisters of 20 July, albeit with many variants and shades to its authoritarian element, was a deep distrust of what, even before 1933, neo-conservative writers had denounced as 'mass democracy'. The opposition overestimated the political weight behind the National Socialist mobilization of the masses in the early years of the regime and the significance of the electoral successes of the NSDAP in 1930–1933, which were largely attributable to agitation and indoctrination. The plotters saw the experience of National Socialism not as a contrast to that of Weimar, but rather as a logical extension of it. The one-party system of the Third Reich seemed to be no more than the multi-party Weimar state taken to its utmost extremes. In the perspective of political history, the reference-point of the plotters was rather the opportunity, missed in 1918–1919, of establishing a comprehensive new order, which they related to the Prussian reforms of 1809 or – with a typical shift of emphasis – to the German uprising against Napoleon in 1813.

On the other hand, the majority of the conservative-nationalist resisters – in clear contrast to the core of the Kreisau Circle – saw no reason to envisage a fundamental reshaping of society and politics. Instead, they wanted to put into effect the 'right' ideas of National Socialism and save them from perversion by corrupt, unscrupulous and incompetent wielders of power. They wanted to establish a 'true' national community in place of the chaotic oligarchy of Nazi parvenus, and to safeguard Germany as a major power, indeed the leading power in central Europe, in the face of Hitler's military adventurism. It was from this standpoint that Schulenburg spoke of 'the coming Reich' (see p.155); the whole idea of a national awakening, which he claimed had been turned on its head by Nazism, was of considerable importance. This may also explain the ambivalence of a number of the plotters, hovering between collaboration and resistance – one thinks of Adam von Trott's activity as an expert on the Far East,[17] of Schulenburg's late memoranda sent to men as high-ranking as Himmler, and of the loyalty of the military in matters directly affecting the conduct of the war.

Only a few plotters wished to see the complete collapse of the existing political system. But Moltke and Yorck characteristically saw this as the necessary precondition for rebuilding society on secular and ethical principles. Therefore they initially restricted themselves to planning for the long-awaited Day X. Despite their misgivings about assassination and thus about deliberate intervention in the historical process, from 1942 onwards the two men actively dedicated themselves to overthrowing the regime. Once aware of the full extent of the impending moral, military and political catastrophe, they saw they could no longer merely wait on events.

Under those circumstances the boundaries between piecemeal criticisms, open opposition and active resistance were necessarily fluid. For this reason it is fruitless to attempt a conceptual distinction between active resistance and other forms of non-co-operation and anti-Nazi behaviour. This may be possible in respect of the members of the communist resistance, leaving aside the interlude of the German-Soviet Non-Aggression pact. But when we come to the socialists, it is much harder to make the distinction. With groups working outside the political system, any blanket judgement is bound to be misleading, especially in borderline cases like Ernst von Weizsäcker and Wilhelm Canaris. [18] The power to determine what should be classified as resistance in the narrower sense lay basically with the Gestapo which, even after 20 July was relatively broad and arbitrary in defining the circle of those to be pursued, quite apart from the subsequent wave of arrests in the 'Storm Operation' of 22 August 1944, which rounded up thousands of potential opponents of the regime, especially figures from the Weimar Republic.

While the circle of those in the know, of sympathizers and part-time advisers was remarkably extensive, the group of truly active plotters remained extremely limited and, to a very great degree, politically isolated. Often, as in the case of Schulenburg, the dividing-line cut right through families, and we find the same thing in working-class resistance, where parents went in fear of denunciation by their children, indoctrinated in the Hitler Youth. Despite numerous foreign contacts and experience, suggestions from abroad were scarcely ever taken up intellectually, and the plotters harked back instead to the mindset of the 1920s and early 1930s. In psychological terms this produced a marked 'introversion' in their ideas for a new order and thus set them apart from the émigré opposition. This isolation in a hostile environment meant that, even at meetings of like-minded people, any open discussion was generally avoided for security reasons, a fact that encouraged misunderstandings, such as the misreading of Field-Marshal Rommel's position.[19] Hand-in-hand with this isolation went a deep, albeit often unexpressed, doubt about the political maturity of the average German citizen.

Plans for a new order were designed to break the electorate down into manageable local units, in which the candidate for election would not be some anonymous party placeman but a respected local citizen – someone who had already achieved prominence in a neighbourhood context through community-building initiatives and sensitivity to the immediate interests of voters. Direct elections were only to take place at this level, which meant that the other representative bodies, reliant on indirect elections, would be in the hands of oligarchies. The influence of ideology and propaganda was to be removed as far as possible, as was the role of party officials, and policies would be restricted to the concrete needs of people on the ground. This was not just a reaction against the plebiscite-like propaganda appeals by the NSDAP; very similar modifications to the electoral system had earlier been put forward by Baron von Gayl, the Interior Minister in von Papen's cabinet. The conservative-nationalist resistance also aspired to a sociological and cultural 'de-massing of the masses'. This blended romantic, agrarian notions with the idea of halting or even reversing urban sprawl; there was even the controversial suggestion that the results of Allied bombing might be exploited to this end. Added to that was an economic policy with a pronounced middle-class flavour, with comparable reforms in the field of education.

The array of alternative conservative Utopias, which was now opened up and offered with varying emphasis by the individual factions and representatives of the conservative-nationalist resistance, shows the dilemma of a political position that ultimately placed the Weimar parliamentary system in a direct line with Nazism. The informing of communist resistance by instructions from the Comintern has concealed certain elements in its political thinking, which it shared with the neo-conservative *Kulturkritik*, for example in the contemporary writings of Ernst Bloch.[20] It was significant that the range of ideas held by the socialists involved in the resistance movement was altogether comparable with that of the conservative-nationalists who, with the concept of a 'Third Idea', the synthesis of western individualism and eastern collectivism and their call for a Christian form of personalism, stood in a uniquely German tradition. It was from this intellectual construct that the Kreisau Circle drew their own often fascinating, if utopian, conclusions. Some of these, like the principle of neighbourliness, the emphasis on regionalism as the basis of future trans-national structures to supersede the nation states of Europe, and not least their ecological concerns, are of increasing relevance in the present decade. However, this does not alter the fact that the various programmes of reform put forward by the German resistance largely ignored the needs of an advanced industrial society.

It would be wrong to deny the fundamental thrust of anti-Nazi thinking which, if not exactly backward-looking, was explicitly anti-liberal, and which, even in supporters of a liberal economic system, like Goerdeler, was blended with pronounced elements of social paternalism. This reveals the fundamental helplessness of non-communist opponents of Fascism when faced with the manipulative exploitation of key elements of the nation's culture by Nazism, whose technocratic aspects certainly suggested a potential pseudo-democracy. Even the language of the opposition chimed in some ways with that of the Nazi Party, and in many respects their panaceas had the same historical provenance as the alluring propaganda of the regime, though the latter admittedly obscured the reality of a society in the process of internal disintegration. Faced with the evils of the Third Reich, the objectives of a Christian society – a state founded on the rule of

law, and a public administration free from corruption – carried
weight and had to be taken seriously. It was for these objectives
that the plotters were risking, and in some cases sacrificing their
lives. But the concrete proposals for imposing these values do
appear comparatively unrealistic, particularly since they were
expressly claimed as more than mere blue-sky thinking.[21]

To say this is not to devalue the conservative-nationalist
resistance politically or morally. It is not easy to admit that Nazism,
or some of the goals for which it stood, had become so deeply
ingrained in the thinking and behaviour of the German masses
that the forces of resistance could only be mobilized through deeply
religious and ultimately utopian thinking. Yet we know that
pragmatic politicians like Konrad Adenauer or Theodor Heuss[22]
lapsed into a mood of resignation or believed they could see no
point of departure whatever for realistic action.

At no point in time could the circle of plotters count on finding
wide support among the population. Father Delp's careful research
and Leber's enquiries showed that the mass of the industrial
workforce was relatively loyal in its support of the regime. Fear of
defeat in war and a rise in the social status of factory employees
operated hand in hand. Opinion surveys from the days following
the attempt on Hitler's life showed a temporary rise in the Führer's
popularity, even in the traditional 'red' strongholds like Berlin's
Wedding district. The communists actually found that the attempts
to expand their underground organization beyond the circle of
former party cadres and to address middle-class and Christian
groups were almost hopeless and merely ran the risk of Gestapo
intervention. It was the younger generation in particular, exposed
to the indoctrination of the Hitler Youth, who, with the exception
of the 'White Rose' group of Munich students, stood aside and
posed a potential threat to any aspirations to overthrow the regime.

However, what most typified the internal situation under the
Third Reich was the fact that the broad middle class had completely succumbed to the undertow of Nazi propaganda. Representatives of skilled trades, commerce and industry, and even the
liberal professions, were completely absent from the resistance.
True, Goerdeler picked up some indirect support from Bosch and

Krupp, but it is noticeable that the business community pointedly kept its distance, or at best, like Hermann Abs,[23] was only
active on the periphery. Furthermore, macro-economists like
Günter Schmölders and Konstantin von Dietze, who were brought
in as experts, held views on social policy which were scarcely distinguishable from those of the Nazi regime, however much they
condemned it in other areas. The *Ordo-Liberalen*,[24] whose ideas
were related to those of the Kreisau Circle, tended to be involved
in the conformist planning for a post-war economy, which Otto
Ohlendorf, as permanent secretary in the Ministry of Economics,
had called for without Hitler's knowledge, in order to have something to put up against the post-war plans from the Allied side.

The upper-middle-class representatives of the resistance, led by
Carl Goerdeler, therefore acted as a 'classless bourgeoisie', with
no confidence in their own kind. This is one explanation for their
almost total rejection of the liberal tradition and for their
continuing efforts to bring back the monarchy. And in view of
the lack of willingness among the Hohenzollern descendants to
make themselves available for such an experiment, this proved to
be a completely utopian objective, though one which had the
important role of indirectly legitimising the desired authoritarian
form of government. Following the publication of Hermann
Rauschning's essays,[25] Hitler was regarded as the destroyer of the
German middle class. It is probably more correct to describe him
as the incarnation of those middle-class strata in Germany which
denied their own tradition. For no serious impulse to resist came
from that quarter; it was the senior civil servants who, as they had
in the *Vormärz* (the period from 1815 to 1848) and in the
revolutions of 1848, appointed themselves champions of the
national interest.

The conservative-nationalist resisters' plans for a new order reflect these facts. They present a largely static structure in which
conflicting social interests were to be harmoniously reconciled in
committees drawn from professional groups and based on equal
representation. Largely independent of these, the executive power
would protect the theoretical interest of the state *vis-à-vis* society.
Given the limited 'popular participation at all levels', the formal

emphasis on the rule of law did not prevent unilateral interests from making claims on power, though this was quite contrary to the intentions of the majority of the plotters. It is true that the conservative-nationalist opposition, impressed by the transformation of the communist resistance through the founding of the 'National Committee for Free Germany',[26] recognized the need to secure the anti-Nazi revolution by anchoring it more broadly in the populace as a whole and widening the basis of its legitimacy. In the months before the attempted coup, this aim was to be met by the highly controversial concept of a 'non-party popular movement', which represented the neo-conservative counterpart to the trend, emerging at this time, towards all-party government and the block system. Yet it is significant that, in this respect, the preparations for the coup did not go beyond draft programmes, which were the subject of continuing dispute.

The social isolation of the resistance, which was true of all its political factions, is another reason why its activities were largely focussed on drafting schemes for a new social and political order. At first glance it would have seemed normal to return to the Weimar constitution, which the Nazis had never formally abolished, though after the death of President Hindenburg in 1934 the last legal link with it had been lost. Nor would it have been surprising if they had pragmatically restricted themselves to the immediate measures necessary to stabilise government after the overthrow of Hitler's regime. However, from a psychological standpoint, this was out of the question; they needed the vision of a fundamentally new order, one which in a certain respect picked up the myth of national awakening from the early 1930s.

Furthermore, in the relatively depoliticised atmosphere of the Third Reich, the plans were given a markedly technocratic character, which ignored the real interests of society and the nascent party groupings. This demonstrates how even those who kept the Nazi regime at arm's length saw its first successful years as making a clean break with Weimar. Thus, the political ideas and values of the anti-republican elite during the Weimar years represented the only resource from which a political alternative to Hitler could be assembled. At the same time, the programmes of the communist and leftwing socialists, and even the vision of the National Committee, with its pared-down 'democratic' block system,[27] would have found no worthwhile support among the working population.

Marion, Countess Yorck, who attended the meetings of the Kreisau Circle, has made the telling comment that Claus Schenk von Stauffenberg would not have taken the decisive step towards the meticulously-planned assassination attempt, to be followed by the imposition of martial law, if behind it there had not been a comprehensive conceptual alternative to Hitler. This is characteristic of the self-image of the military plotters, in which the actual initiative did not come from the responsible army commanders but from the (usually younger) officers of the general staff. However much one may respect their convictions and actions, these men lacked the revolutionary spirit. They were still affected by the trauma of the November 1918 uprising. The fear that the overthrow of the regime, combined with an inevitable defeat in the field, might provoke an uncontrollable situation, like that at the end of the First World War, was one of the forces driving civil opposition in their comprehensive plans for a new order. These were simultaneously intended to legitimise the proposed overthrow of the regime and to free it of any taint of merely serving narrow military and social interests, as was claimed both in Nazi propaganda and by Winston Churchill in his momentous speech to the Commons.[28]

The Plot of 20th July 1944, remaining as it did within the intellectual and political horizon of an independent 'German way', must be assigned to a historical epoch which came to an end with the collapse in May 1945 of National Socialism and the Fascist movement – though a few of its tendencies ran on until the founding of the Federal Republic in 1948–1949. Consequently it had no practical political influence on the establishment of democracy in West Germany. Those of the resistance who survived saw themselves in continuing political isolation and some, like Theodor Steltzer and Paulus van Husen, mourned the path being taken to multi-party democracy in Bonn. In East Germany the communist resistance groups found themselves largely sidelined, though not as completely as the middle-class democratic members of the resistance. In both halves of Germany the political initiative fell again to the political elites that had become prominent in the Weimar years. The subsequent evoking of the resistance tradition, which had been variously reinterpreted to suit the prevailing parliamentary democracy or one-party state, thus represented a fundamental distortion of the intentions of the anti-Hitler opposition and the conditions under which they struggled, as well as a suppression of the deeper social causes of Nazi dictatorship.

Looking back from a greater distance in time and with the help of careful study of the fragmentary evidence that survives, we must now counteract this by emphasizing the intellectual, political and ethical independence of the conservative-nationalist resistance in particular. It was not the democrats, nor the suppressed political parties of the Weimar republic, nor even the institutional churches, who attempted to defend Germany against Hitler and to avert the political, military and above all the moral catastrophe, which the unchecked rampage of the last years of Nazism would bring about. No, those who took the decision to risk a rebellion, in unspeakably difficult circumstances and ultimately in the knowledge that their prospects were hopeless, were in many respects outsiders and, after 20 July, outcasts from the community of national solidarity. While the great majority of the nation and its elite remained silent, the resisters set their face against the tyranny of absolute inhumanity which Hitler embodied.

The actions of the plotters of 20 July, as of the many who opposed the regime in their own way – by sheltering Jews, helping Soviet prisoners-of-war, spreading knowledge of the criminal policies of the regime and protesting against euthanasia and the destruction of human life – offer a challenge which has not been satisfactorily met by the return to freedom and democracy. Helmuth James von Moltke once pointed out that the important thing was to restore the image of humanity 'in the hearts of our fellow-citizens'. What remains particularly relevant today is the call for inner renewal on the basis of individual social and moral identity, as the prerequisite for freedom and social justice, for the reviving of neighbourly and human relationships, for greater willingness to accept responsibility and for individual initiative in a society characterized by the growth of anonymous bureaucratic controls.

The conservative-nationalist resisters were themselves a symptom of the crisis in culture and society of the 1920s and 1930s, which they saw as being the principal cause of the Nazi rise to power. Even today Germany has not fully emerged from that crisis, intellectually or politically. After a period of suppression there are once again signs of a tendency to adopt arguments and positions which originate in the inter-war sense of crisis, although the history of the German resistance clearly demonstrates their inherent contradictions. It is to be hoped that the historical reappraisal of the German opposition to Hitler will replace the facile yea-saying with a willingness to come to grips with the deeper historical and political reasons for its inevitable failure.

3

The social vision and constitutional plans of the German resistance

I. The sociology of the resistance

Helmuth James von Moltke[1] was convinced that the task of the resistance to National Socialism was not limited to the physical removal of tyranny, but that it should proceed to a radical reshaping of the foundations of social and political life. 'We can only expect to get our people to ditch this regime of fear and terror,' he wrote to Lionel Curtis,[2] 'if we are able to show them a picture of something beyond the terrible despair of the immediate future'; in other words, something worth working for, worth starting again for. For Moltke, erecting an 'image of humanity in the heart of every German citizen' was 'a question of religion, upbringing, the ties of work and family, of the proper relationship between responsibility and rights' – and thus also a question of the state of society as a whole. Awareness that the struggle against Nazi tyranny must be waged from the position of an independent social policy was not limited to the Kreisau Circle. The specific historical starting-point of German resistance can be defined by the growing belief of all groups within it that, in addition to a change in the system of government, comprehensive social reforms were necessary.

The question of the social policies of the resistance touches on their specific historical and political content, which went beyond extreme moral protest against lawlessness and violence. They went on to engage with the problem of whether there was a *realistic* alternative to the parasitic subversion of German governmental tradition, which ultimately led to rule by the satraps of an emaciated dictator, cut off in his bunker from the realities of the Reich. Could it be that this proxy tyranny by a corrupt clique had its origins in a deep-rooted aversion in German society to the pluralistic structure of 'mature' social systems? If there *was* an alternative it had to be made visible in the German resistance. The group of individuals involved in the 20th July Plot has been regarded as an actual political elite, a secret governing class. Their political thinking appears to represent those forces that were called upon to adapt German society from the inside to the requirements of a highly industrialized civilization, and to mould it into a political shape suitable for those circumstances.

George K. Romoser[3] and Hannah Arendt[4] have expressly rejected this possibility and claim to see in the German resistance nothing more than a continuation of the anti-democratic opposition to the Weimar Republic. The view that the political character of the resistance was essentially 'reactionary', has been expressed by other authors too. It has a dialectical connection with the hitherto predominant tendency among German historians to see the resistance as prefiguring the re-establishment of constitutional democracy and to make it the father of the Federal Republic or – which is basically the same thing – to claim it, under the banner of communism, for the nationalist mission of the German Democratic Republic. Whether the latter is at all true, even of the resistance groups of the extreme left, would require more detailed examination; however that would go well beyond the framework of this study, which is limited to an analysis of the non-communist resistance. At the same time, it would be wrong to discount the communist resistance, for reasons of ideological convenience, from the overall phenomenon of anti-Nazi opposition in Germany.

Both Romoser's supporters and his critics succumb to the temptation to pass judgement without reference to the specific conditions prevailing at that time; in doing so they erase the historical dimension in which the political thought of the resistance must be situated, and which reveals an unmistakable conflict with present-day theories of democracy. On the other hand, we have to question the assumptions of the resistance and how it saw its historical role, without letting ourselves be forced into the conceptual 'progressive-reactionary' matrix. When we pose this question, the boundary between 'mental emigration' and political non-involvement on the one hand, and active resistance on the other, becomes less important. So does the question, which the German opposition found extremely difficult to answer, of when collaboration should give way to uncompromising opposition. Finally we need not concern ourselves greatly with how much political weight to assign to the different political and religious centres of resistance. Our investigation is restricted to those groups with a direct or indirect connection to the events of 20th July. It does not encompass the communist resistance, nor the émigré groups, whose ideas on social policy differed fundamentally from those which evolved in the atmosphere of a totalitarian state and out of the will to bring about political change from within.

Spokesmen for the resistance have repeatedly stressed that it included representatives of all political persuasions and all 'levels of society'. However, the lower middle class, which almost to a man supported the National Socialist experiment, played scarcely any part in the resistance. At the same time, despite the active participation of some leading socialists, the 20th July Plot was isolated from the mass of working people. How they would react in the event of a coup was a matter of surmise; opinion surveys organized by Father Delp produced little encouragement, and Trott confirmed the view of the Kreisau Circle when he reported in his foreign policy memoranda up to 1944 on the widespread apathy of the working class. The main reason for this was the prompt and effective smashing of illegal socialist and communist organisations, which convinced Theodor Haubach[5] that subversive activity could only be continued on the basis of personal friendships. Leuschner's description of Germany as a 'vast prison' illuminates the fact that the resistance was of necessity a resistance without 'a people'. Uncertainty about the possible reaction of the population, which for the most part gave its allegiance to Hitler, was a major influence on the political thinking and plans of the opposition – in contrast to the resistance based outside Germany.

The active resistance displayed a relatively homogeneous social structure. The overwhelming majority of its members belonged to the upper class and felt personally qualified to assume political leadership – in the face of the regiment of dilettantes they were fighting against. The distinctions between the *bürgerlich* (moderate, middle-class) and socialist oppositions were fluid; Reichwein, Mierendorff and Haubach did not simply represent the typical 'social-democrat intellectual'. Leber was the exact opposite of a socialist functionary; Leuschner and Hermann Maass[6] had, through political activity and their experience under the Nazi system, grown out of their class-conscious thinking. Nevertheless, the group of former labour unionists adopted a rather special position; with the creation of the United Unions executive, they had taken the first step towards a corporatist solution to the labour union problem. However, hopes of reaching an accommodation with the Nazi regime were dashed by the intransigence of the DAF (German Labour Front). Unlike most of the conservative conspirators, their disillusionment came early, but in general they did not join the underground socialist resistance groups.

With the exception of Leuschner, the resistance lacked personalities who could be considered typical representatives of the Weimar Republic. The socialist resisters were those who, in the closing stages of the republic, had taken a clear stand against the leadership of their party and had sharply criticized the Weimar party system as a whole. This meant that, when it came to political planning, none of the inner circle of the resistance, except for Leuschner and Leber, were experienced parliamentarians. Even in the outer groups, parliamentarians were under-represented, a fact which is only partly attributable to their persecution and exclusion from politics. On the other hand, the number of overt or covert opponents of the Weimar republic within the resistance movement was remarkably large. Romoser's thesis, that the resistance represented the continuation of the 'conservative revolution', is true of a section of the conservative-nationalist opposition, although the intellectual representatives of neo-conservatism only on rare occasions took part in anti-Nazi plotting and, as in the case of Ernst Jünger,[7] were of marginal significance at best. The complete discrediting of the Weimar Republic even in the eyes of its former supporters – including those close to the parties of the Weimar coalition – contributed to the paralysis of their will to resist actively. On the other hand, there were members of the inner opposition who remained stubbornly loyal to the republic in the face of considerable reprisals. It must be said in their justification that it was not only psychologically easier, but also easier given the strictures of the police state, to join the resistance having previously collaborated with the regime, than to do so from the identifiably pro-Weimar camp.

Active resistance, where it involved outright conspiracy, demanded both availability and a certain level of material security – the requirements stipulated by Max Weber for the professional politician. The overwhelming majority were members of the upper class, with a conservative or authoritarian attitude, and to that extent were well placed to form the seedbed for an underground resistance that could exploit its position of power in politics and society. Until well into the war they were far less exposed to the impact of totalitarian *Gleichschaltung* than the middle and lower classes. Their monopoly in the provision of top-flight recruits to the diplomatic, civil and armed services had not been decisively broken during the republican era; although the upper class was not in fact socially exclusive, it embodied a definite social stance, which was not easily shifted by demagoguery or political pressure. Its internal solidarity is demonstrated, for example, by the fact that anti-Nazi opinions could be widely circulated yet remain confidential. The individuals who belonged to the inner resistance circle were linked by direct and indirect social ties, long before they decided on conspiracy. Their mental withdrawal from the Nazi system was initially less a question of political conviction than one of personal style; the casual and cynical violation of hitherto accepted social norms by Nazi officials at all levels must have seemed all the more repugnant when combined with incompetence and corruption. Private criticism of and distancing from aspects of the regime seemed natural in a very wide circle of those who knew what was going on, and spread to sympathizers whose opposition grew from disillusionment with the reality of Nazism. All this had great significance in providing a shield for active resistance. Hence the Gestapo tended as a rule to discount statements of anti-regime opinion, and often only intervened when it became absolutely unavoidable and where there would be no political repercussions.

Thus, in the first few years of the regime, the upper class did in fact enjoy a degree of freedom of political opinion. It is for this reason that Ralf Dahrendorf[8] has described them as authoritarian but certainly not totalitarian. The German opposition to Nazism has often been criticized for its lack of determination to embark on genuine action and of being over-optimistic in assessing their chances of removing the regime. This can be explained by the mutual loyalty of the upper class, which proved to be increasingly misplaced, and to the marked hostility and boundless distrust shown towards them by the Nazi 'upstarts'. The social origins of the resistance are one of the reasons why it never took the form of a collective movement and never gave itself a name – the term 'German Freedom Movement' did not catch on. Not until 1943 did efforts to form a broad 'popular movement' begin. To this extent the resistance was not a political 'movement' with the declared aim of gaining a popular majority, of winning over latent public opinion and thus at least fictively representing it. The men who made contacts abroad for the resistance groups presented themselves as honestly intentioned men of some status, and cited support from existing and former institutions – the Army General Staff, the former political parties and the labour unions. As a political elite, who felt unquestionably legitimated by virtue of their social position and political responsibility, they claimed to represent 'the whole nation'.

The preparatory calls for support and the various constitutional plans clearly show that among the members of the resistance the question of political legitimation was not seen as a major problem. In discussions about a future new order the idea of possibly later convoking a constituent assembly played only a subordinate part. Nor did Leuschner have any doubts that the governing group that he envisaged for the labour unions would be accepted by the membership, and it was significant that arguments in favour of proportional representation cropped up in this connection. The impulsive demand made by Goerdeler in 1940, that the revolutionary government should immediately be legalized through a plebiscite, was firmly resisted by the other plotters, who did not share his 'sanguine hopes' about the outcome of such a vote. Very much in the manner of later 'bloc' politics, legitimation of the new government was sought through bringing in all political tendencies seen as still relevant, though initially excluding the communists, certainly those controlled by Moscow. The sharpest critic of this approach was Popitz who, from a strongly *étatiste* standpoint, saw Goerdeler's 'coalition-building' as parliamentarism, though this was necessary if the revolutionaries were to maintain control of events once the coup had succeeded. A 'revolution from above' was dictated to the plotters by the conditions of a totalitarian state; on the question of how far a 'revolution from below' would support their revolution and would be bound to give it legitimacy, opinion in 1944 was divided.

The internal situation of the Third Reich restricted the revolutionary resistance movement to a group of men from the upper class, who were bound together by personal ties, but it also included some labour unionists committed to resistance and a considerable number of members of the officer corps still beholden to Prussian traditions. This had its impact on the planning of their social policy. After the Nazi government's ruthless persecution of opponents on the political left, which its conservative coalition partners supported, it was to be expected that resistance would crystallize in centres which can best be described as 'residues'. It was precisely because of the persistence of strong traditional links with the epoch of Bismarck and the Kaisers that these centres stood apart from the Nazi policy of *Gleichschaltung* or were largely spared from its effects. The relative homogeneity which this produced enables us to reproduce a model of the society envisaged by the resisters, on the basis of their memoranda, plans and personal statements. While many individual aspects of this social vision remained in dispute, its basic outline is astonishingly cohesive and uniform, despite the fact that its concepts were often developed in isolation. However, there were occasional acute differences on domestic policy that could never really be bridged.

This vision of society is characterized by the relatively little importance given to public opinion; also by the notion of an 'organic' body politic, which did not permit social and ideological antagonisms to take root, but converted them into mutually beneficial stimuli, and lastly by the idea of a 'conflict-free' government. This social model, which is distinct from the principles of democracy and modern pluralism, appears to represent the political thought which was continuing to exert a clandestine influence in Nazi Germany. Although this model had a number of features in common with the programmes of resistance movements based abroad, the conservative resistance in Germany was very strongly committed to an independent 'German way'.

II. Overcoming the mass mentality

Ralf Dahrendorf has sought to demonstrate that all groups within the resistance, with the 'sole exception' of the communists, can be described as 'deliberate or unwitting defenders of the *ancien régime*, that their 'rebellion of tradition' was also a rebellion of the 'illiberality and authoritarianism of the past influencing the present'.[1] Nowhere, he says, have morality and liberalism so visibly diverged as in Germany, and we have to question whether the resistance, had it been successful, would not have led to an authoritarian form of government. Dahrendorf thus highlights a key problem in the historical assessment of the resistance; however, it lies not so much in the tension between 'authority' and 'liberalism' as in the conscious and unconscious orientation towards a 'conflict-free society'. Here I am adopting the term used by Dahrendorf to characterize the German political tradition. The social vision of the active resistance was not in fact of a 'restoration'. It did not aim, as Dahrendorf suggests, for a return to the 'values and institutions' of the Weimar era; all groups rejected a simple reversion to the *status quo ante,* at least in theory. The political thinking of the resisters was borne along by their desire to find new solutions to the intellectual and political crisis, which they perceived as a pan-European phenomenon. But in their search they often harked back to the experience of history. To a great extent this thinking combined traditional elements with social utopianism, a fact which distinguishes it from 'restoration' pure and simple, while still giving it markedly conservative features.

Yet it would be wrong to identify the resistance with the inherently problematic concept of a 'conservative revolution'; the resistance represents a broader current embracing both nationalism and the 1920s critique of civilisation, as well as the dawning idea of a united Europe. It thus stood outside the traditional polarity between 'left' and 'right'. The youth-movement, experience of the trenches, and Nietzschean and neo-Kantian philosophy, all had as much influence on the resistance as they did on the intellectual foundations of the rise of National Socialism. These shared experiences and convictions should be regarded as more important than the differences in mentality between the generations. The older generation remembered the Kaiser's Germany and saw its collapse in 1918 as the beginning of the end; the political ideas of the younger generation, on the other hand, were formed in the period when the traditional party-system was apparently being remoulded by reformist efforts ranging from the *Volkskonservativen* (right-wing populists) to the intra-party opposition within the Social-Democrats (SPD). The conflict that originated from this differing point of departure in political history, and which broke out in the final weeks before the July coup, was masked by the experience, shared by all the conspirators, of being condemned to inactivity or, more accurately, to futile action.

The common thread that runs through the testimony of the conspirators, whether it be Leber's diary, the letters of Haubach and Leuschner or Dietrich Bonhoeffer's 'final report', is the painful awareness that, as the 'intermediate generation', they were forced to sit on their hands, at a time when there was so much talk of 'commitment' and 'action'. They were waiting, perhaps in vain, for an impalpable future in which they would be called upon to play a part. Both the Kreisau Circle and the socialists directed their thoughts towards the shaping of this future. They wanted –

and this is where the generations parted company – a new beginning, a clean break with history up to that point. Moltke spoke of
a 'new chronology', Hans Schlange-Schöningen wrote: 'We must
build a new state, not in order to repeat the vicious circle of German history, but to begin a *new* history. It is not true that we are
at the beginning of an age of dictatorship, we are at its end.'[2] This
will to renew is most clearly seen in the overthrow of traditional
ideas about the nation-state in favour of European solutions. It is
found as much in Leuschner, Haubach, Mierendorff and Leber,
as in Moltke, Yorck and Trott – and it forced the formerly *völkisch*
and nationalist conservatives to rethink their position.

Nonetheless, social policy thinking was largely governed by
the conflict, as yet unresolved in Germany, between traditional
social structures and a levelled-down mass society. The fundamental motivation of the youth movement at the beginning of
the twentieth century was its criticism of how technology and
depersonalisation were undermining social and intellectual life.
It raised the urgent question of what creative forces in society
could be mobilized against 'atomisation' and 'collectivisation',
against 'the urban mentality', against domination by 'materialist
concepts of utility', against the loss of a 'sense of quality', against
'promotion-chasing' and 'the cult of stardom', against the mind-
less 'haste' of modern life; at the same time it attacked what
were seen as the outward trappings of a 'bourgeois' lifestyle. With
varying emphasis on the causes, the *consequences* of extreme industrialization were condemned by all resistance groups under
the general term of '*Vermassung*' ('loss of individuality'). They
were anxious to find a new way forward, which prevented the
forces capable of shaping society from being suffocated by the
unchecked development of technology and big business, and
which ensured that a sense of individual responsibility and management of one's own life was not worn down in 'hydra-headed
organizations' and anonymous bureaucracies.

This kind of critique of civilization found its most extreme
confirmation in the reality of society under Nazism, a system which
itself had originally exploited the same irrational and anti-
modernist tendencies, and had been hailed as the vanquisher of

the forces that were subverting 'the life of the nation'. The massed processions, the cheering crowds whipped into a frenzy by propaganda, the paramilitary organization, in which stereotyped social behaviour was imposed under the slogan of 'comradeship' – all these appeared to justify fears of a 'mass mentality'. The former socialist youth leader, Theodor Haubach, believed the paintings of Breughel foreshadowed 'the consequences of the mass-age': 'the mass that has broken loose from the bonds and discipline of the Divine, turned in on itself, estranged from the gods, mutated into grimacing masks and ghosts.' *Vermassung* seemed to be the underlying cause of religious, cultural and political decline; it seemed bound up with the prevalence of a purely 'materialistic' way of life and the abandonment of all values that transcend the perspective of consumption. Dietrich Bonhoeffer[3] posed the alternative choices: either to 'head towards an age in which the best would be chosen, in other words an aristocratic order, or towards one of uniformity in all mental and physical aspects of the human condition.' He spoke of a 'process of vulgarization (*Verpöbelung*) at all levels of society' and saw the real task as one of 'rediscovering the buried experience of quality'. Only in this way, he said, could 'every form of *Vermassung*' be opposed; the job of the church was not forcibly to impose the principle of equality, but to resurrect the 'feeling of space between human beings' (*das Gefühl der menschlichen Distanzen*). In saying this Bonhoeffer was prepared to be reproached for his 'unsocial attitude'.

Thus, 'de-massing the masses' (*Entmassung der Masse*) was the central theme of all plans for political and social reform. In a memorandum written by Horst von Einsiedel[4] for the Kreisau Circle, we read: 'In direct contrast to the human type of the past, firmly moulded by his life's work, the mass type is to a large extent unstable,' someone whose occupation in modern industry no longer gives him inner fulfilment. Even a politician like Goerdeler, close to liberal thinking, saw one of the causes of the crisis in the 'deadening effect of the work process', while Lothar König[5] blamed the progressive 'depersonalisation' and 'subduing of mass-man' on over-hasty and unplanned industrialization. These symptoms, which can be summed up by the Marxist term 'alienation', led most of the Kreisau Circle to conclude that the answer lay in 'personal socialism' and to call for the material and spiritual subsistence of the working classes to be guaranteed. 'The revolution of the 20th century,' Fr Delp wrote, 'needs a definitive theme of its own and the opportunity to create for people a renewed and dependable social context' – a secure social environment and the conditions for individual intellectual and spiritual development. As long as people have to live a life unworthy of humanity, Delp said, they will succumb to their circumstances and will neither pray nor think.

Indeed, the process of levelling and the dissolution of the traditional stratification of society, were key factors in the crisis, since the pace of change was too fast for those affected to adapt their expectations to the new situation. Many in the resistance movement saw this as an inevitable historical process, which began with the breakdown of centuries-old social ties and threatened to march relentlessly onward into the nightmare of Bolshevism. For the Kreisau Circle a root cause was the loss of people's religious security. Theodor Steltzer[6] criticized the 'secularised but unpolitical individualism' of modern life, which denied any metaphysical element in the workings of the mind, and attempted to construct human civilization from purely rational elements. Steltzer's use of the word 'unpolitical' in the sense of 'hostile to the community' is characteristic, since he saw the collectivisation of the masses, rule by 'mass bureaucratic controls' and people's search for 'security within the mass', as no more than the counterpart of rational individualism. Similarly, Eugen Gerstenmaier[7] claimed that secularisation had brought about the collapse of 'communal structures that have evolved naturally through history'.

Alfred Delp, probably the most productive mind in the Kreisau Circle, analysed this process in more detail. He traced it back to two interacting developments. First was the external development of the 'technological, social, scientific and economic world', which was simply putting too much strain on people already caught up in a shift of their spiritual centre of gravity. On the other hand, man as an individual was thrown back on his own resources by the inevitable process of rationalization, but lacked the strength to resist manipulation by external forces. Man, who now only saw himself as a *vegetativum et sensitivum* (a sentient being) must therefore be brought back to awareness of himself as a 'person', and must learn to take himself seriously as 'an ordered design'. Delp saw that individualism – 'the shift of man's spiritual centre of gravity'- had its own historical logic and consistency; in this he differed not only from Steltzer, but from the Cologne Circle around Otto Müller[8] and others who, starting from a more traditional interpretation of Catholic social doctrine, called for a 'Christian pattern of communal life' and of 'life as a whole', which was not free of authoritarian traits. Delp did not believe that simply returning to religion, to the 'Christian state', was a real solution. It was necessary for man to rediscover himself in a real sense that embraced all aspects of life – to overcome his self-alienation – before he could be reintegrated into 'community' and 'nation' and become responsive to a religious message.

Moltke and Yorck attributed the problem of *Vermassung* to the disintegration of medieval universalism and the progressive expansion of the agenda of the modern state, which was, in effect, institutionalised rationalism. This had reached its logical conclusion in a totalitarianism that had succeeded in laying claim to 'the entire man'.[9] They maintained that all loyalties and attachments other than those to the state had been absorbed in the growth and development of the nation-state, and that all 'energies committed to small communities' had been placed in the service of state structures, which in turn presented an anonymous, bureaucratic face to the individual and destroyed his 'emotional attachment to the state'. Moltke felt that this process had led to absurdity in a totalitarian state which turned all 'forms of expression' – art, education, language – into propaganda media and had relativized all normative values. The inevitable collapse of this system would necessarily bring with it 'the destruction of the state idol' and leave behind a vacuum requiring the formation of a new political cohesiveness on the basis of 'the largest possible number of the smallest possible communities', in which men and women would be taken seriously as individuals. For Moltke, overcoming the mass mentality meant abolishing the state in its modern, mechanistic and technology-driven form. Instead, areas of life had to be created, which were free from state intervention, and were to be filled by spontaneously formed communities and autonomous bodies.

This concept, which is reminiscent of Proudhon[10], required the reintegration of isolated individuals into groups of a manageable size, in which the 'sense of personal responsibility' would be revived and a 'blossoming' of true community spirit would take place. Moltke also wanted to reawaken the feeling of emotional commitment to religious and metaphysical values, which the state's claim on the individual had relativized and restricted. 'A mass without faith can be corrupted by any statesman, but a solid rank of believers cannot,' Moltke wrote in 1939. This notion led him away from the usual paths of German Protestant tradition. In a very similar way, Fr Delp criticized the hierarchical bureaucracy of the Catholic Church, which he said had lost sight of human beings as the subject and object of ecclesiastical life. The two men formed the focus of the Kreisau deliberations and had a decisive impact on the Circle's thinking.

Overcoming the mass mentality, not through a return to liberal individualism, but through the creation of a synthesis, which placed the 'community-committed individual' at the centre of things, thus formed the point of departure for Kreisau. As we read in Trott's memorandum of late 1942: 'The key to their joint efforts is the desperate attempt to rescue the core of personal human integrity. Their fundamental ambition is to restore the inalienable divine and natural right of the human individual.' This was expressed most profoundly in Delp's personalist concept of *theonomer Humanismus* ('god-guided humanism'). Similar thought-processes are to be found among nearly all the resistance groups. Leuschner was engaged in an intellectual exchange with Elfreide Nebgen and Jakob Kaiser,[11] and through them came into contact with the ideas of Ludwig Reichhold,[12] regarded at that time as a workable solution. In 1942 Leuschner remarked that after the age of individualist man, the age of collectivist man was dawning, and added: 'There is, however, a third possibility beyond individuality and collectivity, which is not a compromise but something different and higher: the person.' That was exactly how Kreisau expressed it.

By contrast, Julius Leber[13] was more pragmatic. He did not believe that the masses had been turned into automata, and attacked the 'downright grotesque notions of rule by the masses' within his own Socialist party, considering authoritative and energetic leadership of the masses as indispensable. But he was no less forceful in criticizing the anonymity of bureaucratic political operations, which excluded the 'combative personality', and he regarded Marxism's acceptance of historical inevitability as a fundamental error of socialist theory. 'It necessarily diminished the value of the individual personality, whose contribution was no longer sought in creativity but only in organizational activity'; the socialist concept of 'the masses', Leber said, ignored the fact that man was not a predictable factor. Marxism and liberalism both fell into the same error of underestimating the irrational attachments of human beings. Although Leber, like the Kreisau thinkers, called for greater space for the personality to develop, what distinguished him from Kreisau was his constant relationship with the working man. Perhaps because he did not overestimate the masses, he did not share Kreisau's mistrust of them, which bordered on hostility, and we do not find him using that overworked term, *Vermassung*.

Moltke made great efforts to involve representatives of the working class in the work of the Kreisau Circle and, after the death of Carlo Mierendorff,[14] he tried to persuade Julius Leber, whom he code-named 'Neumann', to collaborate with them. However, Leber kept his distance. While sympathizing with many of the Kreisau ideas on social policy, Leber rejected the concept of 'small communities' and the consequences that flowed from it. Mierendorff and Haubach, considerably influenced by Christian Socialism, came closer to Kreisau thinking, which saw the revival of Christian convictions as a means of defeating the 'mass mentality'. Fr Delp went further, linking political reform with a call for fundamental reform of the Church, such that Catholicism would be able once again to fulfil its fundamental social tasks. He accused the Church of failing to provide personal leadership: 'This law, by requiring its leaders to be nameless and faceless, has contributed just as much to the *Vermassung* of our lives as have the anonymity of big business and the faceless bureaucracy of the state, the economy and the political parties.' In a similar vein, Trott called for the asserting of 'new, personal forces'.

The resistance was convinced of the need to get out of that rut where political life was in the hands of functionaries and to overcome the class-based limitations on social action. In this they were continuing with initiatives from the 1920s. In November 1931 Trott stated that a new philosophy was needed, one which did not, like Hegel, magnificently reinvent an outmoded model of the world, but would 'begin by giving reality to a new idea of human personality.' Clearly this meant that the essential nature of the state would have to be thought through afresh.

Although Goerdeler was starting from a very different political position, he too bemoaned the increasing 'fragmentation' of humanity in modern society; he attributed this to the withering of religion in daily life, the 'overvaluing of the material content of life', the prevalence of specialization and an 'ever more excessive urbanization'. The advances of modern science and technology, he said, had led to the loss of spiritual ties and had shattered the unity of mind, body and soul. He sensed vaguely that his somewhat patriarchal model of the state was thrown into question by this, without of course blaming the state tradition itself for this development. With the loss of a sense of the 'totality' of the human personality, he believed that the basis for a harmonious policy that made equal use of all the nation's forces had also been lost. Therefore the restoration of a political and social order, which had been turned completely upside down since the departure of Bismarck, was essentially an anthropological problem. In his 'Political Testament', Goerdeler says that people's lives had to be put back on to a broader foundation. His image of man in society was of someone religious, close to nature, unspoilt by sophistication, but practical, energetic, and ready to take on public responsibilities, Given his basically optimistic standpoint, he did not doubt that the picture he had sketched out could become a reality.

In one of his memoranda Goerdeler presented the alternatives: 'The question is not: capitalism or socialism, but: individualism or collectivism.' He came down in favour of individualism, but of a kind that assumed the integration of the individual in the 'community'. His liberal creed was linked to a strong, almost patriarchal, sense of obligation to provide social care and welfare. He was unambiguous in his social-Darwinist views, stating repeatedly that life was a struggle and that Nazism had done the service of making this clear. It was, however, 'a struggle ennobled by the observance of God's commandments.' Yet at heart he yearned to return to a harmonious social order, free of conflict. The family governed by Christian principles seemed to him to be the model for the life of the state; it is no surprise that he called for people to be educated to have a 'sense of national community free from class bias' and spoke of the need for a 'national reconciliation'. When he was in prison he reproached himself for having abandoned his family, and that demonstrates the tragic contradiction in this figure, who reflects the mutually conflicting tendencies of the age to which he belonged. Goerdeler was closer to the personalist thinking of the Kreisau Circle than one might be led to believe by his terminology. Nonetheless, he was more emphatic than them in seeking the solution to social problems through recourse to the historical experience of the nineteenth century, which he saw as a 'happier' age.

III. National Socialism and Bolshevism

The ordering of state and society, which the resistance hoped to achieve in different ways, was to be founded on the autonomy of the individual. Bolshevism was a complete inversion of that. It was taken to express the total dehumanisation of all social and political relationships. In the minds of nearly all the plotters against Hitler, 'Bolshevism' was synonymous with complete and anarchistic *Vermassung*. It is characteristic that their judgement of Stalinist Russia was predominantly influenced by the clichéd images put about by rightwing and Nazi propaganda. Even those in the resistance who initially greeted Hitler as the vanquisher of communism, came to equate the tyrannical Nazi regime more and more with the Soviet system. As Trott put it: 'What in Germany manifests itself as a filthy brown concoction, we encounter in Moscow as Asiatic ruthlessness and brutality.' National Socialism was seen as the rebellion 'from below', as a radical force arrayed against the western Christian tradition, as destructive potential, which consciously strove, in Schulenburg's words, to 'atomise the masses'. Criticism of the system was focussed not on the authoritarian but on the parasitic elements of domination by the Nazi clique. Beck[1] – and after him, Goerdeler – countered the slogan of the 'total state' with the concept of the 'totality of politics'. Goerdeler looked at the system from the aspect of its 'splintering' effect and thereby characterized it more correctly than has usually been attempted in theories of totalitarian dictatorship.

This equating of National Socialism with Bolshevism strongly influenced resistance thinking and turned the resisters into defenders of a mature social order. This can be seen from how completely they overestimated the impact on domestic policy of the Soviet-German Non-Aggression Pact of August 1939. Late in 1939 *Korvettenkapitän* (lieutenant-commander) Liedig drafted a memorandum[2] that sheds light on the views of the circle around Oster[3] in the Abwehr (military intelligence) and also typifies the political thinking of Beck and Halder.[4] Liedig portrayed the grim vision of a Bolshevist Germany. The Nazi Party, he wrote, was well on its way to a 'second revolution', its apparatus was no more than the 'backdrop to the subversion of old national structures', official Nazi ideology had been downgraded to a mere means of leading the masses and anti-Bolshevism had become an empty formula. It did not prevent Hitler from succumbing to the attraction of 'the nihilistic vacuum of ideas outside the European community of nations'. National Socialism, Liedig prophesied, would be 'swallowed up in the vast Russo-Asiatic region, ... intellectually no less than geopolitically'. Hitler would only be able to maintain his position by becoming a 'satrap of Stalin', his 'Russian viceroy in Soviet Germany'. Furthermore, 'Germany would at best survive as one of the Bolshevist Russian satellites, if indeed it did not sink into a state of helotry to Russia'.

This prognosis, growing out of hate and underestimation of the enemy, was coupled with shrewd analysis of Hitler's political system. 'A revolutionary dynamic that subverts all the historical loyalties and all the cultural affiliations that once made up the dignity and renown of Europe, is the sole and entire secret of his statecraft.' However, the caricature of Bolshevism led to the erroneous conclusion that Hitler had now taken the decisive step towards a 'dynamic long-term relationship' with Soviet Russia; this meant he would be compelled 'to progress in the near future from the first revolution to the second, from the National Socialist to the Bolshevist one'. This idea, though later proved wrong by Germany's invasion of Russia, was a determining factor particularly for conservative resistance circles and the military, prompting the fear of constantly changing forms of 'National Bolshevism' on the domestic front. In a memorandum by Erich Kordt[5] and Hasso von Etzdorf[6] dated October 1939, we read that Germany had 'never been closer to chaos and bolshevism'. At Trott's instigation, a memorandum was sent by Paul Scheffler[7] late in 1939 to the US State Department. This warned in clear terms of the danger of revolutionary repercussions from the fraternizing between Nazis and Bolsheviks, and expressed the hope that this could be averted by a coup d'état. It was fears of this kind that notably strengthened the resolve of the group around Beck, Hassell, Popitz and Goerdeler to overthrow the Hitler regime. But they also provided a lasting argument for the establishment of an authoritarian system of government after the regime's removal. Dietrich Bonhoeffer saw the threat of bolshevism as emphatic confirmation of the need for an 'authoritarian though non-fascist regime' in the post-war period.

It would be distorting the position of the conservative resistance, if one did not at the same time make it clear that behind these fears lay persistent social antipathies, which doubtless led to acute internal tensions within the active resistance. Hassell's remark about the inevitability of 'internal Bolshevisation' of the National Socialist system alluded to the wiping out of the Russian upper class by the Bolsheviks. Hassell spoke expressly about how 'socialism in Hitlerian form' was aimed at smashing the upper classes and reducing the churches to insignificant sects. This kind of thinking amounted to no more than a continuation of middle-class anti-communism. The obvious significance of this in the initially unquestioning acceptance of Hitler and his rise to power cannot be overestimated, and it paralysed conservative forces until well into the war.

A few days after the death of President Hindenburg in 1934, Halder wrote to Beck that 'Hitler's naked determination, carried along by the momentum of idealism' was in practice becoming a distortion. Those ready to rebuild Germany were being opposed by a group – hiding unjustifiably behind the authority of the Führer – which was about to 'destroy existing values'. That group was the embodiment of the 'communist threat'. Halder therefore considered the 'Röhm Rebellion' to be 'only one and not the most dangerous abscess' in Germany; in it he saw communist forces at work, and thus made no distinction between the social-revolutionary forces in the Nazi Party and the communists – this simplification was typical of his political thinking. Even Beck believed, as late as 1938, that it was possible for the General Staff to make a concerted move to free Hitler from the 'Cheka and the commissars' and thus prevent the 'revival of communism'. The passive acceptance by the generals of the murders of June 1934, can be explained very largely by this simplistic comparison between traditional 'idealistic' values and communist 'materialism' and was characteristic of not only Beck and Halder. It was a reprehensible simplification of the problems of social policy. It is also revealing that the anti-Hitler generals, with few exceptions, did not resolve to take unconditional action until the Bolshevist threat took on a military form.

Of necessity the rejection of the Bolshevist system was bound up with the question of what position to adopt *vis-à-vis* anti-communist socialist forces. Hassell simply pushed the problem of socialism to one side as 'another cuckoo's egg that Nazism has laid in the German nest'. However, Adam von Trott saw the accommodation between socialism and tradition as the crucial problem in domestic politics and, at root, also in foreign policy. At an early stage he directed his thoughts towards overcoming class conflict. His attempt to replace the Hegelian tradition of government with a sociological initiative of his own, placed him alongside socialist groups, with whom he worked closely both before and after the Nazis seized power in January 1933. Incidentally, he was also in touch with communists. In February of that year Trott confessed to his father that, in his view, 'the positive rights of the individual' could only endure if at the same time the rights of the masses were 'held sacred', something which he saw little prospect of under the rule of Papen and Hitler. As he saw it, Hegel's 'right to free will' had to be replaced by the 'right to work', meaning self-fulfilment in the widest sense. Here there is broad agreement with Delp's 'personal socialism', from which we may conclude that Trott had a decisive influence on the Kreisau plans.

In 1933 Trott feared that neglecting the rights of the masses would provoke 'a severe reaction', and as late as the spring of 1937 he believed that a popular uprising was certainly on the cards. This was a remarkable, but not unexpected misreading of the political situation under Nazism. Like Schulenburg, he may have harboured a certain sympathy towards the Strasser wing of the Nazi Party.[8] At all events he considered that the conflict had yet to be fought out between the socialist elements of the Nazi movement and the newly forming stratum of mediocre, lower-middle-class Nazi functionaries and capitalist exploiters of the system. From his own point of view, Trott could not have wanted to see a workers' uprising, since that would have made it vastly more difficult to stabilize society. In this context he feared that conflict beyond Germany's borders would hinder or render impossible the resolution of the 'social and economic crisis in Germany', and he tended to underestimate Hitler's aggressiveness in foreign policy. Trott believed that the unwise attitude of the victorious powers at Versailles had driven the German people to an extremism that had now reached fever pitch; hence a war would lead to 'total catastrophe'. In Trott's eyes Nazism was just as much the result of frustrated nationalism as of the social and economic crisis. He believed that a firm but certainly not aggressive stance by the western democracies would bring Nazism to heel within Germany, whereas a repeat of the foreign policies of the 1920s would drive the masses into 'National Bolshevism'. For domestic policy reasons, Trott was a convinced supporter of appeasement. What was going on in Germany, he wrote in 1938, was 'a European phenomenon', and – from a certain patriotic sensitivity – he resisted blanket condemnation of Germany by other countries. He was convinced that totalitarianism was a symptom of the general crisis affecting the democracies as well, a crisis which could be traced to the insufficient social integration of the broad mass of the people. 'It is my opinion that this pandering to the instinctual side of human consciousness, as much by democracy as by totalitarianism, is what has led to the sterile and cynical defeatism that lies at the root of Europe's intellectual chaos.' Exploiting the emotional suggestibility of the masses had become a habit in all political systems; and Trott felt that cynical manipulation of the popular will through propaganda and an appeal to the instincts was the defining symptom of crisis, not only in German but in European society as a whole. He therefore doubted whether the axiom of individual liberty could be realized even in a democratic system built on capitalist foundations. As he wrote to an American journalist, Sheila Sokolow-Grant, with whom he had a close friendship:

> You have not satisfactorily answered my argument, that it is possible that capitalist and imperialist democracy may use liberty simply as a cloak for a policy that relies very much on compulsion, whereas some aspects of 'authoritarian systems' could provide a basically more genuine guarantee of human rights in modern industrial society.

Trott was convinced that the formal principle of democratic freedom had no impact on the extent of real social freedom and that the exposure of the individual to political manipulation could not be prevented even by a liberal system of government. This led him to reject all forms of rule based on the popular vote. The history of the previous ten years, he stated in 1939, showed that 'indiscriminate trust in the judgement of the masses is no use… One way or the other, popular movements have led to despotism'. Trott called for a return to conservative principles and a strict authority anchored in a constitutional framework; every socialist state must to a certain degree be authoritarian if it wants to survive. 'Go and write me an essay on Tradition and Socialism!' he told Julie Braun-Vogelstein. Trott was thus a long way from approving the transfer of western democratic principles to Germany. This view corresponded to that of the socialists; Leber's verdict on the men of the 1918 revolution was a crushing one: they had no concept 'of the new German community that had to be established' and had let themselves by guided by the example of the western democracies, 'without seeing that their inner nature had long since ceased to match their outward form'.

Trott rightly doubted that the American ideal of the 'pioneer' was practicable in the long term, and the conditions of modern society caused him to break away radically from the now meaningless 'middle-class ideology'. He sought a new social order on a European basis, which was to achieve the 'liberation of the masses from economic need' and secure their integration into an authority-based order informed by the Christian spirit. He warned against a formal proclamation of the principle of individual liberty, which violated 'the realities of [Germany's] national history, geography, culture and religious belief'. In a memorandum he wrote in 1943 we read: 'An exclusively rationalist upbringing has made us fail to understand both human nature and the realities of mass society, and we have come to ignore the demons which the *Vermassung* of mankind has released.' In these words Trott expressed the basis of the resistance's thoughts on social and constitutional policy. They demonstrate how the profound crisis of liberal democracy, on which the triumph of fascism and Nazism was built, had infected even its advocates and had convinced them that in the age of industrial society the principle of liberal and parliamentary democracy was doomed to failure.

IV. Agriculture, regional planning and policy for small businesses

An emphasis on tradition, the preservation of historical continuity and the rejection of a confrontational society were the chief features of opposition thinking. Their essentially defensive attitude towards the process of social levelling emerged most strongly in the treatment of agricultural policy. The fact that the Kreisau Circle devoted such attention to it can be explained by the landowning background of the group's founding members. However the other resistance groups showed a similar interest, since it was the agricultural crisis, and especially its impact on the large estates east of the Elbe, which had been a decisive factor in the downfall of the Weimar Republic. At the same time, this interest had been aroused by more profound convictions. 'The questions of agricultural policy will always be an integral component in any discussion about rebuilding the state,' Einsiedel wrote in a memorandum to the Kreisau Circle. The defeating of *Vermassung*, which, he said, must be the basis of the reorganization of Europe, required the creation of a mentality 'which affirms personal worth and the presence of a sphere of individual freedom and at the same time combines these things organically with a natural sense of community'. It was in rural society, Einsiedel claimed, that the roots of organic life were less damaged, 'the natural foundations of a cohesive social life' had been preserved and the sense of personality had not yet succumbed to the mass mentality. For this reason, in the new ordering of society, the greatest importance must placed on 'a strong, well-integrated rural population'.

Opinions of this kind were shared by all political persuasions among the resistance. In the 'provisional constitutional code' drafted by Popitz, agriculture was described as 'the most important source of the nation's strength'; and in the programme of 'Socialist Action' outlined by Mierendorff the guaranteed livelihood of the 'farmer on his soil' was listed as one of the preconditions of social justice and liberty. Goerdeler put the case for maintaining a healthy farming community, 'for reasons of biology, sociology and national policy'; in this he was prompted – as was Schulenburg – by the problematic notion that the farming community had to be looked on as an asset with regard to heredity and population policy: 'The German people must have a viable farming class, not so much for reasons of national security as to preserve the health of the nation.' All groups combined a neo-romantic idealisation of the 'natural country life' with an 'organicist'[1] model of society. 'The development of industrial capitalism and fascist attempts to impose order on it,' declared Einsiedel, 'are taking people away from an organic way of life and placing them in a life of routine; this inevitably fragments people's lives and downgrades their work to a technical and partial function within the rationalized total work-plan.'

This fundamentally anti-rational and anti-individualistic attitude, already emerging as an element in resistance thinking in connection with the causes of *Vermassung*, was not restricted to Einsiedel; we frequently find Goerdeler contrasting 'organic' forms with artificial 'organization', which he picked out as a characteristic of the Nazi system. Einsiedel and also Delp, Gerstenmaier and van Husen[2] were influenced by the romantic concept of *Volk* and the doctrine of the 'independent *Volk*'. In a telling phrase we read that the 'citizen-*Volksgenosse*[3] is no longer an organic limb of a living national body with a government adapted to its needs, but a mechanical component of a state machine geared to materialism and controlled by rationalism'. Steltzer, who was influenced by Friedrich Naumann's 'national social' programme,[4] held very similar views. Even in the narrower circle around Stauffenberg, there were reflections of this kind; and Wilhelm Ahlmann[5] turned his attention in particular to 'the future of the farming community in an industrialised society'.

The resisters varied in the degree to which they rejected technological and industrial progress. Einsiedel went so far as to warn against large-scale mechanization of agriculture, since it was destroying the seasonally determined rhythm of rural life and its elements of 'tranquility and leisure'. He strongly disapproved of 'turning rural life into an "economy"'; likewise, when Mierendorff's action programme called for the safeguarding of agriculture, he pointed to the danger of it 'becoming a football of capitalist interests'. This in effect meant that the liberal principle of free competition should not apply to the agricultural sector. In general, the view was put forward that the 'landscape' had to be kept free from the pernicious impact of urbanization. Cultural institutions, especially schools, should therefore remain independent and not be adapted to urban conditions. In this way the efforts to improve national education in the 1920s, of which Reichwein was a champion in the Kreisau Circle (see Chapter 10) were taken up again, albeit with an ideological emphasis that is problematic.

The matter at issue was essentially that of keeping the large estates intact. Einsiedel defended this on the ground that large estates encouraged the forming of natural centres in the country. The 'representation of rural values' should be in the hands of independent people of high cultural standing, 'who provide an adequate counterweight to other sections of the population, especially commerce.' On this point, however, opinions diverged. Moltke had broken up and distributed part of his estate and thus exemplified the idea of voluntary renunciation. According to some reports, Stauffenberg had also considered dividing up his estate, an idea that seems to have led to plans for comprehensive land reform. Among the keen advocates of breaking up the great estates were Goerdeler, Trott and Leber. A script for a radio broadcast, which Goerdeler drafted early in 1944, contained the promise that where conditions of ownership had become unviable there should be no compensation from the public purse, and that the 'German people's need to be settled on the land... would if necessary be met at the expense of unhealthily large landed estates'; in a speech intended for broadcasting, Leuschner also called for the dissolution of the great estates. Trott went even further; he was thinking in terms of comprehensive land reform, of 'rural communism', and had a patent dislike of the grandees beyond the Elbe. He made it very clear to Yorck that he rejected the 'whole ducal style'.

The supporters of the status quo were outnumbered by those who urged the creation of an extensive category of medium-sized farms. Significantly, Steltzer argued strongly against the law of inheritance, which favoured the owners of large farms as opposed to medium-sized ones. Moltke reflected on whether, when the time came for demobilization, independent farmers and skilled agricultural employees should be the first to be released from military service. Fritz-Dietlof von der Schulenburg called for a comprehensive resettling of farmers, which he compared to the German colonization of Eastern Europe, without coming out decisively against large landholdings. Although he was not actually hostile to industry, when it came to agricultural policy his thinking was deeply romantic, and he considered how senior officials might be bound to the soil through leasing agricultural property from the state. The sound tradition and close links to the native soil, which Schulenburg thought of as basic conditions for a stable and ordered state, could only be formed over an unbroken succession of generations, and that was something found only in the countryside. His call for farming settlements chimed very closely with Nazi ideology, though it did not really square with the concept of a 'new feudalism', which was not to be driven by the profit-motive but grounded on a sense of public responsibility. We can fairly say that Schulenburg 'dreamed' of a landed élite which was to hold its estates in quasi-feudal fiefdom, and manage them in the service of the whole community. Unfortunately, Schulenburg seems to have been unaware that the Third Reich had successfully adopted the traditional method of securing the loyalty of the ruling class by means of generous land grants, which had begun with the Neudeck estate.[6]

The concrete measures advocated by the resistance were aimed initially at combating the 'flight from the land', particularly since the view was that the rural population should not drop below a certain proportion of the total population. On one hand, the flight from the land was to be stemmed by specific structural improvements – cultivating rural cultural institutions, building homes for farm workers, developing craft skills and protecting small and medium-sized enterprises; on the other hand, farm produce prices were to be raised and agricultural wages brought up to a level with those in the industrial sector. The question of how this could be combined with the concept of an economy based on 'performance' was apparently not discussed in detail. Goerdeler fought energetically against ideas of self-sufficiency but was an equally staunch opponent of state subsidies. He considered the problem would be solved automatically by the levying of tariffs to protect agricultural output and saw no contradiction with his outline plans for closer European economic cooperation. There was a lack of agreement as to how this 'energetic rural policy' could be effected and agriculture's share of the German economy stabilized. Within the framework of their European concept, the Kreisau Circle seem to have been aiming for a European economic community isolated from the world economy and, since the total agricultural output of Europe was lower than corresponding demand, there appeared to be no necessity to limit Germany's farm production.

The overall agricultural policy of the resistance had broadly the same social motives as their programme for regional planning. This programme had the negative aim of combating the concentration of the population in a few industrial conurbations, and the positive one of creating healthy living-conditions through house-building and resettlement. As the writers of a Kreisau economic memorandum stressed: 'Despite the increase of affluence brought by the modern industrial economy,' people were living cheek-by-jowl in dreary industrial suburbs and this hindered a 'healthy national life'. The large-scale destruction of big cities during the war and the displacement of a considerable part of their populations provided the opportunity for comprehensive reform. This was something that Schulenburg in particular strove for – partly in connection with his work at the Reich Ministry of the Interior. Schulenburg thought it was perverse to rebuild the bomb-flattened cities, which had long undergone rampant expansion and had become detached from the healthy foundations of life. The task, he said, could not 'consist in restoring the cities, which physically increase national morbidity, mentally encourage the phenomenon of *Vermassung,* politically increase the opportunities for all kinds of demagoguery and culturally lead to a progressive decline'. Goerdeler also rejected metropolitan culture for biological and intellectual reasons: 'Long-term residence in a big city ruins the family.'

The ideas of the resistance on the measures needed were not original, were often not fully thought through, and frequently were realizable only – if at all – given unrestricted powers of state intervention. They did, however, include a fair number of notions that deserve consideration. This is true of Schulenburg's idea of establishing orbital and satellite-towns and of Goerdeler's proposal to locate administrative headquarters in small and medium-sized towns, in order to pave the way for a decentralizing change of structure. For practical reasons Goerdeler came down against the idea that the cities should only be partially rebuilt, since, in spite of the destruction, the huge investment in sewerage and energy supply had to be fully exploited. He did, however, call for lower housing density, for slum-clearance and for blocks of salubrious apartments to be built for rent. Schulenburg, Goerdeler and Popitz shared the view that the growth of cities should be restricted by banning the location of industrial companies in towns over a certain size (the figures vary between 100,000 and 400,000 inhabitants). Sensible and practical ideas were mixed with unrealistic ones; the idea that the process of urbanization, which had taken place over a century, could be reversed by state intervention, betrayed an inadequate knowledge of the needs of modern industrial production, completely disregarded the interests of those affected and were redolent of paternalism. Schulenburg considered dismembering the industrial giants, while Goedeler wanted to oblige businesses to obtain state approval for taking on more than 100 employees. Both men liked the idea of 'reshaping Germany's heavily industrialized regions along the lines of Württemberg';[7] Schulenburg had attempted to put this into effect in his plan for East Prussia and during his time in Silesia (see Chapter 5) and had in fact introduced successful regional planning measures in the Ruhrgebiet.

The desired structural improvements were to be achieved by government legislation and administration and amounted to an extensive policy for resettlement, house-building and the provision of low-rent local authority accommodation. This was advocated both by the Kreisau Circle and the groups around Goerdeler and can be found in the programme developed by Bergsträsser for Leuschner. Schulenburg considered 'the most important economic and national need' was to build small housing estates for workers, to create 'homes of their own' in a garden setting; Goerdeler, who cared most about these things, looked forward to a new relationship between man and nature, leading to an enhancement of moral and community-building forces. In fact, this programme echoed the planning policy put forward by the Nazi party in 1933 and 1935, which did not, however, get beyond the initial stages and fell victim to accelerated rearmament. Instead of a resettlement and housing programme, the Nazis concentrated on building cheap working-class tenements and autobahns.

In their entirety the proposals sketched out for a structural policy added up to the idea of curbing the unpleasant excrescences of modern industrial society, on one hand by reinforcing a rural community consciously isolated from urban life and on the other by extensive thinning-out of population-centres and the shift of industry and commerce into hitherto predominantly agricultural districts. The desire to avoid, as far as possible, anonymous organizations and vast mass-production plants in the industrial sector, led logically to a proactive policy for smaller businesses. Goerdeler repeatedly drew attention to the damaging consequences of the closure of retail businesses in wartime and stressed that the *Mittelstand* (smaller business owners) were the natural reservoir of top management and hence the most valuable resource a nation could possess. Goerdeler's emphatically middle-class and liberal ideas overlapped with Moltke's concept of 'small, manageable communities' and the creation of a broad stratum of economically secure individuals. Moltke, too, considered measures to protect the small businessman and the skilled craftsman, in a way that was analogous to the agricultural programme. Indeed, the self-government which Goerdeler, Schulenburg and the Kreisau Circle identified as the central pillar of their constitution, presupposed the formation of a new, broad class of 'prominent citizens' (*Honoratiorentum*).

It is worth noting that in debating the questions of regional planning and reconstruction, the groups in the resistance were keen to tackle an urgent set of problems, which the Nazi regime seems scarcely to have given serious thought to. It is indicative of the lack of any guiding principles in Nazi domestic policy, that Schulenburg's memorandum formed the basis of a list of questions which was presented to Popitz and Goerdeler in prison, for them to answer in detail. This probably aroused considerable interest within the Reich Ministry of the Interior. Both the Permanent

Secretary, Stuckart,[8] and his deputy Ehrensberger, had been in very close contact with Schulenburg for years. There is also a good deal of evidence that Himmler himself considered making use of the resistance's proposals. Much is revealed about the internal crisis of the National Socialist system by the fact that it had to have its political plans worked out by its staunchest opponents.

V. Economic and social policy

In the criticism of industrial society there emerged – as is usually the case in the transitional stages of a political crisis – considerable areas of agreement between the different factions. As we have seen in the earlier sections, the Kreisau programme combined conservative reformism with socialist-style thinking. The desired synthesis was expressed by Delp in his term 'personal socialism'. Criticism of mass society came both from the liberal and the *étatiste* sides; the large measure of agreement between Goerdeler's objectives and those of Schulenburg demonstrates this, as does the united front presented by Popitz, Hassell and the Kreisau Circle towards economic liberalism in the traditional sense. The crucial differences lay in how they attributed the defects of an industrial society to liberalism and even saw economic planning as an indirect consequence of liberalism, since it was an attempt to escape the economic anarchy provoked by private capitalism.

The Kreisau Circle drew the same conclusion in blaming liberalism for the triumph of 'purely materialistic notions of utility'. The fundamental right of the state to intervene in the economy was something that Moltke did not question; whether the state took the route of economic freedom, or that of economic compulsion appeared to be a matter of expediency. There was agreement that 'a return to the former economic laxity or even total freedom as advocated by extreme economic theory' was unthinkable. They rejected the complete freedom of the individual in the economic sphere if only because it was incompatible with the 'great and organic tasks of the future'. However, at the same time they came out firmly against any form of 'collectivist' economy, since that destroyed 'the vitality of the individual'. Basically they were looking for an economic model that would lead them between the Scylla of *laissez-faire* and the Charybdis of the planned economy to new structures which, in the words of Günter Schmölders,[1] would connect with the 'layer of the personality and of social awareness that lies above pure materialism'. Schmölders was thinking of a 'system of social advancement', which would elevate 'achievement to be the yardstick of social position, giving entitlement to responsible participation in the formulation of political objectives'. As we shall see, this was a construct that incorporated some of Moltke's ideas, though it drew a distinction, which was difficult to realize in practice, between 'gainful activity' and 'the need for social recognition'.

It was very much the intention of Kreisau to prevent individuals or groups from gaining positions of economic dominance, and to prevent state economic policy from serving particular business interests. Hence, any kind of lobbying was rejected. In pushing through its restructuring plans, and especially comprehensive regional planning, the state was to have considerable powers at its disposal. Nonetheless, it was to achieve its aims predominantly by influencing the economy indirectly with measures of fiscal and economic management. This was entirely in line with Goerdeler's views. In his statement *Das Ziel* ('The Goal') he wrote:

> Overall economic policy must be directed at the strongest possible containment of cartels, syndicates, conglomerates, trusts etc. and their break-up into independent companies, in order to win freedom of action for creative, responsibly-minded individuals.

Goerdeler was determined, just as much as the Kreisau Circle was, to prevent unjustified profit, which was not based on real performance, was made at the expense of the German economy, and harmed the interests of society. Despite his links with Bosch,[2] Goerdeler's attitude towards big industrialists was extremely critical; he repeatedly pointed out their tendency to call for state aid in times of crisis and to abdicate responsibility for the economy as a whole. No one was more severe than Goerdeler in condemning the omnipotence and lack of character among senior executives, whom as a class he viewed somewhat differently from the owners of capital. It is characteristic of him that he was deeply distrustful of anonymous public companies and expressly called for rights of consultation for employees.

Schulenburg's formula, 'Ownership is the mission of all society', was something that Goerdeler could fully subscribe to, and he took for granted the social obligations of ownership. In a speech intended for broadcasting in 1944, he wrote: 'We are determined to deprive capitalism in all its forms of any scope for monopoly and abuse for political or other non-commercial ends.' To that extent Goerdeler considered state intervention to be justified and necessary, but he was convinced that the state had to lead by example with a clear and prudent financial policy. He considered the normal fiscal and financial armoury sufficient to maintain a well-ordered and competitive economy, but rejected any further state economic controls. The Germany economy, he said, would grow and prosper, 'as long as the state or another political union leaves as much risk as possible with the individual and takes as little risk as possible away from him'. However, since Goerdeler contemplated only a gradual dismantling of the Nazi command economy, we cannot say that there were any fundamental differences between his concept and Kreisau's. Both wanted to see an economy built on performance, partial public ownership and with state intervention restricted to indirect means. Even on the supervision of cartels and monopolies there was no difference between them; neither denied the positive role of cartels.

However, in 1943, as Hassell and Gerstenmaier tell us, sharp differences of opinion arose between Goerdeler and the Kreisau Circle on this question as well. Turning things rather on their head, Hassell remarked that Goerdeler was 'a kind of reactionary after all'. In his economic objectives, Goerdeler did not basically differ from the macroeconomic advisers to the Kreisau Circle – Schmölders, Blessing,[3] Abs and von Trotha.[4] It does not explain the growing tensions, which were more to do with terminology. Goerdeler believed that the state had to bow to the 'natural' (i.e. liberal) laws of economic life, whereas Moltke, in clear contrast, thought the state should be 'master of the economy'; yet in their application the two concepts led to very similar results. Although

Popitz and Hassell acted as intermediaries in this dispute and in general supported the Kreisau standpoint, it was an unnatural alliance; for them and for Schulenburg, starting from their pointedly *étatiste* position, far-reaching state socialism was a natural conclusion, though it meant an extremely authoritarian solution.

A compromise was made more difficult by the fact that Goerdeler's interlocutors could scarcely assemble between them any experience of a non-*dirigiste* economy, and thus they seriously overestimated the opportunities for state intervention in the management of an economy based on individual initiative – something that both sides wanted. This revealed a basic contradiction in the Kreisau plans, which lay in the fact that they combined a restriction of the state agenda to the social and political fields with the greatest possible powers for the state in economic matters. On the questions of regional planning, measures for restructuring, the decentralization of industry and not least agricultural policy, which Goerdeler also wanted to protect from the play of free-market forces, there was no essential difference. Gerstenmaier tells us that 'Goerdeler's professorial glossing-over of conflicting views' had a provocative effect; however, Goerdeler was by nature too frank to overplay principled disagreements for tactical reasons; in his view, either such disagreements did not exist or they resulted from his opponents' lack of knowledge of the subject.

On the other hand, the differences between Goerdeler and the representatives of Kreisau in the area of substantive social policy were unbridgeable even at a practical level. Goerdeler objected to the term 'social policy' and wanted to replace it with 'compensation policy'; this was a clear expression of his leanings toward harmonization of social conflicts. He considered existing legislation to be adequate, saw the real task of social policy to be that of improving the structure and opposed social insurance legislation that was too broadly conceived, since it crippled the individual's will to work and led to a false sense of security. On these questions Goerdeler's attitude was extremely dogmatic; he remained essentially wedded to the views he put forward in 1932, which largely corresponded to the policies of the Brüning government.

They were highly paternalistic and hard to reconcile with the rest of his thinking, since they lacked any understanding of the roots of class conflict. In Goerdeler's eyes social policy was a morally requisite 'compensation for hardship', not a deliberate revision of the relationship between capital and labour. His only solution to the economic crisis was to lengthen the working day without any increase in wages. The extent of his political naivety is shown by his proposal that the building of social housing, which he considered necessary, should be set in motion by reducing wages in the construction industry.

Goerdeler's dogmatic reliance on lower wages and longer work-ing hours as a remedy for the unemployment that he considered to some extent inevitable, is shown by his devastating criticism of the New Deal, the Beveridge Plan and the 'Marxist theory' of the eight-hour day, which we find in his *Thoughts of a Condemned Man*.[5] He could only partially be dissuaded from the idea that the workforce should have to fund its own unemployment support scheme. He drafted a complicated and retrograde system whereby the state would be largely relieved of its responsibilities at the expense of the insurance contributors and professional groups. These ideas, which even in the conditions of 1932 were politi-cally unrealistic, explain Goerdeler's attitude to the labour un-ions; even at that time he wished to see a merging of all the un-ions in each different industry or profession, either into 'work communities' (*Arbeitsgemeinschaften*) or self-governing 'guilds' (*Arbeiterberufskammer*) with compulsory membership. He wanted to hand responsibility for social insurance, including unemploy-ment benefit, to these bodies and thereby force them 'consciously to share the burden of the state'.[6]

In this way Goerdeler abandoned even the basic idea of Bismarckian social policy and clung to the notion that social advancement for the working class in modern industrial society was possible in principle, albeit not in the course of a single generation. As his 'economic manual' shows, he saw the remedy in greater economic education of the masses; he shared with Leuschner the view that the ghettoising of the working class was due to their lack of education. This was also the view of Haubach,

Reichwein and Jakob Kaiser. However, the alliance between Leuschner and Goerdeler was a temporary expedient; Leuschner expected, as did the Kreisau Circle, that the transitional cabinet would rapidly work itself into the ground and make way for a 'second wave', which would give the socialists a decisive influence. A compromise was politically unthinkable on insurance matters, on Goerdeler's demand for performance-based pay, i.e. piece-rates, on working hours and on pay policy.

Yorck reacted to Goedeler's ideas on social policy by accusing him of being a 'reactionary'. In return Goerdeler labelled the Kreisau Circle 'drawing-room Bolshevists'. The Kreisau proposals for giving employees a share in the profits and capital growth of their company appeared absurd to Goerdeler, because they ran counter to his basic principle of placing responsibility and reward firmly in the hands of top management. He hesitantly adopted the idea of partial nationalization, but only in the case of the energy sector, since he believed that this could be to a large extent placed under the control of local government. He was more sympathetic to Leuschner's proposal for the creation of union-owned businesses; but said these would have to operate under the same competitive conditions as private industry. At the same time, however, Goerdeler objected to 'unreasonably high returns' on capital and was sharply critical of the attitude of heavy industry prior to 1933. He was a man of the 'bourgeois centre' and was one of the few who, even later on, declared allegiance to the policies and person of Gustav Stresemann, a man whose liberalism coincided exactly with his own. What separated Goerdeler from Stresemann and drew him over to Brüning's side,[7] was the 'unpolitical' nature of his own ideas, which were based on the pragmatic requirements of a return to healthy public finance. This was the origin of the divergence of viewpoints within the resistance. While Goerdeler was fundamentally unable to recognize the conflict between different political and social interests and remained wedded to the notion of a 'conflict-free' order, the Kreisau Circle were thinking in terms of new social order, which relied on keeping antagonistic social interests in check, not allowing them free rein.

VI. Community, leadership and a 'new' élite

It was the interpenetration of state and society, so characteristic of Germany's domestic development, which after 1918 prevented the system of parliamentary democracy from taking root. It then appeared to have been superseded by the National Socialist revolution under the slogan of *Volksgemeinschaft* (German national and racial community). There are two reasons why this interpenetration was crucial in resistance thinking. On the one hand, there was the illusion that it was possible to achieve congruence between public action and conflicting social interests. This illusion had persisted in the political thinking of the Weimar period, culminating in the anti-rationalist constructs of Carl Schmitt, and frequently threw the anti-Nazi plotters back on authoritarian solutions. On the other hand, they saw – though not always very clearly – the need to find social policies that would overcome the undesirable dualism of state and society. A symptom of this was the unsatisfactory attempt by Beck and Goerdeler to develop a theory of 'total politics', which would 'harmoniously' unite *raison d'état* and morality, economic interests and spiritual needs. The conservative opposition to Nazism saw in the principle of the 'unity of party and state' the desired means of breaking down the dualism, but discovered all to soon that the opposition between the state and multi-party government had been replaced by the even less controllable conflict between the state and the Nazi Party.

The idea of re-establishing unity in both the political and so-cial fields dictated the thinking and actions of the majority of the plotters. We can see this from the transcripts of Gestapo interro-gations, in which again and again the motive put forward for re-sisting was that Hitler and the Nazi leadership had breached the principle of *Volksgemeinschaft*. Even before 1933 this term was not only used by the pro-Nazi right but was also adopted by Hit-ler's conservative adversaries. In a memorandum sent to Hitler in 1934, Goerdeler called for the establishment of 'a genuine and clearly defined *Volksgemeinschaft*', and in his statement *The Goal*, he wrote about a 'class-free sense of *Volksgemeinschaft*'. The political aims that this terminology revealed, can be linked to what Ferdinand Tönnies[1] called the recognized difference between 'society' (*Gesellschaft*) and 'community' (*Gemeinschaft*). It is characteristic that the term *Gesellschaft* is used only occasionally, usually by Adam von Trott.

The term 'new community', which we find in Goerdeler's memorandum *Practical Measures for the Reshaping of Europe*, is used in various ways by all groups in the resistance. Schulenburg wished to see Bolshevism and 'parasitic capitalism' defeated in a 'new *Gemeinschaftsordnung* (community structure)'; he characterized the officer corps as 'self-contained, detached and hence a genuine community', which possessed the intellectual and moral force to lead the masses in a consistent manner and to free them from the formless law of the mass. This contrasting of the organic *Gemeinschaft* with amorphous 'mass society', which arose naturally from Schulenburg's Prussian-socialist philosophy, chimed with the thinking of the entire resistance. Steltzer defined politics as 'the work of the community', Gerstenmaier talked of 'naturally-arising forms of community', Yorck and Moltke looked for 'the right form of community within the state' (a form of words which makes clear the problem of dualism) and Leber used the phrase 'new German community'. Reichhold saw the victory of the totalitarian state as nothing less than the revolution of the 'community' against class and concluded from this that the labour movement's answer could no longer be one of 'class politics'; instead, he believed the labour movement had to regard itself as one element of the communal whole, enjoying equal rights with the others.

The concept of 'community' embraced the vision of a natural, graduated order, which presupposed the existence of free and self-sufficient individuals. It rejected absolutely the complete absorption of the individual in the community as demanded by the totalitarian state, as much as it rejected an education designed to achieve intellectual and ideological uniformity. The concept was based on the idea of an organically structured society whose unity was determined by historical precedent. It led to a firm rejection of class polarization, but also of any kind of social pluralism. There was an idea that it should be possible to reconcile divergent interests 'harmoniously' in the political sphere by means of sensible social and political structures and at the same time break down the dualism of state and society. Yorck was rather imprecisely adopting Kantian concepts when he formulated this idea in the following way: 'We will have achieved the right kind of community within the state, when our understanding of its inherent function is so strong and uniform that we only need to resort to ethical considerations as a corrective.'

A community requires leadership – and it is perfectly logical that the question of selecting leaders and developing an elite should occupy a central place in anti-Nazi thinking. 'Germany's problem,' Stelzer stated in 1944, 'is exclusively one of leadership.' The catastrophe of Nazism, he said, could be ascribed to the lack of a responsible ruling class. The experience of the Weimar Republic had left its mark, as had the idea, very common in the 1920s, of a personal *Führer* (both a 'leader' and a 'guide' *Tr.*) This was true even among socialists. In the 1930s Mierendorff had turned 'against a system of democratic formalities, which opens the door wide to the political interests of powerful pressure-groups, and thus provides neither strong government nor genuine self-government and co-determination by the people'. Haubach believed that 'our movement must learn to realise that ceremonial, command and firm leadership are in no way undemocratic'. Leber wanted to see a 'statesmanlike personality as leader', whose ethos and inner faith were, he was convinced, the roots of genuine authority.

The members of the anti-Nazi opposition were agreed in their diagnosis that the lack of personal leaders and of a will to lead had been the cause of Germany's downfall. Beck's study of Ludendorff was fundamentally concerned with this problem. Goerdeler's favourite historical theme was the failure of political leadership in Germany since the departure of Bismarck. Schulenburg joined the Nazi Party because he believed 'party politics' to be the opposite of genuine political leadership. Steltzer spoke specifically of the failure of the 'old ruling class', including the military, and traced this back to the same causes that had contributed to *Vermassung*. Goerdeler complained of 'the degrading of political leadership from universality into improvised regional and specialist subdivisions'. This he explained by the ill-defined allocation of responsibilities in Bismarck's imperial constitution and by the inadequate imposition of leadership in the Weimar Republic. Goerdeler was an advocate of the presidential system and was proposed by Brüning to succeed him as Reich Chancellor. As an adviser to President Hindenburg, Goerdeler had argued in favour of a time-limited Enabling Law, and as late as 1941 he stressed the 'sound idea of dictatorially imposing common sense for brief periods'.

At root, this criticism of the failure of Weimar cabinets went deeper, and in this Goerdeler stood for the vast majority of the plotters. He blamed the parliamentary principle and democracy – as he understood them – for the decline of personal leadership in politics. In 1932 he objected to the 'continual disruption of national politics by the provincial parliaments'. He demanded that Prussia be placed under the direct rule of the Reich President 'and his ministers', and declared that the original function of the provincial parliaments had been 'supervisory'. He disparaged democracy as 'rule by the masses', and said that Britain did not represent a true democracy, since the voting system made it possible for a minority party to form the cabinet. But at the same time he talked about how, in Britain too, great leaders were becoming a rarity, attributing this to the 'democratisation' of the state, which brought with it ' a serious diminution of the sense of responsibility, an increase in personal vanity and a growing need for instant popularity'. For Goerdeler, leadership was built on 'trust'. From the standpoint of the successful Chief Burgomaster that he was, he never asked himself the question of how such 'trust' arises; but at all events he doubted that elections were necessary to achieve it. 'We need the stabilizing influence of government leadership that is not dependent on elections,' he wrote in a memorandum entitled *Tasks of Germany's Future.*

In spite of his preoccupation with the problems of leadership in the Wilhelmine era, Goerdeler did not confront the question of how a system should be devised for getting able and responsible individuals into key positions. In this respect he was no exception. Max Weber's work on the necessity of the parliamentary selection of leaders was unknown to the men – with the exception of Leber – who were labouring over a new German constitution. 'It is just a matter of putting the right people in the top positions' – this inept answer to the central problem of the modern constitutional state was characteristic of the prevailing mentality. For Schulenburg, Hassell and Popitz, the natural source of leadership was the higher civil service. Schulenburg, though a pioneering opponent of bureaucracy, thought at least for a time about deliberately turning the civil service into the base for the selection of leaders and to remodel it on the 'shock-troop commander of the Great War'. Almost all the constitutional plans provided for the exclusion of civil servants from the right to stand for election, a fact that reflects an aversion to having a civil service politicised along party lines. Political organizations of all kinds, not just the Nazi Party, were to be prevented from using their patronage in the appointment of civil servants. Goerdeler stood by the demand he had first made in 1932, that the civil service 'should be more firmly depoliticised, just as the Reichswehr was'.

The qualifications required of the governing class were non-political competence, practical expertise and good character. Evidence of this is found in the theoretical discussions between Moltke and Yorck on the question of what a 'statesman' ought to be like – the term 'politician' was never used. Goerdeler did not modify this model when proposing successful local politicians as the preferred candidates for the leadership role. It was his opinion, and that of Steltzer and many others, that local politics was the sphere of practical decision-making and should as far as possible be kept free of the confusing and harmful influence of prestige-hungry political parties. This conception was very much based on Brüning's policy of 'functionalism' (*Sachlichkeit*), and on memories of Baron vom Stein,[2] to whom we will return later. Yet it also contained a contradiction, since both local officials and state civil servants had to be independent of party politics, but at the same time they were expected to display the political qualities of high reputation and trustworthiness, a gift for leadership and critical political judgement. Indeed, Goerdeler lacked a deeper understanding of the workings of central government administration, which was not at all comparable with local government. He thus failed to appreciate the difference between bureaucratic administration and political leadership. We can tell this from the disputes which arose when he joined the second Price Commission, from his calls for the merging of ministries, his criticism of the specialization of administration and his proposal to introduce permanent (specialist) secretaries in ministries, alongside non-permanent personal secretaries to the ministers.

Peculiar to the constitutional thinking of the resistance – again with the exception of Leber – was the view that the plebiscitary component of the modern constitutional state was a sign of degeneracy and was leading – as the example of Hitler seemed to prove – to 'rule by the inferior'. That this slogan, coined by Edgar Jung,[3] applied not only to the National Socialist system but to all forms of parliamentary selection of leaders, is shown by the fact that it was used against the Weimar Republic. However, there were considerable differences of principle on the best way to solve the problem of creating an elite. The group around Popitz and Hassell had no doubt about the mission of the old upper class, from which this group came; and even Goerdeler, who thought on less aristocratic lines, joined in Hassell's repeated complaints that Nazi propaganda pursued the nobility and the upper class with downright hatred. In 1934 Popitz gave an address to the Wednesday Club,[4] in which he expressed the view that it was necessary to establish a governing class. This, together with the criticism of the Nazi 'smear-campaign' against the nobility and intelligentsia, and no doubt also Stauffenberg's view that the historical achievements of the aristocracy should be respected, represented an unmistakable leaning towards the restoration of a socially and politically dispossessed ruling class. Schulenburg, the 'Red Count', was no exception to this; as late as 1941 he was talking about the aristocracy's 'right to exist' as a governing class and he remained an advocate of a historically rooted elite, even if it meant creating one artificially through new land ownership. The Popitz-Hassell group were certainly in favour of openly building an elite, whatever that might mean in practice. In this there is no difference between them and the mainstream of neo-conservative thinking, which rejected the demand for equality of class, whether based on profession or birth.

The Kreisau Circle was diametrically opposed to such ideas, and emphasized the total failure of the old upper class. For that reason they firmly rejected the inclusion of Popitz in any future cabinet. However, Moltke and Yorck were markedly aristocratic in their thinking and it was significant that Yorck talked to Count Alexander Stauffenberg about the historic guilt of the elite for having ignored the social question. Moltke and Yorck were opposed to acquired rights and came closer to the idea of an 'open elite', which was to have intellectual rather than social foundations. Dietrich Bonhoeffer accurately described Kreisau's conception of itself in the following way:

> In the midst of widespread standardization of people's material and spiritual circumstances, the appreciation of the human qualities of uprightness, achievement and courage, which cuts across all social strata today, could provide a new way of selecting the kind of people who are actually entitled to provide strong leadership.

He added, a little acidly, that 'given the justice of history' it would be 'no trouble' to dispense with the privileges of power.

There is no disputing the fact that the Kreisau Circle's plans for a new social order were on weak ground when it came to the institutional implementation of such ideas. They contained many elements that were socially utopian. Yorck and Moltke dreamed of a global elite, of a situation in which 'party loyalties and splits among the people of the planet are only of secondary importance, because the members of one particular party' would be thoroughly committed to the same values as all the others and 'on essential points even enemies would agree'. Psychologically, such a notion can only be explained by the fact that Kreisau was an outlawed group, intellectually isolated and cut off from the outside world. Nonetheless, it was a crucial element in their thinking. In the same spirit, Steltzer complained that the intellectual elite had lost its way and had declined into a society 'whose destruction we are now experiencing'. He hoped for a worldwide class of individuals who would be 'imbued with a new, holistic view of the world and of mankind'. Bonhoeffer echoed this when he talked about 'the birth of a new, noble attitude that unites in one group people from all previous levels of society'.

The Kreisau plans for a new elite were, despite their strongly utopian character, one component of an overall political concept. Initially they reflected the self-image of the Kreisau Circle, which endeavoured to claim legitimacy as the ruling class in its dealings with foreign governments and planned to take charge in Germany in the event of a successful coup. Although Kreisau spent some time thinking about the personnel of a possible government, this was not to be a cabinet in the regular sense, but a trusteeship of the state, in which the terms *Reichsverweser* and *Landesverweser* are found (roughly 'regent' and 'provincial governor' *Tr.*). The constitutional plans say nothing about the relationship between this elite and the political leadership; doubtless the task of the elite was to permeate political and social life both intellectually and spiritually and to represent the conscience of the nation. This was all the more reason for them not to lay themselves open to the suspicion of going after the top political posts.

In very much the same spirit, Haubach proposed creating a 'Council of Elders' made up of personalities who had never played or had ceased to play a part in politics. The task of this council would be to oversee the proper conduct of public affairs. This shows how strong and lasting was the fundamentally apolitical influence of the Youth Movement of the early twentieth century. We are told that among the men around Stauffenberg there had been talk of how 'those in active leadership required the assistance in their deliberations and actions, not of people wedded to office, but of independent minds, of the sort that former rulers of vision frequently gathered around them'. Though Stauffenberg himself may have thought in more realistic terms, it emerges nonetheless that the obsessive German rejection of 'political horse-trading' and longing for a 'supra-political' wisdom in government, continued to exert quite an influence on the resistance.

At the same time, the social utopianism of this concept of a ruling elite is derived from Kreisau's strongly religious orientation.

It presupposed a general Christian revival, comparable to the nationalist awakening of European peoples in the early nineteenth century. It required people to become aware once more of their transcendental commitments. In other words it meant the return to an image of humanity as it had been in Europe before the dissolution of Christendom through secularisation, individualism, the modern state and the undermining of the traditional European economic structure by liberalism and capitalism.

In this connection, Bonhoeffer, Schönfeld,[5] Gerstenmaier and Trott arranged contacts with the world church organizations and Reichwein and Poelchau[6] proposed a 'German Christian Community' to overcome sectarian antagonisms. Steltzer strove to fill out the concept of 'fraternity' with political substance. In doing so he indicated the twin functions of the elite: on the one hand to provide an intellectual lead while not being beholden to any institution; on the other to be a force in shaping the practical political will of the nation. Behind this was the theory of a social order which integrated and gave meaning to all the divergent political interests and currents of thought – a theory which derived both from the German idealist tradition and the Catholic doctrine of natural law.

It was through Moltke's programme of 'small communities' that this concept of an elite was to be put into practice. Even outside the administrative sector there was to be as large a number as possible of spontaneously forming communities which would play a part in the creation of the elite. These 'small, manageable' communities were to grow out of the 'naturally occurring ties between individuals'. Linked to the family, parish and home district, to occupation and workplace, they would not be formed in a 'mechanical, artificial' way, nor would they be 'top-down' organizations, but would be groups assembling from below in a spirit of subsidiarity. They would be characterized by a willingness to share public responsibility and to serve the common good, each in their specific area of activity. Moltke originally thought of granting political privileges to the 'small communities' and their members and considered making the right to vote and stand for election, as well as admission to public office, dependent on activity that promoted community development – e.g. in work camps, social institutions, parish and church administration, co-operatives, study-groups, universities and school associations. In the early stages there would be no freedom of assembly and association except within the framework of the small communities.

Moltke did not underestimate the practical difficulties standing in the way of the realization of these ideas. Which kinds of communities were to be recognized and through which organ of the state should this recognition be articulated? These proved to be insoluble problems, particularly since Moltke intended to equip the communities with extensive rights, including that of levying taxes, as well as the functions of policing and supervision, and even the right to use force against their members. He even had the idea of granting political privileges to members of communities who had rendered service for the public good and giving them 'special advantages in formulating the political programmes of higher bodies'. However, this ran into the inherent contradiction that any kind of formal procedure removed the spontaneous nature of 'small communities' and turned them into institutionalized channels for political demands. However, these reflections of Moltke's were by no means peripheral, as can be seen from the fact that Goerdeler – wanting perhaps to be seen as 'pulling in the same direction' – adopted these ideas himself: 'As in the election of workers' representatives in a factory, groups which distinguish themselves by outstanding reliability and achievement, must be recognized through a qualified voting right.' However, he added that this must not lead to 'preferment in wealth, education and examination results' and that reliability and performance alone should provide the basis of privilege.

What characterized proposals of this kind was not only the implied rejection of an egalitarian society, but most of all the contradiction between the idea of an 'open elite' and its institutional sanctioning. It was obvious that the 'principle of reliability and achievement' would rapidly be replaced by traditional and socially-based sources of legitimation. Even if Moltke did not really intend this, such a concept was bound to lead to misunderstandings. It is therefore unsurprising that

Hermann Maass, a socialist, gained the impression that the 'Group of Counts' and Moltke in particular intended to work for 'the restoration and retention of the privileges of particular, socially restricted group of individuals.' The preferment of an elite which was intended to be set well apart socially, was not only impossible to achieve in practice, but questionable in principle. This was because such preferment required regulation by the state, which was supposed to build *itself* up from those groups provisionally vested with sovereign rights. Furthermore it meant using constitutional regulation to compel the citizen to act for the common good.

Nonetheless, there was something tempting in Moltke's concept. It was related to the idea of replacing the European nation-states by a wealth of smaller territorial units, some of them multinational in character. Europe was to be transformed into a federation of 'self-governing bodies with historic origins', so that the problem of hegemony that had disturbed the peace of Europe over the centuries would disappear. However, the dismembering of the German nation-state, which would result from this, met with opposition in the Kreisau Circle, especially from Delp, Gerstenmaier, Steltzer and van Husen. The struggle that arose over this can be seen in the wording of the *Grundsätze* ('Principles'): 'The Reich[7] *remains* the supreme ruling power of the German people.' It is noticeable that in Moltke's plan federalism and the principle of local autonomy came to mean the same thing and, as with the Kreisau project as a whole, the difference between local autonomy and the democratic formulation of political demands became blurred. These proposals amount, on the one hand, to an extensive undermining of central state authority, very much in line with the socialist idea of a society managing its own affairs; on the other hand they represent a highly progressive attempt to use institutions to bind pluralistic social forces into the natural hierarchies of human society. In this way a potential threat to the existing order would be transformed into a stabilizing force. Moltke's concept was in some respects a conservative variant of the idea of government by 'soviet',[8] a combination of direct democracy and the principle of elitism. The 'godfathers' of this notion were nostalgic for a self-confident Prussian nobility, who considered themselves as equals to the state, indeed as its true pillars, together with the fundamental anti-liberalism of the 'romantic' doctrine of the state.

Moltke protested against the misconception that his intention was to 'atomise' the body politic, and he emphatically opposed 'any weakening of central authority in its own spheres', such as that of economic planning. But this meant that his concept came up against the same dilemma that socialism had been unable to resolve: the contradiction between local political autonomy and economic centralization. Moltke certainly hoped that, by decentralization and local autonomy on the one hand, and the formation of locally-rooted elites on the other, it would be possible to counteract the pernicious omnipotence of the state, whose unjustifiable endowment with moral qualities he saw as the fundamental evil of the German political tradition. 'Once the state is given a moral personality, then in my view we are on the road that leads through Hegel to the deification of the state.' Hence Moltke considered it extraordinarily dangerous to give the state 'a religious explanation and a religious underpinning'. He wanted the state to be regarded essentially as an amoral institution, in order that 'no one shall attempt to hide behind the state'. Consistent with this, he called for the complete separation of Church and State. Thus he even attempted to convince Cardinal Faulhaber[9] that the 1933 Concordat between Hitler and the Vatican should be revoked.

Moltke rejected any form of recognition of the state as an end in itself. His professional position (as legal adviser to the Wehrmacht Supreme Command) gave him an insight into how the authorizing of terrorism by the Nazis was based on the arrogation of legality for state action – 'the persistent illusion of the authoritarian state'. In turning away from the Lutheran concept of the state, Moltke differed fundamentally from Goerdeler who, it is true, also spoke of the 'poison of state-deification' that had taken hold of the German people. However, Goerdeler saw in the state a divinely imposed order, but at the same time stressed: 'The state is not an end in itself, but a means to provide the citizen with welfare and an ordered life.' Despite his occasionally authoritarian and paternalistic tendencies, Goerdeler's position was fundamentally different from those of Hassell, Popitz, Schulenburg and Beck. These men remained trapped in a philosophy of the authoritarian state. Hassell talked about a 'state-conscious Germany', while Schulenburg raised 'Prussia's continuing claim on the Reich'. Popitz voiced the conviction that the German state must be a '*Vollstaat*' ('a state in the fullest sense'), which 'holds all essential elements of governmental life firmly in its hands'.

In the three different philosophies found in the resistance, the differing attitudes to the state were matched by different ideas on the composition of the ruling stratum in the event of the Nazi regime being successfully overturned. Hassell, Popitz, Beck and Schulenburg clung to the existing elite, committed to maintaining the state; Goerdeler wanted to transfer the ordering of society and government to a class of trustworthy citizens trained in the relevant forms of communal and public administration; and the Kreisau Circle wanted to create a new intellectual aristocracy drawn from all social strata, which would be bound together by a shared set of fundamental values. The outline constitutions and objectives of the individual resistance groups were determined by how they envisaged an elite, qualified to exercise power. They were anxious to replace mass society with a form of 'community', whose social hierarchy would give expression to the 'values of personality', and they opposed the formation of political demands by plebiscitary means. Instead they proposed a system for forming elites by various institutional channels. In this we can distinguish conservative positions from those which were specifically reactionary.

VII: From the National Socialist *Führer*-state to a fascist-authoritarian monarchy

The constitutional proposals of the German resistance movement were founded on a rejection of the Weimar 'system' – a fact that demonstrates how completely Germany's first republic was discredited. The parliamentary system was seen as a 'western' import; and the 'party state' with its plebiscitary character had apparently led directly to dictatorship. Hence, the constitutional drafts by the resistance looked back to the nineteenth century, especially to the thinking of Baron vom Stein, which they re-interpreted in an 'organicist' and nationalist sense. But the resisters differed from Stein in the emphasis they placed on the *étatiste*, liberal and conservative elements in the historical tradition that began with the Prussian reforms. Over time, the retrograde and authoritarian plans took precedence; the basic ideas of the groups responsible for those plans did not alter significantly, even though apparent compromises were reached between the individual factions within the resistance.

The constitutional plan worked out in the summer of 1938 by Oster, Schulenburg and Friedrich Heinz[1] provided for the restoration of a 'German monarchy'. It combined a *völkisch* and nationalist agenda with Prusso-German socialism and no doubt owed something to Friedrich Naumann's concept of a 'democratic imperium (*Kaisertum*)'. The constitutional programme which Erich Kordt and Hasso von Etzdorf developed in late 1939 also had traits of extreme authoritarianism. It called for a 'governmental structure which reflects decency, probity and the true Prussian tradition', provided for 'participation by the people in the formation of public policy', 'as befits the free German male' and strove for a 'just and genuinely German (Prussian) socialism', as well as a 'Christian and moral renewal'. The state's adherence to the rule of law was to be guaranteed by means of a *habeas corpus* act. Significantly, the problem of effective control of state power was not raised.

Not long afterwards, those proposals were supplemented by a memorandum from the group within the *Abwehr*, which took is-sue with the political arrangements to be introduced following the coup d'état. In it a lawyer named Etscheid refers to the need for 'true authority', which was to replace Hitler's demand for 'blind obedience' by the people. He professes the view that the 'surviv-ing strata of the middle class' and also 'all workers and employees formerly organized in non-communist unions' would themselves have to accept tough and perhaps unwelcome decisions, so as to ensure that 'our people, along with 180 million Bolsheviks, are not thrown into the melting-pot of further political and social experimentation'. The masses, he claimed, were gradually becoming aware that the National Socialist system had run onto the rocks, after having put up with it on the understanding that 'the collapse which followed the 1914–18 war could only be remedied by very active self-discipline and strict organization, which other politicians, parties and movements had failed to provide'. There was 'a vague feeling that the democratic and parliamentary institutions of other countries did not represent an appropriate system of government for the German people'. On the other hand 'the absolute dictatorship of one individual, or of a narrow and completely isolated group', was not capable of solving either domestic or external problems. 'This has inevitably led to an awareness of the need for conservative institutions and methods to uphold the state – a realization which often finds drastic expression in demanding the heavy but just truncheon of Friedrich Wilhelm.'[2]

This call for a restoration of the monarchy was based on a questionable analysis of the mood of the masses. It illustrates how far the resistance group in the *Abwehr* was trapped in class-based thinking and beholden to the governmental tradition of Prussia, which excluded any affection for the Republic. Their general political stance was characterized by emphatic anti-communism, which explains their acceptance of the Hitler regime in the early years. It was the reason why Etscheid concluded that, given a few days' access to the mighty German propaganda machine, it would be easy to show the German people that there was no other course of action open 'but to adopt a belligerent stance against Bolshevism'. This was consistent with their equating of Nazism and Bolshevism, mentioned earlier. Recognizing this situation, the memorandum goes on, the population would be ready to accept 'a strict, even disagreeable authority', provided it guaranteed justice and 'security of existence'. The general staff, and especially Halder, regularly argued that the popular mood was not yet ripe for a revolution. This was countered in the *Abwehr* memorandum by the assertion that, while 'a broad popular movement was certainly preferable to a "top-down" revolution', the former assumed military setbacks which would necessarily put pressure on 'the military leadership now at the height of its power and standing'. This in turn would mar the internal and external conditions for a coup d'état. In Etscheid's view it was necessary to act without reference to current popular opinion. In general they could, he said, count on ' the willingness of the masses to accept the decisions of men acting responsibly in such exceptional circumstances.' It should also be possible 'to use propaganda skills to present the motives and objectives of their action as being in the interest and therefore in the name of the people as a whole'. 'The tough determination of the intervention would be recognised even by those opposed to it as proof of [our] sense of authority and qualities of leadership.'

In this way the dilemma over whether a coup should be attempted was glossed over. There was now a clear presumption about the attitude of the people, but considerable resistance was anticipated, which could probably be defeated only by a strict, authoritarian system. Beck was of the same opinion when he later said that 'we should not let ourselves be too influenced by responding to moods among the people'. It was, Beck said, appropriate to 'take over considerable parts of what has been created by the National Socialist state in its restructuring process and to secure them for the long term'. This was in line with the draft constitution produced shortly afterwards by Hassell, which contained the proposal that Nazi institutions such as the NSV (*Nationalsozialistische Volkswohlfahrt*, a national welfare organization) the Labour Service, the German Labour Front and the industrial federations should be retained, at least in principle. This meant a partial recognition of the *Gleichschaltung* (Nazification) of society that had been achieved by the Nazi regime. Furthermore, the statement that this would bring about a 'synthesis of hitherto divergent forces' represents a fundamental rejection of the plural interests and party politics in favour of a state-sponsored unity of social forces.

The same memorandum also adduced foreign-policy considerations to justify a 'conservative governance'. This can be attributed to Hassell, who believed he had discovered that British foreign policy favoured a conservative system and the establishment of a constitutional monarchy in Germany. The draft constitution which Hassell submitted in January/February 1940, in consultation with Beck, Popitz and Goerdeler, did not expressly provide for a restoration of the monarchy. However, its vesting of executive powers in a three-man regency council certainly pointed to a solution of that kind. 'A monarchy is very desirable, but is something only to be dealt with in the second act,' Hassell stated in late February 1940. He was following Popitz who, as Hassell remarks, 'initially wanted to postpone' the monarchy question. Goerdeler, on the other hand, was all for being frank about this. The programme was probably also supported by Schacht,[3] Oster and Witzleben, though the initiative came from Popitz.

Hassell's programme expressly limited the transitional solution, which would apply only until such time 'as it will be possible to rebuild a normal constitutional life', but it is pretty clear that this did *not* mean a restoration of parliamentary democratic institutions. The constitutional council to be put in place by the regency would be given the task of 'restructuring the German unitary state in both its political and economic aspects with special regard to historical precedent; and to guarantee participation by the people in the political life of the nation (*Reich*) and the control of the workings of the state on the basis of local and corporate self-government'. In an age of popular sovereignty the formulation 'participation by the people' (*eine Mitarbeit des Volkes*) was notable for its reticence. Indeed a central parliament was not envisaged; Hassell talked of 'control of the life of the state through some kind of body based on the professions (*irgendein berufständisch gegründetes Organ*)'. He called the system envisaged 'an organic and legally constituted state with controls'.

We can be reasonably clear about the genesis of the draft constitution. It was predominantly the work of Hassell and Popitz. Hassell noted: 'Popitz and I always in agreement.' Goerdeler's proposal that a referendum should be held after the coup was energetically rejected by both men. Popitz, in particular, called for 'immediate reform of the Reich', in other words the implementation of his highly centralizing programme, which we find in the instruction to dismiss the provincial governors (*Reichstatthalter*) and transfer executive powers in the provinces

(*Länder*) to the local military commanders.[4] It was Hassell who pointed out 'the necessity to build the state on local and corporate self-government (the "filter system")'. Shortly before this he had developed the idea in an article about 'Stein's organic ideas on government'. In this the whole vexed question of the 'Stein renaissance' in the German resistance becomes clear. The constitution was to take account of the uniqueness of Germany's historical development. In a memorandum which Hassell wrote a little later, on a new order for Europe, he established the principle that 'effective control of state power by the people [must be] in a form appropriate to the nation in question'. Similarly Popitz insisted that 'German tradition founded on "Christian morality"' should serve as their 'lodestar'.

The draft constitution is notable for its proposals for the reform of the professional civil service, which were directed primarily against the Nazi Party. However, it retained the original tenor of the law on professional civil servants, the reduction of the influence of political parties and the rejection of a political bureaucracy. It is no coincidence that there was no mention of the forming of political parties or associations; on the other hand, in connection with control of the written word, there was a return to the all-too-familiar formula 'protection of state and people', with a characteristic change of emphasis. On the subject of press freedom we read that after the war 'new regulations' would be introduced 'on the basis of press freedom in the context of national security.' It is very clear that the programme planned early in 1940, for an overthrow of the Nazi regime, contained no elements that would enable the German state to become a democracy headed by a monarch on the British model. A guarantee of future general elections was also missing. The draft constitution meant a retreat from the principle of parliamentary democracy and could only have been imposed with the open use of political force. Goerdeler was closely involved in its development, but as we shall see, his ideas differed fundamentally from those of Hassell and Popitz, even if at times the men were in formal agreement as to their intention. The programme of early 1940 was not a realistic alternative to Hitler; it would have amounted to a military dictatorship on the lines of the illusions prevailing in 1934.

This verdict also applies to later drafts by the same group, especially Popitz' 'Law on the restoration of regularity to government and legal affairs'. This is closely linked to Hassell's 'programme' and in its substance goes back to the discussions of 1939/40. This document, too, promised an order that befitted the nature and history of the German people, and the 'involvement of people at every level of society' in establishing a definitive constitution. This suggests representation of different professions and occupational groups, and government that had to be 'close to the people', to use a phrase which cropped up later on. It also shows the very conservative nature of the system of government that the Popitz group aspired to. Unlike the 1940 'programme' it does not prejudge the future constitution, other than to give an assurance that that once the general livelihood of the German people had been put on a firm footing, 'the creation of a system of *broadly-based* popular representation' was envisaged – in other words, one not based on the principle of universal suffrage.

The draft was described as a 'Provisional Basic State Code', a title which indicates it was intended to be fairly permanent, and by no means a short-term, transitional set of regulations for the months following a coup d'état. It contains measures for the appointment *and* dismissal of the Reich Chancellor and provides for the appointment of members of a Council of State, 'for a term of five years'. This basic state code predetermined many constitutional questions in a *de facto* manner and was only transitional in the sense that it kept the door open for a restoration of the monarchy and offered the prospect of a final constitution. The provisions it contained were reminiscent of a state of emergency, yet they would represent normality for years ahead, while circumstances immediately following the coup would be regulated by actual emergency legislation to be passed at the same time. The draft has rightly been described as 'absolutist'; not only does it provide for the ruthless imposition of central authority and a general ban on political assemblies, but it contains a general clause to the effect that every German must act in such a way that he 'does not harm the common good nor impugn the honour and good name of Germany.' This clause is situated in the context of the necessity to avert 'external influences' and 'internal subversion' and may have been adopted by an able jurist, as Popitz himself was. The clause cancels out the introductory guarantee of a series of basic rights, which in any case did *not* include freedom of assembly, privacy of correspondence or telephone conversations, freedom of expression or freedom of the press. In contrast to Hassell's programme, research, teaching and practice of the arts are only restricted to the extent 'required by internal and external security and the reverence due to the intellectual and moral assets of the nation'. Their borrowings from the Nazi regime were not merely in terminology, as can be seen from the fact that the cleaning-up of the civil service was to be carried out 'by appropriate application of the law of 7 April 1933 on professional civil servants'. True, the sections of the German civil service law relating to Adolf Hitler and the Nazi Party were to be repealed. However, the provisions governing the treatment of Jews and 'sound heredity' would only be suspended 'pending definitive regulation'.

The Basic State Code gives unlimited powers to the *Reichsverweser* (Regent) as 'head of state'. True, the Regent requires the counter-signature of the Reich Chancellor or the responsible departmental minister; on the other hand he appoints the Reich Chancellor in consultation with the Reich government, and ministers in consultation with the Reich Chancellor. The Regent is also commander-in-chief of the armed forces and takes direct responsibility for financial policy. He presides over the Council of State, whose members are appointed by him from names put forward by the Reich Chancellor. As a rule the Council of State is allowed to express its view on bills before they are passed, but has no right of resolution, and is very similar to the 'Greater German Senate' proposed by Hitler's Minister of the Interior, Wilhelm Frick. Thus the system proposed is a dictatorship with the 'sweetener' of assurances about the rule of law. It is a '*völkisch Führer*-state' without Hitler. There can be no doubt that the draft constitution corresponds fully to Popitz' fundamental position and cannot be explained as a tactical response to an exceptional situation. Popitz was a fierce opponent of universal suffrage. He fought with determination against the party state, and consciously supported a presidential system as a means of defeating parliamentary government. All this, and his demand for a non-elected second chamber, placed him on the extreme right even before 1933.

In this context its is of particular significance that Popitz, like Carl Schmitt, to whom he repeatedly referred, fiercely rejected any form of pluralism or 'polycracy', as he called it. In a lecture to the Wednesday Club in the spring of 1933 he welcomed National Socialism as 'defeating pluralistic forces tied to material interests' and hoped for the emergence of a 'ruling class, founded on knowledge and a sense of responsibility, committed to and serving the people'. He was in favour of a constitutional structure which suited the individual nature of the German people. His 'social' attitude, as he himself stressed, was basically defensive. At any rate he remained trapped in the erroneous Bismarckian belief that the workers could be pacified with social welfare instead of equality of political rights. He rejected Goerdeler's programme of industry-wide labour unions, because he saw in them – with some justification – 'a power-centre of the first order', a 'state within the state'. To the last moment before his arrest in October 1944, he went on warning Stauffenberg about Goerdeler's plans. His intervention in favour of workplace-based unions was a tactical move; he was really thinking in terms of solutions modelled on those of the Third Reich, but he was in favour of the Kreisau programme of profit-sharing for employees. The tax policy that Popitz was considering was aimed at raising the living standard of the lower sections of society.

Though opposed to any form of federalism, Popitz accepted a certain degree of self-government. However, he was not prepared to follow Goerdeler's programme completely. It is significant that Goerdeler's demand for the abolition of the executive presidency (*Regierungspräsident*), led to strong personal animosity between the two men. We can be sure that Popitz was not simply protecting himself when he told the Gestapo that a rigorous unitary state was necessary 'to counteract internationalism, the 'judification' of the Weimar era and the intolerable series of crises caused by parliamentary parties'. In the foreign policy sphere, too, his mindset was comparable with that of the Nazis. He talked about Germany's 'mission' in central Europe and called for a 'nationally homogeneous people, imbued with a sense of community'. His political position cannot therefore be described simply as 'tradition-orientated'. As his contacts with Himmler show, Popitz wanted to make use of the 'Praetorian Guard' of the Third Reich. Hence, Kreisau firmly excluded him as potential member of a post-Nazi cabinet, whereas Goerdeler put his personal differences to one side and wanted to bring Popitz into the post-coup government, because of his practical qualifications.

VIII. The constitutional plans of Carl Goerdeler and the Kreisau Circle

The constitutional plans of Popitz, Hassell and, in the early years, Beck reinforced the governing role of the existing upper class, in as far as its members were not clearly compromised by executive participation in the crimes of the Nazi regime. There was absolutely no provision for a democratic choice of those who were to govern. Alongside these, the two most important draft constitutions produced by the German resistance were Goerdeler's detailed constitutional plan and the Kreisau Circle's 'Principles for the New Order'. In their social policy, both expressed specific objectives. The genesis of Goerdeler's plan can be traced in numerous extant memoranda. These differ in detail and enable us to recognize the influence of various political factions within the resistance; they can, nevertheless, be seen as an integrated model that is clearly distinguishable from the proposals of Popitz and Hassell.

Goerdeler's plan, first developed in his document of late 1941 entitled *The Goal*, was based on contacts he had already had, through Hassell, with Trott, Yorck and Moltke, whereas his closer links with Leuschner did not come about until after *The Goal* had been written. Goerdeler submitted it early in 1942 to the Hassell group and apparently won the approval of Beck (whose thinking he had adopted in some areas). However, Hassell himself rejected it as 'doomed to failure in its attempt to nullify a *fait accompli*' [i.e. the Nazi experiment. *Tr.*] and saw it as a kind of 'reaction'. This made sense to the extent that Goerdeler was not prepared to take over the institutions of the authoritarian *Führer*-state without question, but wanted, as Popitz and Hassell saw it, to return to 'parliamentary' forms. Thus, particular authoritarian traits in Goerdeler's constitutional model can be attributed to his wish to adapt to that group's ideas, but it should be stressed that to a great extent Goerdeler broke free from their 'reactionary' thinking.

The 'Principles for the New Order' arose out of the first and second Kreisau conferences. Drafted by Moltke, they can be traced in particular to the ideas of Stelzer, Yorck, Trott, Delp and Moltke himself. They do not contain any detailed draft constitution and can be interpreted in different ways. However, they have to be seen as founded on the social policy ideas already sketched out by the Kreisau Circle. Like Goerdeler's plan, they rely on suppressing the egalitarian components of the democratic system and strongly emphasize the principles of subsidiarity and self-government, as well as shifting political initiative to the manageable sphere of autonomous local communities.

The anti-egalitarian direction of these constitutional deliberations clearly emerges in the provisions on electoral rights and procedures. Both Kreisau and Goerdeler held to the principle of universal suffrage, but Kreisau fixed the voting-age at 21 and Goerdeler variously at 24 or 25. Both plans provide for additional voting-rights for fathers of families. Kreisau proposed one additional vote for each child below voting-age, while Goerdeler wanted to give a double vote to fathers of at least three legitimate children. This amounted to a strong emphasis on the family as the basic unit in the life of the state. The minimum age at which people could stand for election was set at 27 by Kreisau. Goerdeler chose the age of 28 or 30 for borough and district assembly seats and 35 for the Reichstag. In both schemes members of the armed forces were excluded from standing for election at any level, as were political civil servants in elections to the provincial assemblies (*Landtage)* and the Reichstag. Goerdeler excluded all civil servants as well as clergy of all denominations, but apparently not officials of autonomous communal bodies. This is explained by their anxiety to avoid the politicisation of the civil service and the entry of representatives of centralized power into elected bodies. Kreisau did not grant women the right to stand for election. Schulenburg's proposal that the right to stand in local elections should be dependent on a property-qualification and marital status, was not taken up.

These provisions tend to favour the typical *Honoratioren*, that is to say socially accepted citizens of independent means, respected for their services to the community. Goerdeler drew his inspiration from the municipal institutions of Baron vom Stein, whereas Kreisau leaned more towards the 'small communities', although Stelzer and Delp, in particular, also placed strong emphasis on the Stein tradition of local self-government. Goerdeler was keen to link the right to stand for election with permanent residence in the constituency, as a means of combating the nomination of 'extraneous' candidates by nationwide associations. Kreisau did not require this in so many words, but the quorum necessary for putting up a candidate was intended to serve the same purpose. In both cases what mattered was that the people standing for election should be known to the voters, just as the constituencies were to form units of a 'manageable size'.

The negative experience of the Weimar Republic with proportional representation and list-voting led to the wholesale rejection of this system by all groups in the resistance. Leber summed up the arguments against it like this: 'It is not in any way capable of fulfilling its actual function of choosing suitable men and monitoring the trust between people and government; instead it merely transfers the hard climb up the party ladder onto politics as a whole.' Proportional representation prevented the forming of 'broad currents of ideology' and encouraged the fragmentation of parties. It was these considerations that led Ludwig Bergsträsser, in a draft constitution he produced for Leuschner, to opt for a system of voting for candidates rather than parties. Goerdeler and Stelzer took their criticism even further: proportional representation, they said, forced parties to put programmes and not personalities in the forefront and removed the sense of responsibility of the deputies towards their electorate; Bergsträsser objected to the devaluation of the 'democratic compromise' contained in such statements. There was an inherent contradiction in this which was typical of the mentality of Leber, Goerdeler and Stelzer On the one hand they wanted 'pure', ideologically based parties, while on the other they reproached them for letting ideology dominate politics.

The principle of *relative* majority voting [i.e. where the winning candidate must merely receive more votes than any other, as in the British 'first-past-the-post' system. *Tr.*] was intended to guarantee the 'organic connection' between the electors and the elected and make possible the creation of small constituencies. Hence, Kreisau provided for the breaking down of town councils in larger municipalities into a series of representative bodies of equal status. In large cities these bodies would elect city councillors indirectly. It is not clear how this would work at the borough level, since they were not on an equal footing with the *Länder* (provinces), which were planned to have populations of 3 to 5 million. Nor was the matter of nominating candidates clarified in the Kreisau draft; apparently the plan was for this task to be handed over to the 'small communities'.

Difficulties of this kind arose because both drafts were anxious to prevent the formation of political parties, at least in the inaugural elections. As Steltzer stressed, 'corporatist' self-government assumes a guarantee against domination by centralist parties which inevitably bring their political differences into the smallest village, thereby *destroying* the feeling of corporate responsibility. This accorded with Goerdeler's view; he had always felt that party activity in local politics was a disruptive influence. Hence the solution he was working towards was similar in principle to that of the Kreisau draft. Goerdeler breached the principle of small constituencies in that one quarter of the councillors were to be elected by the whole municipality, not however on a list basis but by a relative majority of the most wards. The final quarter were to be elected by the Chambers of Commerce. He later abandoned this approach and limited the number of candidates to stand in each ward to four. These were to be nominated by business groups, the *Deutsche Gewerkschaft* (a putative single labour union) and the 'political movements'. In this he differed fundamentally from the Kreisau Circle, who wanted at all costs to avoid the involvement of 'organizations', especially a centralist organization like the *Deutsche Gewerkschaft*. This restriction of the right of nomination would have been intolerable in practice. It arose from the consideration that election by relative majority not only presupposed the existence of fewer large parties but also favoured their creation. However, since the associations responsible for putting up candidates were democratically-based, in Goerdeler's view, this proposal was really nothing more than the application of the Kreisau concept to the realities of society; the privileges extended to Kreisau's 'small communities' were equivalent to those granted to the professional (*berufständisch*) associations as conceived by Goerdeler; in the place of 'small' constituencies there was to be election by the officers of professional and trade associations.

For all of these reasons, the question of candidacy for election to municipal councils (and in Kreisau's plan, also to district assemblies [*Kreistagswahlen*]) was of central importance, because for the most part indirect elections were proposed for the higher-level representative bodies. Under the Kreisau scheme, members of the provincial assemblies (*Landtage*) or the city councils of equal status to them were elected by district assemblies (*Kreistage*) or the councils of towns that did not form part of a *Kreis*. The same principle applied to elections to the Reichstag.

Goerdeler's system was more complicated. He proposed a three-stage indirect election: from the municipal council to the district assembly, from the district assembly to the provincial assembly (known under the Third Reich as the *Gau* assembly) and from there to the Reichstag. This was a real 'greasy pole' of a process and would inevitably have meant that only a limited number of people would be available for representative duties, especially since Goerdeler required candidates for the *Landtage* to have served for five years as a municipal councillor or district assemblyman and Reichstag candidates to have served for five years in honorary public office. The purpose of this was to guarantee the selection of an elite capable of governing. This error was to some extent avoided by Kreisau, in that half the members of the *Landtage* were not allowed to belong to any of the electoral bodies. From another point of view this was rather a questionable provision, since in practice the subsidiary election became a method of co-opting. For election to the Reichstag this was only to apply 'temporarily', simply because initially the constitutional structure could not be achieved in any other way. Goerdeler took a route that was essentially the same, though it differed technically. He wanted to have half the deputies in the Reichstag chosen by direct election. The retention of the privilege of associations to nominate candidates and the clause requiring the deputy to be resident in his own constituency and to be distinguished by his service to the public, would guarantee that people voted for the man, not the party. Behind all this was a strongly centralist mode of thinking, whereas the Kreisau Circle deliberately made the federal-style *Landtage* the hub of political activity.

Nevertheless, a large degree of agreement on practical points can be found between the two plans. Goederler started from the concept of *Honoratiorenliberalsimus* [the liberalism of the respected citizen *Tr.*], while Kreisau thought in terms of the organic representation of professional interests. Both plans wanted to avoid domination by professional parliamentarians and to replace 'functionaries' and demagogues by men rooted in the local community; and both were anxious to achieve a 'harmonious' articulation of political demands. There was to be no electioneering in the grand old style. The election would be restricted to the selection of trustworthy representatives who, before the election, laid their personal programme before the electors, relating to matters to be dealt with in the municipality or district. Both plans combined the representational principle of classic liberalism with a kind of direct democracy at the lowest level. However, in Goerdeler's plan, direct democracy was made more or less illusory by the rule that democratically elected bodies, including the *Landtag*, were only to be convened at specific intervals. In boroughs with more than 12 deputies, in districts and provinces, standing committees were to be elected, whose role was to assist the executive authorities in an advisory capacity and which would for their part have the right to make decisions in certain areas. In practice, therefore, they were a further stage of indirect election at all three levels. These committees were to meet *in camera*, whereas the elected representatives of the borough would meet quarterly, the district bi-annually and the province or *Gau* only once a year. Their principal task was to decide on budgets, with the restriction that items of expenditure could only be approved if matched by equivalent revenue. Here Goerdeler was directly following the proposals he had submitted to President Hindenburg in 1932. They demonstrated his aversion to large quasi-parliamentary committees, which had a habit of reaching political decisions through trade-offs. At the same time we can see clearly in them how strongly Goerdeler held views on financial policy which place him in line with Brüning and how much his constitutional thinking was coloured by his experience in local government.

With his recurrently paternalistic tendency, Goerdeler took his basic idea of stimulating the citizen's interest in self-government to an absurd degree. He was worried that parliamentary procedures would allow 'demagogic' elements, with no direct interest in or knowledge of particular matters, to dictate the political decisions about them. This forced him into elaborate arrangements whereby the people's representatives, having been duly elected to power, would be left with only an advisory function. He was opposed to the 'unfettered and over-democratic parliamentary system', but in practice removed any accountability of government to parliament and drew up a political system that would have satisfied Papen's most extreme ambitions: the Reich Chancellor has the authority to lay down initial policy guidelines in cabinet; the ministers, analogous to Bismarck's Reich constitution, are not responsible to parliament. However, they and the Reich Chancellor must be dismissed by the *Generalstatthalter* (Goerdeler's term for the head of state), if this is demanded by a two-thirds majority of the Reichstag or by a simple majority of the Reichstag and *Reichständehaus* (Reich House of Estates, or Upper House) combined and if at the same time a new government is proposed. The government can at any time issue decrees with the force of law on any matter except the budget, financial legislation and treaties with foreign countries; these decrees must be repealed if this is called for by a majority of both houses or a two-thirds majority of either.

This means that Article 48 of the Weimar Constitution was applied as a matter of course and at the same time was logically carried over to the formation of governments, which lay entirely in the hands of the *Generalstatthalter*. This procedure deprived parliament of the initiative in electing chancellors and forming governments, leaving it as nothing more than a constitutional 'brake'. It has been mistakenly described as a 'constructive vote of no confidence', analogous to Article 66 of the *Grundgesetz* (constitution of the German Federal Republic). However, under Goerdeler's scheme, parliament cannot compel the *Generalstatthalter* to appoint a government it has proposed; where there is no vote of confidence, there cannot be a vote of no confidence. In practice it was highly improbable that the *Reichstän-dehaus*, made up in part from senior members of professional associations of all kinds, partly from representatives of unions and employers and partly from 'the great and the good' appointed by the *Generalstatthalter*, would openly challenge the government on key political questions. In any case parliament required a two-thirds majority in order to overturn legislation or bring down a government. In principle, therefore, a government could be a minority cabinet; the two-thirds majority required to bring it down meant in practice that even for the proposal of a new Chancellor there had to be the majority required to amend the constitution (under the terms of the Weimar constitution). This, together with the *Generalstatthalter*'s right to dissolve parliament, ruled out effective parliamentary opposition. The Reichstag was to have no independent right to legislate; to pass laws it required the approval of the non-elected *Reichständehaus*. Laws with financial implications could only be introduced with the Chancellor's prior approval. 'The head of state thus has it in his power, by replacing ministers or the Chancellor... or by a renewed appeal to both houses, or by calling new elections' to push through necessary political measures.

The Kreisau system – as far as we can tell from the outline – is more flexible by comparison; the second chamber or *Reichsrat*, though appointed similarly to Goerdeler's *Reichständehaus*, plays no part in legislation. Unlike Goerdeler's plan, the powers of the Reichstag are not limited. However, as regards the forming of governments the arrangements are similar. Admittedly, the Reich Chancellor is appointed – though ministers are not – by the head of state (in this case called the *Reichsverweser*, or Regent) with the approval of the Reichstag, but the Regent may dismiss a Chancellor at his own discretion, if he simultaneously appoints a new one. The Reichstag, for its part, has the right, with a qualified majority, to demand the dismissal of the Chancellor, provided at the same time it proposes to the Regent the appointment of a new Chancellor. Like Goerdeler, the Kreisau scheme deprives parliament of the initiative in legislation and this is extended to the forming of governments. This has the same disadvantage that, in the case of conflict, the Regent is in a position to use his right of dismissal to force the acceptance of a Chancellor convenient to him.

It may seem a little unfair to impose the test of practicability on these fragmentary and not fully developed drafts. Nonetheless, by doing so we are able to place them in their intellectual sequence. Their lack of precision is due to the fact that none of those involved had a clear idea of the practical function and effect of the constitutional principles they were proposing. For this reason it is not really possible to say much about the specific form of government they were striving towards. Steltzer talked about a 'modified parliamentary system', yet this is only to a limited extent true of the Kreisau draft. The head of state is the *Reichsverweser*, the Regent appointed for a 12-year term on the recommendation of the *Reichsrat*, the upper chamber of parliament. His position is so strong that at the least we must say that sovereignty is divided between the head of state and parliament. The indirect election of its members denies the Reichstag the possibility of gaining public support through the medium of large parties. Furthermore, it is counterbalanced by the *Reichsrat*, the majority of whose members are appointed by the *Reichsverweser*. This would tend to reinforce, rather than reduce, the disadvantage of the presidential system, which became clear with the fall of the Brüning cabinet –

namely the government's dependence in practice on the head of state. The parliamentary principle only appears in the provision that the Chancellor is appointed with the approval of parliament; but in practice the government's dependence on the confidence of the majority in parliament is illusory, since parliament can only insist that the Chancellor be replaced in the event of clear conflict and then only with a qualified majority, which probably means a two-thirds majority. These constitutional arrangements can therefore not be equated with the 'constructive vote of no-confidence', in today's Federal parliament, which merely has the purpose of preventing negative opposition majorities. In Goerdeler's plan parliament is restricted to a mere monitoring function. It is true that it shares with the *Reichständehaus* the right to legislate in competition with the government, but the upper chamber is largely appointed by the head of state. Furthermore, legislation with expenditure implications cannot be introduced except with government approval. Goerdeler claimed that that he was not looking for 'a repetition of Bismarck's Reich, nor of Weimar, nor of the Third Reich' but for something which combined the merits of all three. This remark, written when he was in prison in 1944, was his answer to the severe criticism levelled against his constitutional plan, before the attempted coup, from the most varied of quarters. Until immediately before the bomb-plot was carried out, Popitz warned against Goerdeler's plan, so that Stauffenberg was made to fear that a return to the 'Weimar system' was envisaged. Josef Wirmer[1] passed on Goerdeler's 'new and constructive ideas' and emphasized that 'in no respect would they be a re-hash of the old arrangements'. Still, a certain mistrust towards Goerdeler remained. The criticism from Leber and the Kreisau Circle was even more outspoken. Yorck said outright that a coup led by Beck and Goerdeler would bring in a thoroughly reactionary regime. It would necessarily require the reestablishment of the old parties and labour unions, thus recreating the conditions of 1932. Goerdeler's plan was damned as a 'Kerensky solution,[2] which shows how great was the fear of the Bolshevisation of Germany in the wake of its defeat. Yorck's prognosis was in part justified, as Goerdeler's outline constitutional plan shows.

Goerdeler was too greatly influenced by his experiences in the Brüning and von Papen administrations and until his death he believed that had he joined von Papen's cabinet he could have averted Germany's fate.

But did Goerdeler really want an authoritarian system, possibly modelled on that of Hungary or Bulgaria? Despite the high esteem in which he held the personality and historical achievement of Bismarck, his constitutional plans reached further back, taking the Prussian reformers as their model, but with a historical interpretation that was predominantly nationalist. Goerdeler was a staunch advocate of a return to the reforms of Baron vom Stein and the German tradition of self-government. He was not alone in this view. The German resistance were trying to create a reformed constitution, which took account of their country's unique historical development – and was suited to the 'German nature' – at the same time rejecting western constitutional models. As the thinking of the 1920s had foreshadowed, this would inevitably lead to an attempt to adopt the reformist ideas of Stein and his colleagues. Given the psychological conditions under which the resistance were working and especially in view of the 'lost connection with the thoughts and feelings of the outside world', the system of parliamentary democracy seemed to be historically completely outmoded. Thus Bonhoeffer was able to express the view, in a memorandum to groups abroad, that for quite a number of European countries, including France and Italy, a return to fully developed parliamentary democracy would be impossible. For the men plotting against Hitler, the memory of the rise of Prussia was a living and powerful motivation. They drew the strength to rebel from an unbroken historical tradition and what mattered to them, as Trott put it, was not the upholding of the German army and German power, but above all 'the preservation of Germany's historical continuity'.

The appeal to Stein is a genuine component of resistance thinking. Whereas Popitz and Hassell focussed on the conservative aspects of Stein's view of the state and Goerdeler stressed Stein's 'liberalism', Steltzer, Delp, Moltke, Trott, Haubach and Mierendorff picked up the idea of *Genossenschaft* (partnership) which clearly emerged from Stein's reform plans. Leuschner called for 'self-government in all spheres of social and economic life'; he and Leber read Stein's writings while in prison. The tradition of self-government that began with Stein was also affirmed in Bergsträsser's memorandum, mentioned earlier. The reforms, which had shared origins, nonetheless bore very different features. Steltzer held the view that what Stein had envisaged - 'the municipality as a moral and intellectual community of free and upright men' – had got lost in the process of industrialization and *Vermassung* and he therefore believed that a determined revival of public-spiritedness was necessary. He quoted Stein's dictum that what mattered was not the 'organization of the constitution' but the 'perfecting of human nature': 'It is the character of the intention that must be shaped, not only the knowledge.' Self-government, as defined by Steltzer, was 'democracy in the structures upon which the life of the state is built'.

By contrast, Goerdeler believed that self-government had remained alive and that even in imperial Germany it had 'displayed a coherence that had been the admiration of the whole world'; and that it had held its ground in the Weimar Republic 'despite the extreme democratisation of electoral rights' and 'far-reaching subversion of the political parties'. To him, self-government was not the creation of the Prussian reformers but was a continuation of the 'old Germanic tradition' – as indeed Stein himself had believed. Goerdeler considered self-government as a *sui generis* principle of statehood and one which was directly opposed to the democratic idea, which he regarded as plebiscitary. Steltzer held similar views. 'Self-government and democracy are quite separate forms of organization and different in their effect,' we read in the surviving fragments of *Thoughts on a New Order of Self-government*. 'Democracies are anxious to suppress self-government, because the party headquarters, engaged in their struggle with one another, cannot tolerate the conciliatory influence of self-government at the practical working level.' Hence Goerdeler, in the memoranda he sent to Hitler, was able to make the point that it was the *Führer-* state which most of all needed thriving self-government, if it was not to succumb to intellectual atrophy caused by rampant bureaucracy and fall victim to the subversive influence of individual group interests hiding behind the cloak of the Nazi Party. Later he expressed the view that states without self-government, such as 'the USA or the Soviet Union', would fall prey to internal subversion or – as the example of France showed – would become a political wasteland.

Goedeler's terminology has a paternalistic flavour and he praised self-government as a nostrum for all political systems. Nonetheless, the Kreisau Circle assigned to self-government the same constitutional function, that of foiling the egalitarian and plebiscitary trends in modern society and putting public-spirit-edness in the place of specific interests. Moltke, on the other hand, regarded the form of the constitution as secondary, though for good reasons he considered a return to monarchy impossible. The arguments which Kreisau mobilized in favour of self-government were the same as Goerdeler's. The difference was that Kreisau saw self-government more in the sense of partnership than as cooperation in a political community, not just as a check on and adviser to the executive – i.e. the elected officials as executors of community decisions – and not as a city council as that was traditionally understood. However, both concepts coincide in their desire to restrict the formation of political demands to the sphere of rational decisions on practical matters, to eliminate as far as possible the power-struggle between groups and to replace it with a principle of proportional representation reminiscent of the block system.

Goerdeler and Kreisau both took account of this idea by granting self-government to labour and employers' organizations, which fed into the indirectly elected Reich Economic Council. Both envisaged that employers and employees in the relevant business sectors would be represented on an equal footing in the Chambers of Commerce. This kind of twin structure of political and occupational (*berufständisch*) self-government, which was again sought in the second chamber, seemed designed to achieve a harmonious reconciliation of divergent social interests at each regional level.

The prevailing mindset of the resistance, which saw policy formation as participation by lay citizens in public administration, is clearly expressed in the identification of the principle of self-government with federalism. Neither Goerdeler nor Kreisau settled the question of how far the *Länder* (provinces) were to be described as 'self-governing entities' with the character of independent states. This is particularly true of Kreisau, although the institution of *Landesverweser* (provincial governor), alongside the *Landeshauptmann* (provincial premier), has a federalist character. Paradoxically, Goerdeler, who conceived of the *Länder* as self-governing units, was in favour of granting them wider areas of competence than intended by Kreisau. In Goerdeler's scheme the provincial *Oberpräsident* (prefect or governor) was only to have powers to oversee and direct the authorities placed under him. By contrast, the Kreisau plan gave central government wide powers to intervene in economic and social matters, as well as in questions of regional planning, a fact which in practice would have imposed lasting restrictions on local government at borough and district level. This went counter to the main thrust of Kreisau thinking; originally it seemed that they wanted to remove the financial sovereignty of the Reich. However, mainly on the advice of Schulenburg, this course was abandoned.

Goerdeler's concept of strong government with a wide measure of self-government not restricted by competing spheres of authority, made the elected members of self-governing entities and especially the provincial premiers, into a strong intermediate ruling elite within the state. This was in no way true of the Kreisau plan. Their *Landesverweser* (provincial governor), elected for 12 years and simultaneously a member of the *Reichsrat* (second chamber) had the right to nominate candidates for the post of provincial premier, as well as overseeing the provincial administration and being responsible for implementing Reich policies. He had to be confirmed in his post by the *Reichsverweser* (regent). Hence, the position of the provincial premier was significantly weaker than in Goerdeler's scheme, whereas the provincial governor had to represent national interests. However, this unintentional design flaw was attributable to Kreisau's overvaluation of the partnership principle, which simply did not meet the demands of modern government. This prevented Kreisau from conceiving of a truly federal structure, so that in this too they looked on the National Socialist *Gleichschaltung* of the provinces as a *fait accompli*, just as – unlike Goerdeler – they thought in terms of a completely new territorial arrangement, which destroyed the old *Länder*.

IX: Parties, labour unions and a collective 'democratic' movement

The plans for a new order put forward by the German resistance were a continuation of the situation created by National Socialism, in that they did not strive to involve *parties* in policy-making, in the way that is necessary in a modern parliamentary system. An exception to this is the constitutional plan developed by Ludwig Bergsträsser, though even he only recommended a return to the parliamentary system in the long term. He warned against holding elections too soon and sought to achieve a reawakening of political life through building up local self-government with the help of the churches and the labour unions. He too envisaged a second chamber formed by means of indirect elections from the self-governing bodies. This was intended to counterbalance the domination of parliament by the parties. All the other plans regarded the political parties as particularist forces, lacking any close connection with the people, without democratic legitimation and posing a threat to the unity of state and 'community'.

It is this rejection of party politics, inspired by 'organicist' or *étatiste* thinking, which may explain why Steltzer remarked in 1949 that the parties had not overcome their ideological origins and were still trapped in partial perspectives. Before the convening of the Parliamentary Council[1] he had recommended the adoption of the Kreisau scheme on the grounds that only a structure of that kind could secure democracy against the claims on power by centralist parties. Those parties, he said, 'demand supremacy over the state, thereby making it impossible to build a sound and healthy state'. Steltzer called Germany's post-war democracy 'party-based totalitarianism in a veiled form'. Ideas of this kind were typical of the whole of the resistance, and it is remarkable that they never pointed out the qualitative difference between the Nazi party and the democratic parties of Weimar. Goerdeler was also opposed to the 'party state' and summed up his plans in a conversation with Kluge[2] when he said that what was needed was a 'comprehensive reconciliation without the formation of parties'.

On this point Goerdeler was on unsure ground. He was right in seeing the fragmentation of the Weimar parties as a crucial cause of the crisis. His demand for election by absolute majority (i.e. where the winning candidate must receive more than 50% of all votes cast), echoed by Leber, Leuschner and Kaiser, was a consequence of their experience of the republic. Goerdeler considered the British two-party system to be ideal, but doubted that it could be transplanted to Germany.[3] He groped towards a wide variety of solutions. In late 1943 he proposed that only the three strongest parties be admitted and that the weak ones be deprived of their mandate. In an analogy with the British system, he considered the formation of a conservative, a liberal and a socialist party, while firmly rejecting a revival of the communist party and the creation of parties based on the Catholic and Protestant churches. He was reluctant to do this, but his trip to Bulgaria in 1938 had shown him that a formal ban on parties was ineffective. The only way to avoid party fragmentation was to construct an electoral system carefully tailored to the educational level of the population.

Hans Peters[4] tells us that the Kreisau Circle had also 'scarcely considered a direct restriction of party political activity'; but there can be no doubt that – initially at least – Kreisau had quite consistently refused to countenance any form of policy-making outside the system of self-government founded on 'small communities'. This also explains the tension between Kreisau and Goerdeler and with the union group working with him. Kreisau saw the probable revival of the old, ideologically-based associations as a thoroughly backward-looking policy. This caused Delp to warn one of Goerdeler's close colleagues, Hermann Kaiser,[5] that he was putting forward a 'reactionary' programme and to advise him instead to establish contact with Schulenburg and Moltke. At that time – summer 1942 – the hope was that a fundamental reshaping of political life could be achieved.

The chief area of conflict between the two groups arose over the question of the labour unions. Leuschner's efforts to transform the German Labour Front into a unitary socialist labour union ran up against the extremely devolutionary intentions of Kreisau. Moltke and his friends were not anti-union; but they were keen on the formation of workplace unions. These were not, however, intended purely as organs for employee representation, but also as an 'economic community' within the firm to which the owners of the firm and the entire staff would belong. Thought was given to the rights and obligations of the workplace union, which included jointly nominating representatives of the workforce on the management board, the contractual right of the workforce to be given reliable information about the firm's balance-sheet and profit-and-loss situation and to share in the profits and asset-growth. Such agreements were to be monitored by the self-governing body of the relevant industrial sector. This was a practical application of the idea of 'small communities'. In the workplace union class-conflict was removed; it was a genuine 'business community' based on partnership. This utopian project, which incidentally resulted in a restriction on the employee's mobility, was similar in its ideology to the Nazi labour contract. Nevertheless, Carlo Mierendorff (see Chapter 9) was one of the socialists who gave it his support, whereas Haubach, Maass, and most of all Leber, firmly rejected it. Since it was impossible to do without union labour, a compromise was agreed on: the so-called German Labour Union (*Deutsche Gewerkschaft*) was to be a 'necessary means' of implementing the economic programme which was essential to the rebuilding of the state. However, it was only intended as a temporary expedient. As the *Principles of the New Order* puts it: 'The German Labour Union will fulfil its purpose by putting through this programme and by transferring its appointed tasks to the organs of the state and to self-governing industry and commerce.' It is significant that Moltke never abandoned the hope that this compromise could be reversed. To prevent the growth of a union bureaucracy cut off from the workforce, Yorck and Moltke wanted to make it compulsory for union representatives to carry on their regular occupation for at least half of each working day. This idea was typical of their social utopianism and was resisted even by Mierendorff. Trott sided with the socialists on this.

By contrast, Goerdeler and Leuschner were certainly more realistic and it is no surprise that some of the Kreisau Circle accused Leuschner of being too caught up in the 'old' organizational thinking. Leuschner had withdrawn from the discussions on this question and had already, in close collaboration with Kaiser, pursued his own plan for a single, catch-all labour union, in the event of Germany's collapse. He succeeded in persuading Goerdeler that it was not advisable to carry over the Nazis' German Labour Front into the new state structure; its assets were to be transferred to the 'German Labour Union', which would act as the sole representative of all employees and would have compulsory membership. In the *Reichständehaus* (House of Estates, or second chamber of parliament), envisaged by Goerdeler, the German Labour Union would have equal status with the employers' federations. Leuschner seems to have been influenced by Goerdeler and also believed that the German workers were satisfied with the German Labour Front as an institution. He seriously pursued the idea of creating a crucial role for the unitary labour union in the new state order and to manage without the formation of political parties. As Goerdeler stated, the German Labour Union was to be an 'organic continuation of the equally all-embracing Labour front'. There is no doubt that from the union side, the German Labour Front was seen as a possible way of solving social problems, and the decision to avoid politically-oriented unions was part of the general criticism of party politics. Leuschner accepted the principle that the labour unions had to be free from the influence of any political group. He adopted Goerdeler's programme, whereby social insurance and employment offices were to be union-run. He advocated not only the nationalization of raw-material production and other key industries, but also independent business activity on the part of the unions, which would enable them 'as producers to exert a significant influence on the shaping of the economy'.

It is easy to see from this why Popitz protested about the extraordinary increase in power that Goedeler's plans gave to the unions. On the other hand Leuschner appears to have overestimated the opportunities these plans gave him to increase his own political power. He turned down the offer of becoming Chancellor after a successful coup, since that would have kept him away from setting up the German Labour Union. He even thought the post of Vice-Chancellor would be a severe imposition. Leuschner was a practical politician; that is why it is very difficult to be precise about the social order that he envisaged. He seems to have been heavily influenced by the ideas of Ludwig Reichhold. From an essay that has survived from 1942, we learn that Leuschner considered Reichhold's rather vague concept of a new order based on occupational 'estates' (*ständische Ordnung*) as worthy of consideration:

> The labour movement represents the political identity of the working class, whose status is equal to the small farmers and the urban middle class. They come from the same roots, are subject to the same laws and exercise the same rights as any class of European society.

These formulations, drawn in part from Reichhold's theories, lean towards a democratic polity of 'estates', in the historical sense of the term.

If we are to make a judgement on the ideas of the resistance on social policy, it is important to note that the tendency to eliminate parliamentary parties from government was not restricted to those groups which were conservative in the narrower sense of the word. Not only Leuschner, but also Habermann, Wirmer and Jakob Kaiser thought in terms of a synthesis of democratic and *berufständisch* elements. Habermann called upon Schulenburg to take responsibility for founding a farmers' party (*Bauernpartei*). This was to be joined by both a middle-class (*bürgerlich*) and a workers' party; the latter would be modelled on the British Labour Party, that is to say non-Marxist and probably union-supported. The Christian labour unions decided against re-founding the German Social Democratic Party (SPD) and objected to the revival of a class-based socialist party. The resistance group in Cologne considered creating a 'party of all economically active people', while Andreas Hermes[6] envisaged a broad, Christian-orientated People's Party.

Yet, as the war dragged on, these plans blended with the concept, discussed throughout the resistance, of a collective, democratic movement embracing all social groups. Leuschner was driven by the emphasis on unions to give consideration to his colleagues from the Christian labour unions. This forced him into conflict with the representatives of social democracy, especially Leber and Mierendorff, though the bonds of mutual friendship led him to conceal this at first. Mierendorff had been involved in drawing up the programme for a unitary labour union. The situation at the end of 1942 was summed up by Maass when he wrote:

> The question remained open as to whether, in addition to the labour union, a specifically political organization should also be formed. A certain degree of unity was achieved on the decision that the former multi-party system was not to be restored; but that at most a *single* party should be formed, drawn from a narrow selection of politically dedicated elements.

From this we can discern some hesitancy on Leuschner's part towards the idea of forming a mass party independent of the labour union. This is confirmed by Bergsträsser's memorandum, in which he assigned the leading role to the labour union and the churches, following the collapse of Nazism.

It was in this notion of a broad, democratic, popular movement in support of the post-Nazi government, that the plans of the German resistance overlapped with those of resistance groups in other European countries. The difference was that in the rest of Europe people were simply waiting for the military rather than the political defeat of Nazism. In Germany the resistance faced the ideological dilemma of not wanting to establish the new order on the basis of a popular vote, although – with the exception of Popitz and Hassell – they believed they could not proceed without the cooperation of the population as a whole. Hence this question produced serious internal disputes between the various groups within the resistance, which brought them close to a complete break. Faced with the progressive political and social disintegration of the Third Reich, there was considerable attraction in the idea of replacing the former mass parties by a single party of democratic integration, bringing together all forces concerned to rebuild Germany. However, the fascist paradigm also played a part. The group around Jakob Kaiser discussed a paper from the Romanian Mihail Manoilescu, who was a supporter of his country's fascist 'Iron Guard'. He proposed 'the single party as the political institution of the new regime' and presented the one-party system as the solution of the future, whereby the necessary formation of an elite in the modern mass state would be taken on by a state party. However, these views met with little enthusiasm and some firm opposition. Nevertheless, Moltke's idea of creating a new political elite could find some common ground here, even though his assumptions were quite different. There is no doubt that Schulenberg also held views of this kind; he had originally wanted to transform the Nazi Party into a quasi-monastic order, whose function would be to select and train a new generation of leaders, but which would not itself seek to exercise political power. Others had similar ideas; the so-called Stauffenberg Oath, whose origins are admittedly far from clear, was a move in this direction.

The notions that bore the stamp of 1920s anti-rationalism retreated before the plan for a 'popular non-party movement', a collective movement that embraced the goal of a 'national community' (*Volksgemeinschaft*). In the spring of 1943 Mierendorff and Haubach together worked out an agenda of 'Socialist Action', which was to unite Christian, socialist, communist and liberal forces in a 'popular non-party movement for the salvation of Germany' (See Chapter 9). The programme included moderate socialist objectives of the Kreisau type; it emphasized the Christian foundations of European culture, demanded a settlement both with the West and with the Soviet Union and called for 'a united front of all the enemies of National Socialism'. This action programme reflected Mierendorff's conviction that the future would have to bring a joining of the two forces which had alone remained resistant to the chaos of Nazism – Christianity and socialism. This can be traced back to his discussions with Moltke and Yorck; Yorck insisted that the planned overthrow of the Nazi regime needed a broader basis – 'bringing in the social democrats, including their left wing'.

A crucial element of the plan was the countering of communist agitation with an effective political force. The Kreisau Circle took the decisive step beyond the creation of an 'emergency control' programme and on to the shaping of political events, by becoming actively involved in the plot to get rid of Hitler. A memorandum was produced on Moltke's orders while he was in Turkey in late 1943. This sketched out the objectives of the conspiracy for the benefit of the Americans and pointed out the danger of a communist-Bolshevist Germany and of German national Bolshevism. There was a danger that a democratically-minded German government could come into conflict with the mass of the workers; therefore an effort must be made to win over hitherto pro-Russian circles:

> A government of this kind must, in order to avoid getting into a hopeless situation *vis-à-vis* the workers and their communist wing, operate domestically with a very strong left wing and actively seek support from social-democratic and labour union quarters.

Furthermore it would be desirable to involve those communists who were men of good sense and not tied to Moscow. This particularly reflected the position of Adolf Reichwein (see Chapter 10), who had informal links with communist groups.

Already heightened by the worsening military situation, the growing fear of a communist revolution was strongly reinforced by the activities of the (communist-inspired) 'National Committee for a Free Germany', whose psychological impact on the plotters can scarcely be overestimated. We can see this clearly in the messages Trott succeeded in passing to Allen W. Dulles[7] in the spring of 1944. The extent of the leftward slide had been astonishing and was getting steadily more significant. In this situation, Trott was chiefly concerned to obtain Allied assurances that would support the position of the socialists on the domestic front. This explains his request for the western Allies to encourage the German workers 'to shape the labour movement according to their own wishes, without any involvement of capitalist groups in the west, with their anti-labour attitudes'. This was very much in line with the 'Turkish' memorandum. At the same time it reflected Trott's own strongly anti-capitalist stance. At a meeting with Dulles a year earlier, he had tried to justify a possible eastward orientation on Germany's part: the Germans had, like the Russians, 'broken away from bourgeois ideology' and wanted a radical solution to their social problems, one which 'went beyond national boundaries.' At the time Trott was hoping for an internal collapse of Bolshevism in Russia and for both nations to return to the intellectual traditions of the Christian west. However, by 1944, this had given way to a clear appreciation of the communist threat.

Goerdeler, for his part, also took up the idea of a 'popular movement'. It was to 'unite all occupational classes and levels of society and all regions of the country' and embrace 'all Germans, from social-democrats on the left, through the centre, to rightwing German nationalists'. This 'popular movement on the broadest of foundations' would initially have to be led by the government but later would be independent of it; the movement would permit opposition groups within it, which might represent the blueprint for future parties. This idea brought about close contacts between all the anti-Nazi groups and forced them to put more flesh on the bones of their conceptual programmes. However, establishing the principles for the formation of the 'popular movement' led to severe disagreement in the spring of 1944. It is clear from Trott's messages to Dulles that the socialist groups had gained political muscle and on this question were able to win decisive arguments. As Otto John[8] wrote, Leber was thinking in terms of 'a kind of new Popular Front made up of all surviving and viable social and democratic forces'. He was not prepared to adopt Christian principles in the programme of the 'popular movement' and came down firmly against the formulation proposed by Mierendorff and Reichwein: 'The Popular Movement declares its faith in German culture and in the Christian past of the German people.' Leber told Leuschner and Jakob Kaiser emphatically that he 'would not allow important principles of the old social democracy simply to be thrown overboard for the sake of desired unity'. He was opposed to the idea that the state they were hoping to create should be given a Christian character, as was the wish of the leaders of the Christian labour unions.

X. The military coup and a 'democratic' popular uprising

The conflicts that had been breaking out since the spring of 1944 can be explained in part by the overwrought nerves of the plotters and their knowledge that the removal of Hitler was long overdue and would possibly be too late when it finally happened. It was reflections of this kind that brought both Leuschner and Leber each to the independent decision not to outflank the other politically by joining a Beck-Goerdeler government. The passivity of the generals, unanimously criticized by the civilian plotters, led Leber and Leuschner to doubt whether the coup would ever take place. At the same time a broad front was formed against Goerdeler, whose members included Leber, Moltke, Yorck, Gerstenmaier, Delp and Haubach on the left, and Hassell, Popitz and Jessen on the right. Though the views of the two wings were diametrically opposed, their objectives were the same. The extreme conservatives held the view that, given the 'completely proletarianized millions now populating central Europe', an attempted Bolshevist revolution could only be prevented by rigidly authoritarian government. They did not believe that Goerdeler, with his innately conciliatory style, was capable of providing this, quite apart from disapproving of his plans for the labour unions.

Leber, Yorck, Moltke and Trott, who had already stated earlier that in the event of a coup 'any whiff of reaction' had to be avoided, no longer considered Goerdeler acceptable in domestic politics. This was partly due to the suggestion that he stood for 'big business', though there was only limited truth in this. They accused him of cherishing illusions in foreign affairs, and this was only too justified since, right up to the summer of 1944, Goerdeler thought it perfectly possible that Germany would emerge from military defeat without any significant territorial losses. By contrast, Leber, Yorck and Moltke were already anticipating the complete occupation of Germany and were prepared to cede territory well within the frontiers as they had stood in 1937.

Meanwhile Goerdeler – like the Nazi leadership – still saw a considerable chance of exploiting the apparent conflict between the Western Powers and communism. Leber toyed with the idea of preparing an independent course of action by the socialist forces in the event of Germany's collapse, and he agreed with Yorck that any post-Nazi government would have to extend leftwards as far as possible.

The man now increasingly recognized as being at the centre of the plot was Claus von Stauffenberg,[1] who thus provoked the mistrust of Goerdeler and, initially, of Leuschner, both of whom wanted to prevent 'the generals from doing anything political'. Originally Stauffenberg had repeatedly emphasized that the Nazi regime would have to be replaced by a government that was positioned 'more towards the bourgeois (*bürgerlich*) centre'. However, his own basic stance was one of pronounced conservatism, strongly influenced by military attitudes. The 'Oath', which has – rather unreliably – been attributed to him, speaks of 'the falsehood of equality'. The justification he gave for planning Hitler's overthrow was that, in the event of a military collapse, the officer corps could not be permitted to fail again and lose the initiative, as they had in 1918. The conclusions Stauffenberg drew from the revolutionary events of November 1918 set him apart from the prevailing opinion in the officer corps. Unlike them, Stauffenberg was convinced that the army *did* bear a political responsibility.

In the same context Stauffenberg remarked that the Wehrmacht was 'the most conservative institution in our state, but one which is simultaneously rooted in the people'. This statement is characteristic of Stauffenberg and puts him close to the conservative-cum-socialist position of Trott. It shows that he considered it necessary to maintain the army for reasons other than national political power and explains why he decided to cooperate with the socialists. It seems that his own plans for domestic politics have not survived, as is true of most information from this final phase of the resistance; but we know that they provoked the mistrust of Maass, precisely because they were kept so general. We can be sure that Stauffenberg's outline was a fervent and highly idealistic synthesis of socialist and conservative ideas. Stauffenberg knew about the deliberations of the Kreisau Circle and aligned himself with Yorck's views. However, there can be no doubt that he followed his own, albeit rather vague, political line and was therefore extremely reticent about his position.

Originally Stauffenberg had opposed the re-establishing of the labour unions, but he must equally be regarded as hostile to any return to the 1932 situation of rule by presidential decree. He was acutely aware of the threat of 'Bolshevism' advancing both inside and outside Germany, but a friendship developed between him and the socialist Leber, due in part to Leber's positive attitude towards the military. For this reason Stauffenberg abandoned his concerns about labour unions. Other factors in this were Stauffenberg's acknowledgement that the armed forces Supreme Command had failed the nation in the First World War and his memory of the alliance between Ebert and Groener[2] – which in his view had been forged too late. Stauffenberg independently built on Beck's initiatives, as is shown by his remark that when 'mere' military men achieve positions of power in government they 'always fail to solve social problems and come to grief over them; they often fail to realise that they are simply eking out their existence on the remnants of an outdated social order.' It was thoughts such as these that convinced him of the need to join the 'left'.

Everything points to the fact that Stauffenberg approved of Reichwein and Leber making contact with the communist Saefkow group.[3] The intention was obviously to test whether there was a chance of winning over any individual communist groups to their side. Leber's first contact led to his arrest, after which he became highly suspicious, since the communists' demands – following the officially announced line – appeared too moderate. The tactical motive for putting out feelers towards the communists was to deter agitation by the Soviet-controlled National Committee. Both Moltke and Trott were afraid that the tendency, recognizable in the programme of the National Committee, to mingle nationalist and Bolshevist elements, would lead to a 'German National-Bolshevism'. As we read in Moltke's 'Turkish' memorandum of late 1943:

> Ultimately we must avoid at all costs any situation that would make it possible to challenge a democratic German government as un-nationalist or anti-nationalist, and to bring about a merging of the nationalist, communist and pro-Russian factions in opposition to it.

Given the experience of the late phase of the Weimar Republic, the fear of such a combination of forces does not seem unfounded. It also played a serious part in Stalin's policy towards Germany even after 1945; at the same time it reflected the thinking of the resistance, who, as we have seen, equated National Socialism with Bolshevism. Communicating with communist groups therefore meant the exact opposite of an eastward orientation; rather it was an attempt, made in ignorance of the close ties between the communist resistance and Moscow, to win over independent-minded communists from the political line put out by the National Committee. Admittedly such a policy was only possible if peace could be made with Russia; this had been called for by Trott, by Moltke in his 'Turkish' memorandum and in Mierendorrf's action programme. Thus Stauffenberg's apparent leaning toward Russia may be explained as a tactical decision, analogous to the Russo-German relationship which developed in the 1920s despite Germany's fundamental rejection of the Soviet system.[4]

Even before Leber's arrest, Stauffenberg had had Leuschner in mind for the Chancellorship and, when Leuschner declined, he had chosen Leber. This prompted Goerdeler, while still in prison, to voice sharp criticism of Stauffenberg's 'unclear political line, seeking support from leftwing socialists and communists'. It also led Gisevius[5] to give Allen Dulles a thoroughly misleading account of the plans associated with Stauffenberg's tactical leftward manoeuvre. In fact the moves made by the anti-Nazi opposition in the early summer of 1944 amounted to a fundamental u-turn. On the one hand, Beck and Goerdeler were basically working for a change of government and associated reforms, the scope and direction of which were the subject of strong differences between them and the Popitz-Hassell faction. On the other hand, Stauffenberg, Leber, Trott, and probably Fritz von der

Schulenburg, together with those members of the Kreisau Circle who were still active, wanted to see a revolutionary uprising
of army and people, which would follow the completion of
Walküre (Valkyrie – codename for the assassination of Hitler).
This would unite political forces with the military leadership
and secure the political overthrow of Nazism. It would be a combination of 'revolution from above' with 'revolution from below', something which was quite incorrectly interpreted by
Gisevius as a 'revolution of workers, peasants and soldiers' in
the communist sense. Within a concept like this, the creation of
a popular democratic front made sense, whereas the implementation of Goerdeler's plan, which was an attempt to impose reforms on the military dictatorship, would have unwittingly ended
as a pale and questionable imitation of the ruling Nazi Party.

It is symptomatic of the different mentalities of the two factions
that Goerdeler took the Prussian reforms as his historical exemplar,
whereas Leber and Stauffenberg evoked the German uprising of
1813. This is not contradicted by Stauffenberg's statement that
Gneisenau's[6] organizing of the popular revolt could not provide a
precedent for the present political situation, and that it was only
permissible to unleash such forces if 'sufficiently strong moral
resilience were present in the structures of state and society'. In
the situation prevailing in 1944, when the collapse of the Third
Reich threatened to lead immediately to Bolshevist dictatorship
in central Europe, such reservations were no longer justified.
Stauffenberg was therefore determined to lead in combined
triumph those forces that had fought each other so bitterly in
1918, and had thus destroyed Germany's freedom of action in
foreign affairs. How strongly Stauffenberg's thinking was rooted
in the events of 1918 is shown by the fact that, unlike Trott, he
urged a diplomatic solution that would avert a military catastrophe
and a repeat of the humiliation of November 1918.

In its final phase, the plot was led by Stauffenberg, Leber, Trott
and Schulenburg. They clearly felt a sense of national responsibility, and a determination to provide clear political leadership and
authority. Aware that history could not be turned back, their actions were taking them into an open-ended future that would lead

to a reshaping of politics. Leber talked about the new state 'for which we must find a new and positive content and a convincing formulation'. But at the same time he admitted that he was unable to define the 'positive goal' that had to be erected in opposition to Nazism. In the same way Trott groped towards a fundamentally new answer to society's problems, one which would overcome the previous sterile party-political formulae. 'Recognizing our own real task,' he wrote in February 1944

> liberates us and gives us a purpose in life. It clarifies the choice among a confusing multiplicity of principles and values that fill the horizon of the modern world citizen. In this task we must throw off the burden and the depressing constrictions of the past century and through severe trials and hard work construct a new framework in which to live. We are still in the early stages, but among the ruins the outline of our task is emerging clearly in black and white.

In these visions, which were no doubt shared by Trott's close friend Stauffenberg, lay the hope of achieving an organic society that would unite, in a lasting synthesis, the qualities of naturalness and directness with the conditions of modern technological and industrial society, and national German traditions with a European consciousness.

XI. The 'German Way'

The social policy ideas of the resistance have to be judged by the assumptions of their own times. This period was seen as an age of transition, of the destruction of forms that had grown up through history, an age that sought new, universal solutions though without abandoning the link with historical continuity. 'With the events of January 1933,' Trott once wrote, 'a revolution took place in *Europe* which, though it has not destroyed our goals, has certainly buried the road which we thought would lead us to them. We have to think about this again.' Trott and his friends saw the Nazi seizure of power as a manifestation of the decline of the European community of nations since Versailles. For them the Nazi regime represented the final stage of a development that was defined by the rise of mass society and the loss of personal values as much as of the moral and Christian tradition of Western Europe.

The thinking of the resistance revolved around finding a solution to the crisis in European society, which was seen in the last analysis as an anthropological and religious one. The solution they sought would surmount former political and social battle-lines in a qualitatively superior synthesis and bring western man back into a direct relationship with his historic heritage and his transcendental destiny. Alfred Delp presented this concept in a lengthy memorandum entitled *The Third Idea*, which has not survived. In place of capitalism and communism which, due to 'too narrow an approach', played off the individual against the community or the community against the individual, he conceived of a social order which would restore the unity of the individual and society. Trott's memorandum, *Germany between East and West*, which has also been lost, started in principle from the same point and sought a middle way between 'the eastern principle of political realism' and the 'western principle of individuality'. A romantic view of Russia that had been common in the 1920s persisted subliminally in these ideas. They saw the way of life of the rural Russian-Orthodox population as simple, personal and yet rooted in the community. It appeared to them to be untouched both by Bolshevism and by technological civilization. It contained both extremes: western emphasis on individual freedom and eastern rationality; and each had to be brought into a proper relationship with the other. Trott spoke of the mission of the German spirit to act as a meaningful intermediary between east and west and concluded that a German element was indispensable in any future peace settlement in Europe.

These tentative attempts to reach a new synthesis typify the resistance's vision of society in that they did not – unlike some of the officer corps, including Oster – stubbornly insist on maintaining an unbroken imperial tradition. Goerdeler spoke of an answer that lay between 'Russian Bolshevism and Anglo-Saxon capitalism'; Schulenburg wanted to see a 'new communal order' that would defeat both 'parasitic capitalism' and 'Bolshevist collectivism';

Leuschner synthesized individualism and collectivism in the term 'person'. As Gerstenmaier expressed it, the attempt to create a new social and economic order that would transcend the old party doctrines, took them down a route between the western forms of democracy and eastern totalitarianism, between the subjective concept of the state and the objective one of the people, between personal economic initiative and the socialist planned economy.

The resistance thinking on social policy was strongly utopian and non-rationalist in character and thus fully reflects the particular intellectual and scientific atmosphere of the Weimar period. Many of the problems discussed at that time were concealed from view by the Nazi system; the increasing isolation of the resistance from foreign contact had a psychological effect even in cases were contact was maintained, and this led to a certain introversion in their political and social thinking. The social model in the mind of the anti-Nazi opposition, if for a moment we consider this as a single entity, contained thoroughly divergent views. Superficially it could be seen as a serious attempt to implement the principles claimed by the Nazis, but morally and politically perverted by them. It could be seen to represent a contemporary development of the ideas of the Prussian reformers, as a decidedly 'revolutionary' return to a view of man that had been in decline since secularisation, or as a realization of the romantically conservative ideals of a 'Christian state'. Nonetheless, in certain fundamental aspects there was a unity in this image of man and society. It was based on a rejection of the plebiscitary and egalitarian trends in modern society and on an attempt to control the pluralism of political interests and social forces through the discipline of an organic community. This notion of a 'conflict-free' society brought their thinking close to the Nazi ideology of a *Volksgemeinschaft* (national or racial community). It was equally bound up with the philosophy identifying the *Volk* with its *Führer*, society with the state, the individual with the community. It inspired their programmes for agriculture and small businesses and had something superficially in common with their idea of a partly institutionalised mechanism for creating an open elite.

There was a general view – even held by most socialists – that parliamentary democracy had been responsible for its own lapse into absurdity. Even those who defended it – Leber, Bergsträsser and, to a limited extent, Jakob Kaiser – saw a necessity for strong leadership to prevail over party rule. To a greater or lesser extent, all the forms of democracy proposed by the resistance restricted the involvement of political parties and even the opinion-forming function of public debate. The failure of the Weimar Republic had taught the lesson that a modern democracy requires a minimum of basic consensus in order to function. This in turn inspired the utopian call for an organic community in which the framing of political demands was restricted to the field of pragmatic decision-making and placed in the hands of indirectly elected representative committees. Their decisions would not arise from a broad public debate about the general direction of policy, but would be made by respected citizens chosen for their record of service to the local community. In this there was a strong trend towards de-politicisation, which is understandable in view of the complete political saturation of all areas of life by the Nazis. At the same time, however, it had its roots in the traditional German inexperience of politics and in the inadequate development of a political science along western lines, as had become clear in the Weimar period.

Even Ranke[1] had rejected western constitutional models as being inappropriate to German nature. This view, explained by the unique historical development of Germany, subsequently made it harder for parliamentary democracy to take root in Germany and contributed significantly to its lack of acceptance under Weimar. It was a key component in the political mindset of the 20 July resistance group. It can be found in Popitz, Hassell, Goerdeler, Bonhoeffer, Schulenburg, Trott, Delp, Moltke, Leber and Stauffenberg and shows how strongly the resistance was bound to tradition and how little German society was emancipated from a social structure dominated by 'respectable' burghers. The unwillingness of the Allies to respond to the overtures of the resistance merely aggravated the anti-western trauma, and this has been described by Dahrendorf and others as one of the causes of

Germany's crisis in the twentieth century. Individual democratic groups in the resistance deliberately distanced themselves from this central current in the thinking of the men of 20 July – despite the hermetic isolation of Germany from other countries. As early as 1937, Brill,[2] the founder of the 'German Popular Front' and co-author of the *Buchenwald Manifesto*, analysed the National Socialist variant of the 'idea of a *Volksgemeinschaft*', as well as the thought-processes underlying and supporting it. He called this 'the German ideology'.

The notion of the 'German way' was developed both by Trott and Moltke as the basis of a consciously European programme, though this was inevitably misunderstood abroad. The emphasis on unity as opposed to 'pluralist fragmentation' was specific to the anti-Nazi opposition's social vision. It was part and parcel of the resistance's 'backward-facing confrontation', as Ralf Dahrendorf so tellingly describes it; they were fighting against a regime in which a parasitic subversion of government institutions was taking place under the cloak of unity and community, carried out by a bewildering number of mutually competing and feuding organizations and cliques. This led to both the suppression and political neutralizing of the functional elites. For that reason the regime was judged by the conservative groups in the resistance to be thoroughly revolutionary, not to say 'Bolshevist'; it was a minority who were determined to oppose the regime, not only with the weapons of 'counter-revolution' but with revolutionary methods that were consciously democratic.

Their fundamentally anti-pluralistic and anti-liberal stance prevented the resisters of 20 July from overcoming their ingrained social prejudices and their assumption that they were the legitimate ruling elite. Thus they were unable to advance towards an open and democratically constituted society, which would avoid ossification of the political process caused by too much institutionalisation of divergent social and political interests. The constitutional thinking of the German resistance failed, in all fundamental questions, to make any contribution to the resurrection of German government and political life after 1945. The surviving representatives of the resistance, though several took up leading positions in political life, found themselves increasingly isolated politically; essentially they were left on the sidelines. The social vision and constitutional plans of the resistance, firmly trapped as they were in the German governmental tradition and its peculiarly unpragmatic conception of politics, nonetheless continued to typify certain characteristics of political thought in post-war Germany, even though they slowly retreated after the founding of the Federal Republic. Similar ideas, derived from the 'German way' model, such as the plan for an 'aligned society' (*die formierte Gesellschaft*) proposed by Luwdig Erhard, to perform the 'tasks of the community', still have an influence today. They remain just as hazy and display just the same distrust, not to say open hostility, towards the plurality of social forces, as was true of the social policy programme of the resistance. They place too great a demand on the political possibilities open to parliamentary democracy in the practical world of technology and industry.

There can be no doubt that there is a close link between the question of the social vision of the resistance and that of the motives which drove them to make the radical break with the National Socialist state and, as Stauffenberg put it, to 'commit high treason with all means available to us'. Those motives found a practical expression in the plans for a new order, but they went further than that, and it would be a mistake to measure the legitimacy of the Resistance only by their social and constitutional ideas, bound as they were to a particular historical situation. The German resistance was fighting for the dignity and Christian destiny of mankind, for justice and decency, for the freedom of the individual from political violence and social compulsion. The resistance waged this battle in an intellectual and historical context in which – not only in Germany – parliamentary democracy appeared to be in a grave crisis, one which made Germany's return to democracy questionable. The proposals worked out by the anti-Nazi opposition remained imprisoned in the tradition of German idealist philosophy, which, as Reichwein repeatedly stressed, made a direct relationship with politics more difficult.

We can learn much about the situation in Germany in those years from the fact that, despite their declared intention, even

Hitler's opponents were unable to escape the isolation of German political thought. The failure of the attempted coup d'état on 20 July 1944 put a tragic end to a heroic enterprise and meant that Germany would have to continue down the road to absolute catastrophe. It finally put paid to the 'German way'. By reason of Germany's traditional political conduct and the narrowness of its political thinking, in turn a reflection of belated social emancipation, German society proved incapable of developing modern and relevant alternatives to Hitler's profoundly reactionary dictatorship. This explains, on the one hand, why in 1933 National Socialism was able to take control of the machinery of state without serious opposition. On the other hand, it was only after understanding and coming to terms with this that Germany was finally able to achieve a spiritual conversion to the western tradition of constitutional politics.

The Kreisau Circle
and the future reorganization
of Germany and Europe

To this day the Kreisau Circle's[1] plans for a new order exert a strange fascination. Our longer historical perspective allows contemporary resonances to emerge from beneath those elements that were rooted in their own time. It seems profitable to present these resonances and present them in their context. Helmut James von Moltke was always concerned to preserve the documents and memoranda relating to the Kreisau programme and from those which have come down to us we can see that it represented a comprehensive scheme for the future. In its boldness and compelling inner logic, it is unsurpassed by any other plans for political reform produced by the German resistance.

The Kreisau programme emerged as a comprehensive alternative to the totalitarianism of the Third Reich, designed to crush it for all time as a force in world history. The Nazi regime appeared to the men of Kreisau to be not the result of a unique concatenation of recent events, but the inevitable consequence of a fateful trend in Western European history that had begun in the late Middle Ages. First becoming noticeable with the German Reformation, this was marked by the disintegration of universal Christendom, the loosening of obligations on the individual and the breaking down of 'natural orders'.

The Kreisau interpretation of history was closely bound up with the thinking of Count Helmuth James von Moltke and Peter Yorck von Wartenburg, who since 1939 had been presenting their ideas to a very close circle of friends, from which the resistance developed from 1940 onward, and which the Gestapo later named after the Kreisau estate. Its earliest origins date back to 1930, though unfortunately the publication of Moltke's correspondence is incomplete and does not make it possible to draw any firm conclusions about this. However, it was only in the late autumn of 1938 that the thinking which led to the fundamental turning point took on a more solid form.

In a letter Moltke wrote in October 1938 from London, where he was preparing for his final law examinations, he spoke of 'the last flickers of the old' and of his fear that Britain might turn fascist and 'the new' be stifled. In November Moltke returned to Germany 'deeply anxious about the future of Europe' and, according to a letter to Lionel Curtis, he occupied himself with the question of how the west could successfully be protected from being taken over by a 'Caesarist' regime. He saw himself faced with a choice: either to return to Kreisau and tend his estate, 'with all the benefits and disadvantages of the rural life and in the absolute certainty that I will never be able to do anything useful again', or to join forces with like-minded people in Britain and do everything in his power 'to defend the faith of Europe against the Caesars and perhaps to give it new expression'.

In February 1939 Moltke wrote to Lionel Curtis that it was his 'duty and obligation to make the attempt to be on the right side, whatever troubles, difficulties or sacrifices this may entail'. It was precisely Moltke's decision not to return to England that gave birth to the Kreisau programme. This phase saw the first plans for a new order, which were mainly set out in the memorandum written in the summer of 1939 and entitled *Small Communities*.

Moltke was very firm in rejecting the accusation that as a 'liberal landed aristocrat' he was merely retreating to the tranquillity of Kreisau. In June 1940 he wrote to his wife Freya: 'It is our duty to recognize what is repugnant, to analyse it, to defeat it through a superior synthesis and thus make it serve our purpose.' At the same time his thoughts were revolving around the question of whether he would be lucky enough to survive the stage 'between intellectual triumph and actual revolution', and he comforted himself by pointing out that in retrospect the time span between Voltaire's heralding of the French Revolution and its arrival had been short.

At the very pinnacle of Germany's successes in France, Moltke described them to Yorck as 'the triumph of evil'. Yorck, on the other hand, did not accept that it would have any deep effect on France – he spoke of the 'melodramatic finale of an epoch' and of signs of something new springing up. Moltke expressed the view that the war, by making a clean sweep, was offering 'a really great opportunity to advance in an age of genuine stability'. At the end of the year he wrote of the 'task of seizing control of the chaos in our midst'. If this succeeded, he claimed, Europe would enter a 'period of secure peace', since 'this is a war that will really decide the burning questions, and will not be followed by yet another war fought over the same issues'. The clear optimism of Moltke's basic position shows through in these statements and informs his vision that with the end of the war would come the opportunity to make a genuinely new start.

In the months following Germany's triumph over France, the decision was made to plan systematically for the approaching future. The fact that the Nazi regime was pushing on towards further external victories, did not put Moltke off his stride. As he saw it, the succession of military successes was bound to overstretch the regime's resources. He saw the Third Reich as standing at the close of a universal process of change which had become irreversible with the rise of the secular, absolutist and institutionalised state. This process had continued under the domination of nationalist thinking, of liberalism 'tainted' by egalitarianism and of a capitalist mass-society characterised by materialism, and had culminated in the mass-hysteria of the Third Reich.

Moltke was convinced that this was an age in which 'natural' social structures, and the potency of religious and cultural symbolism were being lost, an age of political double-speak and escalating social polarities, an age which was heading for perdition. To those who shared his viewpoint, it was clear that the old order must be allowed to burn itself out and that they must hold themselves ready to fill the 'vacuum' left by the 'destruction of the idolized state' – and by that they meant not just the Nazi regime but secularised states in general.

For Moltke the link between theory and practice was unarguable. In his memorandum on 'The starting-point, objectives and tasks', which had already evolved in the spring of 1941 from discussions with a group of close friends, we read that 'the end of the war will offer an opportunity to reshape the world for the better, into something society has not seen since the disintegration of the medieval Church'. From the outset he conceived of this change in a European context.

This vision, which led Moltke to talk of the 'Day X' of a fundamentally new beginning, and of a 'new chronology', is less isolated from the thinking of its time than its unilateral formulation might lead us to suppose. The notion of being at the end of a historical era, or of approaching a fundamental rupture between epochs, can be found throughout neo-conservative thinking of the 1920s. This is also true of Moltke's apocalyptic tone when he talks of the 'terrible dangers that may destroy everything'. The mainstream of neo-conservative thought proclaimed a revolution against the ideas of 1789, against enlightenment and liberalism, but at the same time turned away from the nineteenth century as being the embodiment of bourgeois materialism. It shared Moltke's vision of a seismic shift, which was bringing to an end the individualist age that had begun with the Enlightenment.

In a similar way, but with differing historical perspectives, the champions of the *Reichgedanken*[2] started from the notion that the west had begun to go wrong with the Reformation and the loss of the universal Christian church. This was particularly true of the Viennese social philosopher Othmar Spann,[3] whose ideas were widely accepted in the Catholic camp. And Protestant authors, taking their cue from the writings of Edgar Julius Jung, also adopted this viewpoint. There was a widespread idea that western society was in need of a fundamentally new beginning. In 1945 Hannah Arendt took it up in her philosophy of the 'fresh start'.

Direct influences on Moltke and Yorck cannot be demonstrated, though thought-processes of this kind were current among the Boberhaus Circle.[4] We may assume that the ideas of Eugen

Rosenstock-Huessy,[5] who in the broadest sense can be counted among the conservative revolutionaries, had only an indirect impact on them.[6] The stimulus that Moltke received from the Schwarzwald Circle in Vienna,[7] had more of a socialist flavour. In fact, all the evidence suggests rather that Moltke had no direct literary exemplars but wrote his memoranda on his own initiative, often after developing his ideas in conversation and correspondence with Yorck, Einsiedel and others.

The concept of 'small communities', formulated at an early stage, provided the intellectual core of the plans for a new order and has some wholly original features. However, it is not without antecedents in the history of ideas. It has a certain amount in common with Othmar Spann's theory of the 'organic state', which also based the social organism on small units: the family, occupational affiliations and local ties. It even has superficial similarities with Arthur Mahraun's concept of 'neighbourhood', as propounded in his 'Manifesto for Young Germany', published in 1927.[8] Moltke, and those in the Kreisau Circle who most closely shared his views, took up and enlarged on ideas that were circulating at the time, though no direct intellectual paternity can be proved.

As Moltke and Yorck saw it, the programme they sought consistently to develop was always a 'revolutionary' one, and we must not ignore the fact that they made great efforts to avoid watering it down or accepting compromises on its formulation. Hence Moltke waged a continual battle to persuade his new-found partners to agree among themselves or – as was the case for a time with Mierendorff – to prevent them dropping out altogether. In November 1943 he spoke about a 'fundamental danger-zone, where some people hope that by sacrificing principles they will make the boat more buoyant, forgetting that by doing so they make it impossible to steer'. He was intransigent in resisting such tendencies.

As the war progressed, Moltke was faced with the problem of when the right moment would come for the military coup that he now supported. Originally such thoughts were taboo in the Kreisau Circle, since its members assumed the collapse would be brought about by an internal process. However, as closer relations were established with the group around Carl Goerdeler and the military conspiracy led by Stauffenberg, the question arose as to how far political action, eventually taking the form of the 20 July attempt on Hitler's life, should anticipate the historical process. At the same time the conspirators came under increasing pressure to put an end to the escalation of crime and violence.

Like all revolutionaries, Moltke underestimated the length of time before Day X, yet at other times he feared it would take a lifetime to arrive. However, in the years that followed, his chief concern was that the attempted coup that Goerdeler and Stauffenberg were planning and with which most of the Kreisau members sympathized, should take place at the right moment and in accordance with the principles which had by now been worked out. Despite great efforts to establish a common platform, notably involving an accommodation with the socialists, Moltke was increasingly seen by his closest colleagues as the one who was putting on the brakes. He resisted 'all the hustle and bustle of the others', by which he meant chiefly the activities of the Goerdeler circle. 'Waiting is of course much harder than taking action,' he said early in 1943, when the idea of a coup d'état was assuming a concrete form.

A meeting with Beck and Goerdeler on 8 January 1943 revealed serious differences regarding the execution of the coup. Moltke's disparaging term, 'Kerenski solution', referred on the one hand to the premature implementation of the plan, and on the other to the lack of revolutionary determination in the attempted coup. Moltke noted sarcastically that it would be better if Haeften,[9] Yorck and Gerstenmaier 'do their little number without me'.

The same thing happened at the beginning of March. It was only with difficulty that he managed to restrain his Kreisau colleagues and hold to his 'relatively intransigent line', in the face not only of Yorck and Gerstenmaier, but also of Lothar König and Fr Delp. In a letter to Curtis he explained his criticism of the actions of the anti-Nazi opposition up to that point by arguing that 'we need a revolution, not a coup d'état'. The struggle for 'the right form and the right formula' went on. Early in August 1943 Moltke was once more complaining that 'Leuschner is showing rather unpleasant signs of having joined the grandees' club, a fact which has given such a boost to the reactionaries that we will no doubt slide into the Kerenski solution'. These statements reveal not only the sharp political conflict with Goerdeler but also Moltke's concerns about the timetable.

Indeed, in the spring of 1943, Moltke still did not see any opportunity to act. This partly reflects the fact that the Kreisau plans had not yet matured. At all events he was opposed to hasty action and pointed out the difficulties in an effort to persuade his comrades-in-arms to bide their time. He knew that only Stelzer and Mierendorff were on his side on this question. True, in August 1943 he showed a little more optimism, but only a few days later he was pleading once more for the coup to be postponed. The chances of a 'sound, organic outcome', he claimed, would be ruined by a premature revolution that was no more than a coup d'état. In the half-hearted planning for revolution he saw 'a serious symptom of the immaturity of our nation and our own situation'. By that he meant that as yet there were no signs that Germany was ready for a fundamental new beginning. 'In fact,' he went on, 'much more will have to lie in rubble and ashes before the time is ripe.'

The Kreisau plans for a new order have to be understood from their own perspective of the future. Their essential features were already contained in the memorandum on 'The Principles of Government', which Moltke wrote in October 1940. They were given full shape in the memorandum, 'Starting-point, Objectives and Tasks', which is dated 24 April 1941 and was reissued in a series of revised versions. It can be considered as the basic text of the Kreisau Circle. The document highlighted three principal views – the reawakening of the 'sense of inner commitment' to transcendental values, of the sense of responsibility in the individual and of 'forms of self-expression'. The memorandum had as its aim the total defeat of power-politics, nationalism, racism and the state. In it we read: 'We must aspire to a situation in which party-politicking and divisions among the people of this planet are of only secondary importance, because everyone, gathered together in one party' would be under the influence of the same ethical forces. This could only come about through the restoration of liberty and of a sense of responsibility.

This sounded immensely optimistic, but Moltke saw this revolutionary change of attitude itself as part of the historical process that was being accelerated and brought to its turning point by the war. For there had been a total crushing of all community structures below the level of the state, which in turn had been discredited through its inability to promote peace. The destruction of this state would rouse the 'people's innate need for commitment' and would create a vacuum that had to be filled. The document continued in near-euphoric mode: 'The end of the war will therefore see a mood of reflection and repentance such as has not been seen since the year 999 AD, when the end of the world was expected.'

Moltke's vision bore millenarian features, and in a certain sense it represented a transposing of the 'national awakening' syndrome of the 1920s into the vision of defeating the Nazi 'empire of evil'. The notion that National Socialism was no more than a transitional stage on the way to a fundamental reshaping of society, had also been put forward by Hans Zehrer[10] and quite a number of neo-conservative journalists. What was different about Moltke's projected goals was the fact that he had freed himself from the obsession with the 'German way' and was now placing his emphasis on Europe as a whole. In common with the myths of national regeneration in the Weimar years, Moltke believed that it was the younger generation who would be the mainstay of the new beginning. This contributed significantly to the intergenerational tension within the 20 July movement. Looking to the post-war diplomatic situation, Moltke still did not in 1941 anticipate Germany's total military collapse, but rather a general exhaustion of the combatants. This, combined with a breakdown of Nazi rule, would render the German Reich incapable of continuing the war. He hoped that opponents of the war would come to power in every European country and that they would urge a 'genuinely European peace settlement'. By 1944 the prospect had become much gloomier, but the hope persisted that the victors would also be seized by the burgeoning desire for a new order and that in this way the foundations for a comprehensive fresh start would be created.

Moltke predicted a political unification of the European continent in a world divided in two, where an Anglo-Saxon union centred on the USA would face a European continent augmented by part of Africa. However, this would not include Russia, which would be confined to its former borders. In the spring of 1943 this vision was transformed into the idea that 'Germany's contribution to the European order' would probably have to be made within the 'triangle of tension between America, Britain and Russia'. This would guarantee 'direct and indirect opportunities for preventing an organizational violation of European life'. As we know today, this was an illusion, born in the wishful thinking that the desired new order could still be set in motion.

In 1941 Moltke hoped that demobilization in Europe would result in a 'large common economic organization' made up of self-governing economic bodies. He had the visionary idea that the great nation-states should be replaced by 'self-governing entities with historical antecedents' [i.e. historically identifiable regions such as Lombardy, Burgundy, Bavaria *Tr.*]. These would have a variety of constitutional structures, but would be governed by a directly elected European legislature and a cabinet of departmental ministers. These would be assisted by a cabinet comprised of representatives of the governments of the semi-independent nations of Europe (*Länderregierungen*). It is here that we see the roots of the Kreisau plans for Europe, which were later worked out in much greater detail.

The Kreisau Circle's outline foreign policy consistently aimed for the political unification of Europe. With good reason they called for 'a right of European co-determination' for Germany and hoped they could predetermine a means for articulating political demands in post-war Europe. The Kreisau Circle, or it least its 'left wing' around Moltke and Yorck, was distinguished from the rest of the resistance by its consistent internationalism and uncompromising rejection of any form of nationalism as a political principle. All the same it remains open to question how far Moltke's emphatically federalist position, anticipating the idea of a Europe of regions, was shared by the majority of Kreisau who, like Delp, Gerstenmaier, Leber and Trott, thought in more strongly nationalist terms. In December 1941 Moltke wrote that both he and Yorck accepted that 'the success of our struggle will probably bring about the total collapse of our national unity', but that they were prepared to 'look that in the face'. On the other hand, the principles of the new order held firmly to the Reich as the 'supreme governing authority of the German people'. It is remarkable how willing Moltke was at this early stage to accept the consequences of Germany's distantly looming defeat. Clearly, we cannot accuse him of mere utopianism.

The Kreisau constitutional plans deliberately equipped the *Landersverweser*, or provincial governors, with all the attributes of sovereignty over restored territorial entities, in case the Reich should have no powers of negotiation. This coincided with federalist objectives and incidentally with the hope that at the provincial level it would be possible to evade the destruction of sovereignty imposed on Germany by the victorious Allies. This might win recognition for the reconstruction to be carried out by local initiative. A memorandum written in spring 1943 stated: 'However much Germany's freedom of action may by restricted by the inroads of foreign powers, it will still be necessary for small and intermediate self-governing bodies and functional organisations to continue operating spontaneously.' Germany's 'constructive contribution' to a European peace settlement would have to be the introduction of the 'personal socialism' advocated by Kreisau, as the 'structural solution to Europe's social and economic problems'. Thus their prime concern was, in this way, to guarantee the 'peaceful evolving of national culture' with which, as the 'Principles of the New Order' put it, 'the maintenance of absolute sovereignty of individual states' was no longer compatible.

The inner circle around Moltke never doubted that the principles of domestic policy they had developed together should also be applied to foreign affairs; the terms of a European peace settlement would depend, they believed, on a 'large measure of agreement on questions directly affecting the moral, judicial, social and economic aspects of life'. A memorandum written in advance of the third Kreisau conference traced the primary cause of the current world crisis to 'the way people have been morally and politically deracinated'. No dialogue between states was possible without the 'inward strengthening and outward securing of

individual rights and identity', as well as the 'reshaping of major
and minor social institutions'. With regard to the supposedly
identical nature of domestic and foreign policy we find no sign of
terms like '*raison d'état*' in the thinking of the Kreisau Circle.

'Europe after the war', as Moltke defined it in his famous 1942
letter to Lionel Curtis, seemed less a matter of hydra-headed
organizations than of the restoration of 'the image of humanity in
the hearts of our fellow-citizens'. This phrase, emotive as it sounds,
got to the heart of the matter, since the progressive brutalisation
of the regime and the ever more comfortless wartime conditions,
had plunged German society into a profound apathy, in which
the individual had reverted to a condition of mere vegetative
survival and had lost all interest in higher things. The effect of
this was aggravated by the breaking down of primary social ties
and of mature social milieus, which was partly deliberate and partly
resulted from the enforced migration and re-housing of millions
of ordinary Germans.

If the Nazi regime remained in power for long, it would lead to
the loss of the moral, intellectual and physical core of the German
people and end in a 'Germanic Bolshevisation'. This warning was
contained in a paper written in October 1942 for the second
Kreisau conference. The author was Georg Angermaier, a Jesuit,
but it was also worked on by Alfred Delp and Lothar König. If
the system was to remain in place 'until its internal resources were
exhausted' and it 'collapsed from within', the result would be
'intellectual and moral nihilism' among the broad mass of the
people and it would provoke a 'battle of everyone against everyone'.

Seen like that, there was little point in waiting for the collapse
to happen, and ways of overthrowing the regime had to be
examined. Removal of the Nazis by 'revolts from below' would
only bring 'needless destruction and a false "liberation"', with the
risk that 'new demagogues' would appear. These phrases show that
even among the conspirators the trauma of November 1918 was
still having its effect.

Because of the circumstances just described the only viable route
to be taken – as far as the Kreisau Circle was concerned – was 'the
removal of the system by an ideologically driven and integrated

group' whose success depended, however, on having sufficient time to spread their convictions more generally, and who would collaborate with 'sufficiently powerful forces' which would place themselves at the disposal of the cause. This was an allusion to joining forces with the military opposition to Hitler. Admittedly, a mere military dictatorship appeared obsolete; the principal role of the military was rather to establish a situation in which there would be an opportunity for a genuine formulation of political demands. Thus even when overthrowing the regime, it was necessary to preserve the primacy of politics.

The memorandum went on to define the central objective as that of restoring '*Volk*, Reich and state, which are being internally subverted and threatened' and 'liberating the essential strengths that Germans rely on'. This markedly nationalistic tone shows that the text was not drafted by Moltke and Yorck, any more than the call for a 'genuine democracy' came from their vocabulary. However, the notion that Germans needed 'a new inner mood and attitude', that enabled them to assume 'responsibility for life as a whole', was close to Moltke's and Yorck's thinking. This is also true of the diagnosis that the current situation was characterized by 'the loss of a sense of personality', by *Vermassung* and 'dumbing down', by an 'amoral energy' and a confining of the individual exclusively to 'the primitive business of staying alive and the gratification of basic needs'. The remedy for all this was to be the 'de-massing' of the masses and the forming of 'personal obligations' on the basis of secured rights and property. There was to be a 'restoration of private life' and an 'appreciation of intellectual and philosophical values'. Along with this went the regaining of man's capacity for faith, as Moltke would have agreed. The document went on to say that Germans had become 'a nation on the streets', whose sense of homeland had been destroyed by the policies of the regime.

The document quoted above represents the thinking of the Jesuit group and the parts that follow outline the future political structure for the Reich, to which they aspired. The paper sets out with rare clarity the anthropological assumptions underlying the Kreisau plans. Fr Alfred Delp devoted the greatest attention to these questions, which were closely related to his pastoral duties. He did not shrink from a self-critical admission of the 'impotence of the Church' and the inappropriateness of its theological answers to the 'desolation of mankind'. Delp observed a 'loss of religious and intellectual substance', a progressive *Vermassung* and indeed a 'loss of certainty in natural instincts'. He stressed the need to reverse the general psychological disintegration, which had led to an 'astonishing and frighteningly great disinterest in ordinary human concerns'. The very first things to be done, before politics in a real sense were possible again, were to restore the capacity for individuals to communicate with one another and to create a bare minimum of trust.

Delp was not afraid to talk about 'the agony of mankind', about how people were expending all their efforts 'in the struggle and fear for their bare existence' and were becoming 'incapable of any real emotion'. What was needed was the 'rediscovery of a western way of life'. Here he was picking up on what Moltke, in his earlier paper, 'Starting-point, Objectives and Tasks', had summed up in the term 'restoration of forms of self-expression'. The mood of cynical compromise and moral apathy was spreading, and not only in Germany; it appeared to be as much the cause as the effect of the Nazi dictatorship. It required the conscious re-establishment of everyday social relationships, so as to enable individuals to assume communal responsibility and to accept politics as the expression of communal interests. When facing his trial-judge, Roland Freisler, Delp later gave unforgettable voice to this concern with his prophetic-sounding call for revolutionary intervention: 'This twentieth-century revolution needs its definitive theme and the opportunity for creating a renewed, dependable context for humanity.'

Against this background Moltke's concept of 'small communities' gains a deeper meaning. Its aim was to make all forms of sub-governmental interaction of a partnership nature the starting-point for the political constitution. These included the family, neighbourhood, voluntary associations, study-groups, housing associations, youth groups and social or cultural institutions of all kinds, including social services such as the fire brigade and kindergar-

tens; but also the churches, sects and cultural and learned societies, as long as they served the common good. The inspiration for
all this lay in the Anglo-American world, which gave preference
to private over public initiatives. Hence Moltke became the champion of the greatest possible participation by responsible adult
citizens, who were suspicious of instructions from centralist organizations and bureaucratic structures. Only in 'small communities' could 'the feeling of responsibility towards all others' develop and be transferred from there to the political system as a
whole. Moltke's viewpoint embraced widely differing fields of action, but he considered that the restoration of primary obligations and loyalties and the long overdue reorganization of Europe
were mutually necessary to each other.

The liberation of individual spontaneity that Moltke wanted to
achieve contained an element that challenged the modern
institutionalised state. With the idea of making the activity of
individuals in 'small communities' a precondition for their taking
up political office, Moltke was aiming to restrict the state primarily
to a supervisory function. Domination by the state was to be
replaced by an organic pyramid of self-governing bodies, which,
while remaining private in a legal sense, would be granted electoral
privileges. This can be interpreted as a conservative version of the
Räte (soviet or council) system, yet underlying its position is the
Kantian philosophy of identity, which seems hardly to have been
modified by involvement with Anglo-Saxon pragmatism. A
problem arose with the political implementation of the principle
of 'small communities', because the indirect institutionalisation
it envisaged inevitably destroyed the element of spontaneity and
honorary office holding. For the advantage of the free formation
of elites and selection of leaders intended for the 'small
communities' would thereby be lost. It was not inconceivable that
this would mean the return to a class-based society.

With this concept Moltke hoped to see like-minded people
joining forces across European frontiers and becoming the
standard-bearers of the new beginning. This was what he meant
by the 'party of the like-minded' that he had addressed in the very
first memorandum, a party on whose solidarity he hoped to be

able to build the future Europe. Beyond this, the men of Kreisau saw certain opportunities to introduce, as a constructive contribution to peace in Europe, 'the idea of a personal socialism realized in sound forms of self-government', in which they saw 'a general solution to Europe's social and economic problems'.

The overall objective of Kreisau was to develop new social and political entities, which would replace the former governmental structures. It was this that they saw as their true European task. In one of the Kreisau texts we read: 'All in all, the internal reform of Germany must develop a language of its own, which is not derived from either extreme, capitalism or communism,' so that 'the influence of Germany's internal reform can help to build trust throughout Europe.' The men of Kreisau hoped that with effective support from the Christian churches they could achieve a new beginning for Europe.

For the great majority of Kreisau the goal of restoring a Christian way of life was part of the solution of the social problems which, in their view, had played a significant part in the crisis in western civilization that had culminated in Nazism. To some extent this attitude arose from a mistaken assessment of the causes for the Nazi rise and seizure of power – an attitude that Kreisau shared with a good many neo-conservatives. The social programme that Kreisau developed and which clearly stood apart from comparable plans made by the Goerdeler circle, ranged from the guaranteeing of basic social rights through to the detailed regulation of working conditions; it embraced joint decision-making in the workplace as well as industry-wide consultation and the guaranteed right to employment. To that extent it represented a socialist-influenced wish list that even today has not been completely fulfilled. In this context the men of Kreisau were anxious to avoid the forming of mass-organizations, in other words a return to the traditional labour unions. They were to be replaced by workplace communities in which employers and employees worked in co-operation. Nonetheless, Kreisau ultimately agreed to accept for a transitional period Wilhelm Leuschner's concept of a 'German Labour Union'. In the forefront of Kreisau thinking, as with Goerdeler's, was an economic and social structure that focussed on small and medium-sized businesses. In very large companies the Kreisau concept of workplace unions was impracticable, since it imposed undue restrictions on the employee's freedom of movement. As for their economic planning, it was predominantly influenced by *ordo-liberal* thinking, which was hardly suited to a structural removal of the conflict between capital and labour. Furthermore, an unbridgeable gap appeared between a centralized fiscal authority on one hand, and the idea of local self-government on the other. Kreisau thinking had this in common with the tradition of democratic socialism, which likewise oscillated between local self-government and central control of the economy.

The Kreisau proposals for a constitution in the narrower sense were the least innovative area of their thinking. We find a large degree of convergence with the drafts by the Goerdeler group, produced at the same time, albeit with certain socialist elements. Like Goerdeler, they considered that the parliamentary system had proved itself inadequate and had to be replaced by a constitution of mixed representation, which returned politics to its regulatory role. At the same time, there was a desire to ban the involvement of political parties, whose activities were seen as the principal cause for the emergence of mass emotions and their manipulation. In the early drafts political parties still get a marginal mention, but in later versions they disappear completely. Thus the justification that Theodor Steltzer gave for the desired corporatist self-government was not least that it guaranteed 'security against domination by centralist parties'. He complained that party rule 'inevitably brings political conflict into the smallest village and thereby destroys the sense of corporate responsibility'.

The constitutional model finally agreed upon relied largely on an over-emphasis of the principle of indirect elections; delegates from the parish and county level would sit in provincial assemblies (*Landtage*) and in the Reich parliament, whose authority was however essentially limited to the appointment of the Chancellor. Furthermore, the *Reichsverweser*, or Regent, acquired an unusually (and probably unintentionally) strong position, to which the draft constitution unwittingly gave authoritarian features. Equally unintended was the political weakening of the envisaged 20 provinces (*Länder*), whose populations were to be limited to between 3 and 5 million, and whose remit was extremely limited, in contrast to the strongly federalist programme. The over-extension of the partnership principle meant that the Kreisau plans failed to achieve a structure of federated states, and furthermore they gave the Regent the right of supervision over the provincial premiers. We can be certain that this was not Moltke's intention, since he sought to keep the state within bounds, and his ideas bore unmistakably anti-authoritarian features.

Kreisau's constitutional model resembled 'to a large extent' the constitutional plan by Hans Zehrer, published in 1932 in the monthly journal *Die Tat* ('Action'). Its weaknesses can be attributed to its attempt to combine corporatist and representative elements, and to restrict access to political activity essentially to meritorious (male) notables. One explanation for this lies in the fact that, in avoiding a return to the political atmosphere of the Weimar Republic, they gave disproportionate privileges to the executive. There is very little reason to trace these ideas back to the immediate experience of the Third Reich. Rather, they are an almost unbroken continuation of the broad current of anti-liberalism of the 1920s.

The unique contribution of the Kreisau Circle does not lie in the field of alternative draft constitutions, since these were coloured by the fashionable rejection of the parliamentary principle as completely outmoded, and since Kreisau aspired to historical forms which had not yet 'outlived their usefulness'. Their central objective was to overcome from within the 'spiritual devastation' wrought by Nazi tyranny. However it went well beyond this and by demanding the restoration of conditions for human political discourse it outlasted the specific constitutional debate. The conflict, never fully resolved, with the older conspirators in Carl Goerdeler's circle, concerned Kreisau's ambition for a fundamental upheaval, not merely a change of systems. The members of the inner circle, if not the others, considered themselves 'revolutionaries'. Their aim was not merely to revolutionize attitudes, but to create the social and material conditions in which individuals who were capable of self-determination and public responsibility could exist. In this respect the men of Kreisau must be considered as

dissidents in the conservative camp, who seriously sought to reform society and to place human beings and citizens at the centre
of their thinking.

Nearly six decades after the attempted coup of 20 July 1944 was
crushed, specific elements of Kreisau thought emerge again with
greater clarity. The concept of European regions, the consistent
advocacy of a United States of Europe, the determined confrontation
of Nazism as a political structure, the nostalgia for the shared
European values enshrined in Christendom and humanism – all
these are as much part of their thinking as is the call for spontaneous
solidarity based on the Christian spirit. In our present-day climate,
in which the term 'political disenchantment' (*Politikverdrossenheit*)
is doing the rounds, the fundamental concerns of Kreisau are gaining
in importance. They were endeavouring to define what is needed
to motivate the individual and give him or her the capacity to assume
public responsibility, and to restore credibility to public associations.
Unsuited as these ideas are to the present-day system of
parliamentary pluralism, they still cannot be entirely dismissed as
outmoded. While starting from differing political positions, the men
of Kreisau were united in a hazardous venture – launching forth
together into a new Europe. Had they succeeded they might have
occupied the position, to this day not really filled, of a critical yet
socially progressive conservatism in the constitutional life of the
German Federal Republic. They represented that side of Europe
that did not succumb to the allure of fascist dictators, and they
anticipated the shared aspirations for European unity that have
developed in the past four decades.

CHAPTER 5

Fritz-Dietlof von der Schulenburg and the Prussian tradition

Fritz-Dietlof, Count von der Schulenburg (1902–1944),[1] is one of the most important figures in the resistance movement of 20 July 1944. Long before Claus Schenk von Stauffenberg took centre stage in the plot to overthrow Hitler, Schulenburg was the inner driving force of the conspiracy. To begin with, like many of the conservative-minded resistance fighters, he had given his almost unreserved support to the National Socialist regime. As one of the most talented younger Prussian civil servants, he saw unique career opportunities opening up for him in 1933, which he initially exploited with his appointment as personal adviser to Erich Koch, *Gauleiter* and *Oberpräsident* of East Prussia. Remarkably, the appointment of Koch as Oberpräsident to replace a nominee from the Papen era, Dr Wilhelm Kutscher, can be attributed to Schulenburg's personal lobbying of Daluege[2] and Göring.[3] However, as early as the summer of 1933, the initial illusions had faded and Koch's disappointing leadership style, his tendency to Byzantine intrigue, corruption and almost feudal airs and graces, all drew the sharpest criticism from Schulenburg and led to a breakdown in their previously close relationship.

Schulenburg served as a *Landrat* (district prefect) in Fischhausen (East Prussia), then in 1937 as deputy chief of police in Berlin, and from 1939 as *Regierungspräsident* (provincial governor) of Silesia. In all these posts, he sought to put into practice his principles of effective, corruption-free administration that was open to modern developments and aware of its social responsibilities. However, in June 1940 he resigned his post as governor of Silesia and volunteered for military service with the tradition-steeped 9th Potsdam Infantry Regiment, whose officers were predominantly members of the aristocracy and a good many of whom were personally connected with Schulenburg. As an officer in an infantry battalion he was accepting a rather subordinate position. But he turned down subsequent offers of senior administrative posts in the occupied territory of Russia. Not until he became actively involved with the resistance did he seek a post as a ministerial civil servant in Berlin. He declined Himmler's offer of a relatively senior rank in the SS.

All this shows that Schulenburg was not bent on a public career. For all his cosmopolitan manners and easy adaptability he remained true to his aristocratic Prussian principles, deeply ingrained with the Protestant ethic. Unlike many others, he had never allowed himself to be corrupted, even in minor matters, by the prevailing ethos of the Third Reich. The inner independence of a personality firmly grounded in deep religious commitment, enabled Schulenburg to distance himself from daily events and prevented him from getting entangled in the jockeying for power which typified the inner workings of the Third Reich. Though he repeatedly found himself working in responsible and influential positions, he withdrew from clashes with colleagues – which were far from absent in his service career, and which his brisk and somewhat arrogant manner did nothing to alleviate. Instead he settled for posts which, though perhaps of lesser status, guaranteed him greater personal independence; however, he was not afraid to express frankly the true motives for his decision. This personal independence, which marked him out throughout his life, would have made him exceptional even under the conditions of a normal society. In the corridors of Nazi power, where everything depended on intrigue, personal favours, nepotism and the 'old pals' act', Schulenburg's moral scruples were incongruous and frequently met with incomprehension, even among those who sympathized with his views.

By his own admission this young aristocrat had, prior to his successful entry into the civil service, scarcely concerned himself with politics. Why he joined the Nazi Party at an early stage, and must be considered an active supporter of its aims during the phase of the Party's seizure and consolidation of power, is a question of fundamental interest, and one which goes beyond the details of his personal life and background. It is tied up with the motives that caused the conservatively disposed German elite to place their hopes in Hitler and the National Socialist movement. In many respects, though, Fritz-Dietlof von der Schulenburg represents an exceptional case. While many of his contemporaries, who sympathized with German nationalist and neo-conservatives ideas, took a positive view of National Socialism without becoming personally involved in it, Schulenburg decided as early as 1931 to work actively for the Nazi cause, even though at the time this could certainly have damaged, even destroyed his career. After a brief spell in the *Bündische Reichschaft*[4] he joined the Nazi Party because, as he wrote in October 1932, he wanted to 'play an active part in the political battle'.

Schulenberg's decision to join the Nazis was not wholly surprising, even though it was contrary to Prussian civil service regulations at that time. One of his brothers was already a member, another was in the SA, and Fritz-Dietlof's step came as a relief to his strongly German-nationalist family. We know little about his own motives, but we can be fairly sure that he expected the National Socialist movement to succeed in solving the social problems and overcoming the class struggle in a spirit of 'national community'. Much has been made of Schulenburg's pro-socialist tendencies, which in Recklinghausen, (the Ruhr town where he was posted early in his career) earned him the nickname of the 'Red Count'. However, this motive should not be overestimated. Schulenburg certainly sympathized with the Strasser wing of the NSDAP and he frequently said remarkably favourable things about Gregor Strasser.[5] However, his Nazi sympathies sprang from a general position of protest against the 'Weimar system', for which 'socialist' attitudes represent only one of many causes.

As early as 1928 Schulenburg had spoken of the opportunity for the Nazi Party to help in forming 'the nucleus of a movement for German renewal'. He stressed the need for a 'radical revolution

stemming from a new Prussian attitude to government and a new
German view of the world'. This chimed with the expectations of
many representatives of neo-conservatism, who saw the Nazi Party,
though imperfect and not yet free from its party-political origins,
as the first stage in a comprehensive movement to revitalize
Germany. He told friends apologetically that he was aware of the
'shady side of the Party' and that it was full of irregular goings-on
and dubious individuals. However, he had come to the conclusion
that 'no rallying of the people is possible under any other banner'.
This equated with the notion, widespread among the middle-class
rightwing camp, and deliberately nurtured by Nazi propaganda,
that the 'popular movement' of Nazism was instrumental in the
drive towards a profound, epoch-making and all-embracing
regeneration of the state and *Volk*.

An important factor in bringing Schulenburg into the Nazi Party
was his conviction that – particularly in northern Germany – it
was turning into a genuine 'people's movement' and thus shedding
the characteristics of a political party. At the same time he shared
the view that a seizure of power by the Nazis would provide the
starting-point for a fundamental reshaping of state and society. It
is no coincidence that even in the regime's latter years he repeatedly
spoke of 'the coming state' or 'the coming Reich'. In this respect
he was a proponent of the myth, created by Oswald Spengler[6] and
others, of the dawn of a new 'revolutionary' age that would reverse
the unfortunate developments of the recent past, which had been
caused by individualism, rationalism and the structures of western
capitalism and materialism attributable thereto. At the start of his
career at least, when the influence of Ernst Niekisch and Friedrich
Hielscher[7] is discernible, Schulenburg can be counted firmly
among the 'conservative revolutionaries'. Admittedly he held a
variant of this position, which was moulded by the specifically
Prussian tradition of government. In his proposals for reform we
find the typical elements of neo-conservative philosophy: rejection
of the metropolitan way of life, idealization of rural living
conditions, a deep distrust of the growth of vast industrial
companies and the urge to replace these with skill-based small
and medium-sized businesses. The notion of re-populating rural

areas in the east, which is such an important part of this mindset, is something that Schulenburg harks back to with remarkable emphasis. Despite his administrative experience in the Ruhr region, he felt a deep attachment to Germany's eastern marches, and he shared with many the idea that only in these still quasi-colonial lands could the strength develop for Germany's inner rebirth.

However, the radical quality that imbues Schulenburg's vision of a fundamental reform of the west, is not enough to explain his strong affinity with the Nazi movement, no matter how much its political style, deliberately favouring personal initiative and technocratic 'fixes', appealed to his urge for energetic action and involvement. True, Schulenburg had no time for the Bavarian braggadocio of men like Göring and Röhm, apparent even in the years before the Nazis seized power. In this he was obviously influenced by Gregor Strasser and his north German supporters. However, Schulenburg did not share Strasser's conviction, growing firmer since the spring of 1932,[8] that the Nazi Party should abandon its role of radical opposition and embark on constructive cooperation and serious political responsibility. Instead he believed that the remaining 'time-frame' should be used to 'renew and take the party in hand, by removing the bigwigs'. Purging the Party of opportunistic elements was 'a necessity if the Party is to carry forward the idea'. Such assertions reflect the illusions typical of those factions that switched from the neo-conservative camp to the Nazi Party.

For this reason, in October 1932, Schulenburg rejected as dangerously misguided the idea that the Nazi Party should participate in government following the November General Election, especially if the cabinet was headed by von Papen as Chancellor. This, he said, would 'deal a fatal blow to the party as the political vehicle for the idea of Nazism'. Though based on very different assumptions, this was close to Hitler's position at the time – he too repeatedly insisted on 'maintaining the purity of the idea'. On the other hand, no doubt influenced by Strasser's close associates, Schulenburg expressed definite doubts as to whether Hitler was the 'great statesman', capable of representing the Movement in the 'game of political chess' with a 'sure touch'. He feared Hitler might 'perhaps even lack the ultimate toughness' needed. He regretted Gregor Strasser's resignation from parliamentary office, which took effect on 8 December 1932. He considered Strasser the 'strongest constructive force' among all the Führer's lieutenants and the 'only man of real stature', and he accurately predicted that Strasser would 'not fight out his battle in the rear of the party'.[9]

Another factor in Schulenburg's position was his strong criticism of the social-democratic leanings of the Papen cabinet. This places him firmly on the radical wing of the Nazi Party, which later demanded a 'second revolution'. He roundly dismissed any hasty compromises, which would threaten the desired move away from party-political domination and lobbying by vested interests. He allowed himself the hope that, after a period of upheaval, his vision of a class-free and party-free state would, in the logic of events, come to pass. We do not know whether Schulenburg remained in contact with Strasser and his supporters after his resignation, but Schulenburg must have been personally affected by Strasser's murder in the 'Night of the Long Knives' on 30 June 1934. Schulenburg basically agreed with the idea of a party purge and considered the influence exerted by Röhm to be disastrous and intolerable. In many circles the liquidation of the SA leadership was welcomed as a step that Hitler had to take, in order to rid the Movement of extremists. Schulenburg was fundamentally opposed to Röhm's plans for a militia, and probably considered action against him necessary. It is possible that Schulenburg was himself in danger, due to his close links with Strasser's colleagues, but we know little about how he reacted to the events of 30 June 1934.

Despite certain reservations, when the Nazis seized power Schulenburg expected 'policies that would revolutionize all spheres of life', and he was convinced the Movement would rid itself of its 'party ballast' and take over the state. For the first two years of the regime he devoted his life to playing a part in this epoch-making task. In doing so he concentrated on asserting the principles of the Prussian governmental tradition as he saw it. He considered the National Socialist movement to be the indispensable catalyst for a much-needed transformation, which would lead to a perfectly organized, yet non-bureaucratic, rule by civil servants.

Schulenburg was consistent in his support for the not uncommon idea that the Nazi Party should shrink down from a mass movement to an elite political 'order' (in the chivalric sense). Its function then would consist of acting as the vehicle for 'political will', keeping alive the 'National Socialist ideal', training and educating the nation and selecting new leaders.

Schulenburg combined energetic organizational activity on behalf of the Nazi Party with efforts to serve the interests of long-term reform. He therefore took part in the discussions of the 'Königsberg Circle',[10] whose members included both Party representatives and a number of conservative nationalists. The group examined projects for reform in the light of the 'Prussian socialism' that Schulenburg stood for. This was not, however, something that fitted well with the inclinations of the new regime, which was basically uninterested in that kind of planning.

As head of the political office of the *Gauleiter* of East Prussia, Schulenburg initially applied all his energy and passion for activity to implementing the new Nazi order that he envisaged. While he did not hesitate to intervene in administrative matters, he opposed any reintroduction of the jobbery and patronage that he had criticized so strongly in the Weimar period. With the introduction of the 7 April 1933 Law on the Re-establishment of the Professional Civil Service, a serious conflict over the treatment of civil servants arose between Schulenburg and the *Gau* office for the civil service, which made his position increasingly untenable.

He still believed he could dismiss the mounting corruption and breaches of the law as the inevitable by-products of a transitional phase. It took many years for him finally to conclude that it was impossible to remove the evils of the system from within. In his letter of justification to *Gauleiter* Koch, dated 31 December 1935, he castigated Koch's personal corruption with as little ceremony as he did the errors in his staff appointments. In the same letter, he drew attention to the increasing detachment of the Nazi Party from the myth of the Führer, a trend that was attracting growing criticism from a public that still adulated Hitler. 'If we keep on hearing this kind of unprompted talk from the people, as is widely the case, then it is an ominous sign of how far the people and their leaders have drifted apart in this part of the country.' At the time, Schulenburg may still have hoped that this phenomenon was confined to East Prussia. Even so, he must have had to abandon the illusion that Germany's eastern provinces could become a showplace for the National Socialist revolution. He expressed his approval of, and may even have contributed to the thoroughly constructive 'East Prussia Plan', which was intended to reduce the region's total economic dependence on agriculture. 'East Prussia is historical Prussian territory,' he wrote to the *Gauleiter* in July 1933, 'and as such has the mission to re-establish once and for all the Prussian lifestyle of struggle and toil. There are areas where even we National Socialists have departed very far from that.' At that time Schulenburg's opposition to the spreading corruption in the Party was already becoming apparent, and he ended by summing it up in the phrase: 'With the people and Hitler, and against the fat-cats.' Like many of his contemporaries, Schulenburg was still unable to appreciate that it was Hitler himself who was promoting the accelerating process of moral and political subversion. It was only the circumstances surrounding the dismissal of the *Gauleiter* of Southern Westphalia, Josef Wagner, which removed the scales from his eyes.[11]

Schulenburg's disillusionment with the National Socialist system did not happen overnight; the process was a protracted one and in many respects it appeared contradictory. Thus he was largely in agreement with the foreign policy aims of the regime, much as he condemned the methods applied. This was particularly true of the 'crushing' of the Bolshevist system, which he saw as the greatest task of the age. He agreed with the Nazi concept of *Lebensraum* (living-space). He spoke of the 'grandeur and beauty of the east'. Building it up and filling it with 'new strength' he saw as a 'mammoth task, which will decide whether our nation ultimately succumbs to urban civilization or once more takes root here in the east and rejuvenates itself'. In Schulenburg's war-diary from the summer of 1941 we read: 'We must proclaim the development of the east as a great work of liberation from the confines and poverty of what is now Germany,' and 'drive the German people forward to happiness and greatness.' Certainly we should make some allowances for these rash statements, influenced as they were by Germany's early military successes in Russia, particularly since Schulenburg soon had an opportunity to experience conditions in the occupied Russian territories at first hand. He hesitated before turning down the opportunity to become General Commissioner of the Ukraine, and even his later memorandum on the creation of city 'partnerships' is based on the automatic assumption of a German-dominated Greater Europe stretching from Vilnius, Minsk and Lublin in the east, through Prague and Brno to Groningen in Holland and Liège in Belgium. Schulenburg was still steeped in the agrarian romanticism of the 1920s, as is seen from his call for a comprehensive return to agriculture, for a return to a human society bred in the soil and for what he called 'the swing from the city to the countryside'.

However, Schulenburg differed fundamentally in his view of the political measures required for the creation of a 'new Europe with an eastern bulwark'. The conditions necessary for the 'rebirth of western values' that he aspired to were the prevention of all gratuitous exploitation, protection of the basic freedom of the individual, of ownership, of opinion and religious belief, and the rule of law in place of arbitrary powers. The peoples living under Germany's protection must not be robbed of their 'national character', or of their 'freedom to pursue their own cultural and political development unhindered'. Alongside the policy of developing the east, there must be a thorough cleanup in the 'Old Reich', replacing corrupt individuals by the most able men available. He added the prophetic warning that 'if people and property in the occupied lands were seen as mere objects for ruthless exploitation', it would amount to 'Bolshevism in another form'. This vision, which was far removed from Hitler's intensive plans for a war of racial annihilation, appears in many respects to have been appallingly naïve. What is more, it shows that the troops in the field had little experience as yet of 'criminal military orders' [the standard term for the orders to kill all Soviet commissars and partisans on sight *Tr.*]; we can also see a contradiction between Schulenburg's colonial vision and his assessment of the military situation at that time, which indicates a relatively good insight into the strategic thinking of the German leadership. He certainly did not expect the Soviet Union to be defeated before the spring of 1942, nor that the whole war would come to an end earlier than 1943.

Schulenburg's deliberations on eastern policy follow the official Nazi line on many points. However, they spring from different roots and pursue very different goals. The notion that Germany had a cultural mission in the east was a commonplace of German imperialism before 1914 and reached a peak in the pan-German movement. Ambitious territorial plans to subject (the then Polish) East Prussia to German control were by no means the preserve of the nationalist and National Socialist movements. They were even discussed by those conservative nationalists who, on 20 July 1944, emerged publicly as implacable opponents of the Nazi regime. Germany's *Drang nach Osten* (eastward urge) had undergone a modification through the influence of neo-conservative ideas, particularly Moeller van den Bruck's concept of 'young nations'.[12] From the time he spent in the occupied regions of the Soviet Union, Schulenburg, too, felt that the Russians, and other Soviet peoples with whom he came in contact, represented a young, 'unspent' population, untouched by western civilization, and he drew admiring attention to their simple religious faith.

Schulenburg convinced himself that, once the Bolshevist system had been stamped out, the peoples of Eastern Europe could live in harmony under German supremacy. He also believed, very much in the manner of Oswald Spengler and his followers, that the Reich was destined to assume the task of 'replacing parasitic capitalism by a social order based on communities'. His political beliefs were founded on the idea of a global confrontation between a collapsing, capitalist west and an east that had adopted the principles of 'Prussian socialism'. The idea of a 'common Germano-Slavic destiny', and of its being some consolation for Germany's defeat in 1918, had a profound influence on Schulenburg, often through indirect channels.

That Germany's mission was to lead Europe, Schulenburg was in no doubt at all. Only rarely do we find him worrying that, in seeking an eastern solution, Germany would be resisted by nationalist sentiment among what he called the 'protected peoples'.

Yet his intention was to allow them political as well as cultural autonomy, and he believed that order could be maintained, not by the might of the bayonet, but by superior leadership.

Today it is hard for us to put ourselves inside the minds of the ruling class at that time. Their ideas were characteristically reinforced by an exaggerated anti-Bolshevism and an unreal romanticization of Russia. Viewed objectively, the nationalism and imperialism in these thought-processes is unmistakable; subjectively the intellectuals of the right, by whom the young Schulenburg was influenced in the 1920s, dreamed of returning to a perfectly integrated society, for which Eastern Europe would provide a seedbed. This incapacity for sober political analysis was typical of a whole generation; they were easy prey for brilliant propagandists like Hans Zehrer. In Schulenburg the flaw was combined with the illusion that the magnitude of the task would transform the mediocrity of the means and help to bring about what was seen as a historical necessity.

For Schulenburg was in less and less doubt about the looming internal decay of the Nazi regime and its decoupling from the Prussian tradition of government. In a letter written in spring 1943 he accused the Nazi leadership of acting counter to the 'tradition of the state and its inherent laws'. In earlier years he had believed it would be possible to reverse the irregularities and excrescences of Nazi rule, to impose policies that were based on simple criteria of quality and practicality, and to bring to power a governing class of total integrity. Now, however, he recognized that this was contrary to the whole essence of Nazi tyranny, though admittedly without appreciating the causes in detail. In spring 1941 he told his wife how 'stupid' he had been before; when returning to the problem of selecting leaders it had become clear to him that in the 'coming Reich' a central role would be ascribed to Prussian institutions, 'because the Party will then drop out of the picture'. Under interrogation by the Gestapo he expressed this insight with typical succinctness:

> The more I thought about what was happening, the clearer it became to me that all the features had a single origin: *force without*

restraint, inside and outside. To begin with I looked for opportunities to remedy this evil by reform. But gradually I came to realize that reform would no longer do any good, since everything is interlinked and based on fundamental facts which are immutably bound up with the *nature of the system.*

Schulenburg acted from an internally consistent position. His decision to place himself at the service of the National Socialist movement had the same intellectual foundation that later drove him inevitably into the resistance camp. The coinciding motives for his support of Nazism and for his ultimate bitter opposition to it come as no surprise. What is harder to explain is why a personality of such remarkable human and professional stature could for years hold the mistaken belief that, under the conditions of the Third Reich, it was possible to work constructively and point the way to a new future. It is not easy for those living today to appreciate the psychological power of the myth of a national renaissance, which Nazi propaganda was able to exploit successfully. One can perceive a collective autosuggestion among important sections of the German elite, or a psychological compensation for the years in which it was impossible to articulate any sense of national identity through the Weimar political system. At all events, the myth of a fundamental new beginning, which had failed in 1918 and was now overdue, goes a long way towards explaining the otherwise incomprehensible willingness to give the new system the benefit of the doubt. Under other circumstances they would scarcely have accepted the political Messianism they saw National Socialism to be.

In view of the considerable degree of ideological identity between the neo-conservative movement and the ostensible goals of the Nazi Party, it is not surprising that the neo-conservatives, more than anyone, displayed a political blindness that even the nationalistic euphoria of August 1914 had failed to induce. We cannot but notice that even declared opponents of Hitler and seasoned practitioners of the political trade were drawn into the wake of the apparently self-generated success of Nazism. Julius Leber, as a concentration-camp inmate, was paradoxically shielded from the reality of the Nazi reign of terror and actually believed that Hitler should be given a chance to bring about a settlement between the workers and the state and achieve a lasting solution to the problems of society. It was the academic intelligentsia, vacillating between the party lines, who were particularly prone to wishful political thinking, willing to overlook the obvious weaknesses of the Nazi movement and its Führer; the same was true of the exponents of the presidential system, whether it be Heinrich Brüning, Kurt von Schleicher or Franz von Papen. As a background to this there were seething social resentments, culminating in an exaggerated anti-communism that coincided with the tangible interests of the German upper class. When we read time and again in the literature about the susceptibility of the 'masses' as a factor in the Nazis' success in mobilizing support, we should not overlook the fact that large groups in the upper echelons of society and government were equally subject to an irrational collective neurosis, culminating in the hope that the Nazi Party would, if properly handled, strip off its anarchic garb and willingly take its part in the keenly anticipated 'national state'. Part of this illusion was the widespread hope, which Hitler in fact fulfilled in the early years of the regime, that he would become more moderate once in power and part company with the 'forces of social revolution' in his movement.

As early as 1931 Schulenburg had, in various lectures, presented a concept of fundamental reform that was very closely allied with Oswald Spengler's 'Prussian socialism'. Like Spengler, he rejected outright the Weimar constitution and the parliamentary system. To the young civil servant, the existence of parliament and political parties appeared to be the driving force undermining and breaking down the 'Prussian idea of the state', corrupting the professional civil service trained in the Prussian mould. Schulenburg's invective against the 'hysterical rubbish about Republic, Constitution and Flag', his willingness to repeat accusations that behind the activities of political parties were 'dark powers' alien to the German nature, his frequent support for anti-Semitism – all single him out as a relatively uncritical pupil of Spengler. We find again and again in Schulenburg's memoranda different versions of Spengler's dictum: 'Without the public servant as a class, the German people is not imaginable, either as a race or in its present dangerous situation. Given the circumstances of the twentieth century, the notion of service to the state *must* be developed again, a sense of moral status capable of carrying the state forward into the future.'

Schulenburg believed in the possibility of a social order that transcended class and in the merging of conflicting social interests into a virtual identity of state and people. At the core of his political thinking was a historical utopia, projected into the future. The Prussia of Friedrich Wilhelm I and of Frederick the Great, which he regarded as his lodestar, never existed. In invoking the Frederician tradition, he gave it the same idealistic slant as Spengler had done in his doctrine of 'Prussian socialism'. Moreover he himself embodied much of the Prussian heritage, the core of which, as he saw it, was a selfless, dedicated yet far from subordinate civil service. He idealized the great Prussian public servants of the reform era and measured his own actions against this ideal. An important part of this was firmness of conviction, which included a willingness both to accept contradiction from subordinates and to confront his superiors with unpalatable truths. In Schulenburg, Prussiandom and the Protestant ethic were inextricably bound up with one another.

In the initial phase of the Nazi regime, Schulenburg had looked on the National Socialist movement as merely an interim step to a fundamental restructuring based on the classic Prussian model. He supported the efforts, initiated by the Reich Ministry of the Interior, to achieve a sweeping centralization and fundamental reform of state administration. For a transitional period he considered it essential to fill civil service positions with representatives of the Nazi Party. But he was in no doubt that in the long run their place would have to be taken by a technically well-qualified corps of civil servants who, admittedly, would have been educated in the spirit of Nazism. His aim was to blend Prussiandom with National Socialism. His numerous memoranda and lectures are woven around the problem of how to separate organically the jurisdictions of the Party and the civil service, and how to counteract the progressive fragmentation of political and administrative agendas and the neglect of the professional civil service.

In the event, things took precisely the opposite course. True, there was a constant stream of complaints from Party leaders that all power lay with the state bureaucracy and that the Party was largely without influence. At the same time, with certain exceptions, local and regional offices of the Nazi Party found themselves downgraded in relation to the local authorities. Thus the impression might be gained of an increasing consolidation of state power. However, to an ever greater extent, important fields of governmental action were taken away from the responsible departments and placed in the hands of special administrative bodies that were taking root in the twilight area between Party and state. It was in the most senior positions that the civil service was becoming less and less able to hold its own against unchecked Party influences, and this was Schulenburg's greatest concern. He fought vainly against widespread hostility to civil servants within the Nazi leadership. To begin with he may have cherished the illusion that the aggressive downgrading of the civil service was not the will of the Führer. From 1934 onward, Schulenburg repeatedly invoked Hitler's positive statements in *Mein Kampf* about the role of the civil service, as well as the promise Hitler had made in Potsdam's garrison church that he would honour the Prussian tradition. Yet Hitler had done so only for tactical reasons.

The proposals for reorganization, which Schulenburg had been working on since 1934, were aimed at overcoming the continual tension between the state and Party authorities. He believed he had found a solution to the problem in a merging of staff at all levels of the political and administrative hierarchies. As a corollary of this he called for joint training of young party officials and civil servants. But this would surely not have been a means of removing the permanent institutional conflict. Rather, it would have destroyed the vestige of independence that the civil service had been able to preserve from incursions by the Party. Schulenburg overlooked the rule that dated back to the beginnings of the Nazi movement, whereby Hitler's subordinates were bound by unconditional loyalty to their Führer alone, and were not subject to any form of bureaucratic control whatsoever. This of course ran completely counter to Schulenburg's notion of a modern bureaucratic state. The 'personal leadership' demanded by Hitler and his satraps represents the absolute opposite of administrative action based on the principle of a regulated and devolved bureaucracy. In the same way, the concept of the 'legality' of administration was completely foreign to Nazi ideas. To that extent, Schulenburg's well-intentioned attempt to reconcile the Prussian tradition of administration with the Nazi Führer-principle was doomed to failure.

Schulenburg was certainly willing to go some way to meet Nazi wishes. The public servant, whom he envisaged as representing the class which was the true pillar of the state, was not the average lower-ranking official. He took as his models the *Oberpräsidenten* (provincial governors) and ministers of the age of Prussian reform, in other words the epitome of those exercising high political functions. He also viewed the problems of government exclusively from the perspective of an inner circle of general administrators, even though had occasional opportunities to get to know other branches of government – as when he worked in the Reich Ministry of Economics. The professional civil service in the areas of justice and finance remained largely a closed book to him. He held the classic civil service view, which equated administrative activity with the assumption of sovereign functions. Consequently, he wanted to return the status of the civil service to its original fields of duty.

Schulenburg's ideal of the public servant contained some thoroughly undemocratic notions. This was typical of his personal style of disregarding superficial niceties, administrative rules and occasionally boundaries of authority. The senior civil servant he envisaged was, on the one hand, the counterpart of the military officer, while on the other he was required to possess qualities of political leadership. When people raised the objection that politics meant 'conflict' and this was not part of a bureaucrat's job, he immediately replied by insisting that civil servants, in addition to the classic 'Prussian' virtues, must possess 'heroic' traits. At the same time, the homogeneous governing elite that must be created was to be distinguished by its commitment to the people and its social attitude, whatever that might mean. 'The administrator of the future,' he wrote in 1932, must be something of a 'leader of the people.' He recognized that this could not apply to public service as a whole, and therefore made a distinction between 'senior posts with independent responsibility and powers of decision, and jobs concerned only with administration and organization'. For the latter he wanted to create an 'intermediate type, somewhere between employee and official'.

The civil service of the future was above all to be a community bound together by shared attitudes. Echoing Spengler, in 1931 Schulenburg described the position of the governing elite as derived from 'the circumstances of blood, the soil and history'. In this connection he spoke of 'the chivalric ideal of service to the population as a whole'. Access to the elite corps of public servants was to be open. Training would be provided in specially established colleges. The selection of people for the top official posts was to be based solely on the criteria of performance and strength of character. Schulenburg considered the previous requirement for a degree in law as superfluous. In the interim he, like Johannes Popitz, called for the separate training of civil service candidates, for which the principles of the Prussian general staff were the model. The senior civil servants themselves were to be bound to the countryside through land grants and kept away from the corrupting influences of the big city. These ideas, too, were remarkably close to Nazi thinking, as represented by people like Walter Darré,[13] albeit with far more emphasis on the elitist elements.

This idealized concept of the public servant represented the kernel of the reorganization plans that Schulenburg pursued with such tenacity. He certainly changed the emphasis at times, not least under the influence of his disagreeable encounters with the Nazi leadership. At the same time he drew varying degrees of inspiration from military exemplars. Schulenburg's image of the Prussia of history was permanently shaped by the traditions of the Prussian army, and he never tired of saying how crucially it had influenced the development of the civil service. Like many of the neo-conservative writers by whom he was directly or indirectly influenced, Schulenburg had a tendency to transpose military terminology and experience to the civil sphere. Thus he compared civil servants to the 'shock-troop officers of the Great War', and proposed 'administrative courts-martial' as a way of cleaning up bureaucracy. His analogy was with the military courts-martial held in Prussia after the defeat of 1806.

As late as 1938 Schulenburg publicly advocated a revival of the Prusso-German civil-service state. In clear opposition to Hitler's preference for maintaining the constitutional status quo, he highlighted the need for 'major governmental reforms':

> No one can pretend that our state is in the lean, tough condition that the nation needs for its vital struggle… The strength of the state has yet to be built up organically from beneath and firmly marshalled. The state is still not free from the centralized sclerosis and brittle weakness of an uncreative bureaucracy. Nor has our society been shaped in every detail. The building blocks of the national structure – family, profession, parish – are only just now being put in place.

Schulenburg had in mind a second 'Prussian reform'. This would not simply remedy once and for all the failures of the 'age of the system', but would at the same time put into practice the principles of 'Prussian socialism'.

The various proposals for administrative reform that Schulenburg submitted for discussion among professional administrators, pointed towards a strongly centralized, unitary administrative structure with pronounced corporatist elements. They coincided with the reform proposals of the Reich Ministry of the Interior to the extent that neither provided for autonomy of the provinces (*Länder*), which were simply to be administrative units. However, Schulenburg's system had unmistakable features of a welfare state. One of these was a comprehensive system of economic planning. The key to this would be the highest possible level of efficiency in the civil service. It must be set up to function at the touch of a button. Nevertheless, the individual official would be given a wide measure of discretion and not shackled by bureaucratic instructions.

Originally, Schulenburg's position was strongly centralist – only after a period of transition might it be possible to think about 'making room for municipal and profession-based (*berufsständisch*) self-government'. However, he later spoke out in favour of administrative decentralization. 'Too much centralization would hugely inflate the state bureaucracy and thus increase its political power.' This change of mind had a good deal to do with the conflict that had broken out between the Reich Ministry of the Interior and the regional and city governors (*Gauleiter, Oberpräsidenten* and *Reichstatthalter*). The ministry wanted to introduce a unified administration, which would encompass the 'intermediate level of authority', i.e. the prefecture, and would be subject to instruction from the centre. The *Gauleiter*, on the other hand, pressed for far-reaching autonomy for the 'intermediate authorities'. Until the end of the war there was a dispute as to whether these 'authorities' were at the level of the prefecture (*Regierungspräsidenten*) or of the *Oberpräsidenten* and their equivalents in non-Prussian territories. Both sides invoked the principle of self-government. The Reich ministry demanded it at the level of the borough (*Kommune*) and county or district *(Kreis)*. Schulenburg regarded the question of the relationship between national and regional government as secondary, though he encouraged the trend to regional self-government and advocated the 'home-grown' principle. What he most wanted was a horizontal integration of the different strands of administration into a unified system. He was thinking about incorporating the departments of finance, employment and the economy into the overall administration at all levels; and even the Gestapo was to be subordinate to the relevant administrative head. Beside the Foreign Office, the military high command and specialized technical departments, only the administration of justice, among all the long-standing government ministries, was to retain its independence.[14]

At the time, Schulenburg's proposed solutions were relatively well received; they matched the ambitions of the Reich Ministry of the Interior to extend the remit of the general internal administration. Schulenburg's ideas also overlapped with those of Carl Goerdeler who, from a municipal perspective, also showed a preference for the principle of unitary administration. The horizontal integration of the administrative structure was to be balanced by widening the remit of lower-ranking administrators *vis-à-vis* the centre. Schulenburg believed that in this way he could limit the negative effects of central integration, and reduce the influence of a ministerial bureaucracy that he described as sometimes overwhelmingly negative. At the same time he wanted to expand the discretionary scope of local and regional administrative officers and dismantle bureaucratic routines. Reform along these lines would have placed the officials of the 'intermediate authorities' in a position of exceptional power. Its aim was to introduce the Führer-principle into the civil service. But whether it took sufficient account of the practical demands of the modern bureaucratic state, is open to doubt. It meant reintroducing the principle of departmental administration. That in turn meant making former departments of state into Reich offices (*Reichsämter*), modelled on those of the Bismarckian era. It followed that the *Reichsämter* would be downgraded to mere 'arms of the Reich Chancellery', which was indeed the way things were now going under the Third Reich.

At the same time, Schulenburg was faced with the problem of removing the dualism of Party and state. By aiming to unify political and administrative control at all levels of administration, he lent support to the widespread efforts of the Party apparatus to place general administration under its direct authority. The principle of combining in one person the function of *Kreisleiter* (chief Party official of a county) with that of *Landrat* (chief government official of a county), seemed for a time to be accepted. However, in the eyes of the Party it did not prove successful. On the other hand, the combining of the offices of *Gauleiter* and *Oberpräsident* had broken the chain of administrative authority and had contributed significantly to the fragmenting of administration complained of by Schulenburg. His ideas were closely akin to those propounded mainly by the staff of Hitler's Deputy (Rudolf Hess) and by the *Gauleiter*: they envisaged a *Reichmittelinstanz* (intermediate Reich authority), which would have given the Party unrestricted authority at regional level. This in fact came about in the final year of the war, with the appointment of the *Gauleiter* to be Reich Defence Commissioners. Civil administration was placed under their jurisdiction. Schulenburg did not resolve the basic contradiction that lay in the fact that the selection of senior Party officials did *not* follow the principles that he wanted to see underlying the development of a top civil service corps. In essence, his proposals made the Nazi Party dispensable as the apparatus of political control.[15]

The political system that Schulenburg was working towards was authoritarian in character and had nothing in common with the tradition of liberal constitutionalism. His tradition was that of pre-revolutionary Prussia and his intention was to put adminis- tration in the place of constitutional government. His drafts avoid any reference to elected representative bodies. It is true, however, that the administrative chiefs, at every level, would be assisted by advisory bodies. Schulenburg also wanted the professions to be run by self-governing bodies. These too would be headed by indi- viduals who combined both Party and state functions. Those peo- ple would not be bound by the recommendations of the advisory committees, and they had an important say in the appointment of committee members. The committees' role was to provide a link back to the interests of the population as a whole. As Schulenburg put it:

> The council is an outlet for popular opinion. It must expose mistakes and abuses, and in a spirit of constructive criticism make proposals for remedying them. It will be the express duty of every member of the council to speak his mind freely and to be unsparingly critical on matters of substance.

Schulenburg's proposals for structuring the top echelons of government are very fragmentary. Nonetheless, they show clearly that his reform plans were not, as he claimed, an 'organic governmental structure' built up from the bottom, but a highly *étatiste* counterpart to the Nazi Führer-state. In these plans there is no room for 'decision-making bodies sharing responsibility with the Führer', nor even for the Reich government as a collegiate committee. Governmental and Party leadership were to be combined in the office of Reich Chancellor. Schulenburg did, however, consider that the Führer-cum-Reich Chancellor had to be 'set apart from the administration of government'. There is no knowing whether this thought was prompted by the question, still open at that time, about who should occupy the post of Reich President following the death of Hindenburg. Meanwhile, as early as 1934 Schulenburg envisaged the creation of a European super-state, which would necessarily alter the position of the Führer:

> The 'Führer of the Reich' is to be the supreme representative of the future Reich, and the 'Führer of the Movement' is to be the Führer of the future Movement[16] … The Reich of the future will bring together states, peoples and movements in central and Eastern Europe under one leadership (*Führung*). We must start today seeking the appropriate form whereby states, peoples and movements join the Reich, under the Führer of the Reich.

However, Schulenburg restricted his proposals to the creation of an *Ordensrat* (something akin to a Privy Council *Tr.*), to assist the Führer/Reich Chancellor. Half of the council would consist of *Reichsleiter* and *Gauleiter* and the other half would be leading citizens (*Honoratioren*), appointed by the Führer. Schulenburg may well have taken as his model the Council of State devised by Baron vom Stein, which was revived in a dubious form by Hermann Göring when he was Minister-President of Prussia. Schulenburg's proposal coincided with similar plans from other quarters for creating a legislative Reich senate, or an electoral body to choose a Führer.[17] The difference was that Schulenburg's *Ordensrat* was not to be given any role in government legislation.

It is surprising that Schulenburg, an administrative lawyer who had been through a regular legal training, paid virtually no attention to legislation and its institutional framework and largely neglected the judicature. Even an authoritarian state requires regulated responsibility for legislation, if the uniformity of governmental action is to be guaranteed. Furthermore, we have to wonder why such a gifted and versatile expert on administration, as Schulenburg was, almost entirely overlooked the problem of keeping power in check, even though he vehemently denounced the cynical abuse of power by Nazi officials at every level. He did occasionally talk about how the proposed self-governing bodies would provide an adequate check against arbitrary use of official power. He also wanted to see the Public Audit Office

(*Rechnungshof*) given the right to investigate administrative activity in general, though this was little more than an echo of contemporary overestimates of the effectiveness of Prussia's *Oberrechenkammer* (High Court of Auditors). Such a move would only have created a bureaucratic control-mechanism that inhibited initiative, thus precisely negating the principle of a self-accountable civil service, quite apart from the fact that it only treated a corruption-free administration as a secondary objective.

Schulenburg's reorganization plans suffer from having nothing adequate to match the mechanisms for the partial control of power that had been developed in the modern constitutional state. He was firmly convinced that the strength of character of the men chosen for the governing elite would in itself be a barrier to the abuse of power. He told his interrogators in October 1944: 'We wanted a ruling stratum that would set an example in attitude and action.' The members of this ruling order would be welded together by the most rigorous selection and training and dedicated only to the ideal of the state. Their internal homogeneity would, in Schulenburg's mind, be sufficient to guarantee the avoidance of abuses and the removal of office-holders who violated the code of 'service to the community as a whole'. The notion of an elite public service, set apart from the rest of the population, is frequently found in neo-conservative writings of the 1920s. The methods proposed for recruiting its members were extremely varied and contradictory. However, the predominant view was that this elite should be made up of leaders emerging 'naturally' and 'organically' from their own neighbourhoods. One such concept was Arthur Mahraun's 'Young German Order'. Similar ideas are found in Edgar Jung and numerous other neo-conservative writers, not least Ernst Jünger and August Winnig,[18] who we know had a direct influence on Schulenburg.

The ranking of the 'neighbourhood' and the 'countryside' as basic units of society next to the family and the parish is also found in Schulenburg's memoranda, though without any further explanation.

Both the Kreisau Circle and the Goerdeler group were concerned in varying ways with the selection of political leaders from social units of a manageable size. In this way they hoped to avoid the undesirable consequences of an electoral process which they saw as 'mechanistic'. This notion was combined with a widespread aversion to big cities; their hope was to reverse the increasing population density caused by industrial development, through a comprehensive resettlement policy initially limited to Reich territory. Schulenburg called this 'internal colonization'. The thinking of the *Bündische Reichschaft* was along exactly these lines; it also included the idealization of cultivating frontier lands, the idea of colonization and of *Mitteleuropa*. These notions all culminated in the expectation that the process of *Vermassung* could be reversed. It was hoped that, through direct ties to the soil, the family, the immediate neighbourhood and small and medium-sized firms, the individual could be brought back into a 'natural' order – one which put personal and religious values in place of materialistic consumption and spiritual nihilism.

Fritz Dietlof von der Schulenburg was not a systematic thinker. His role in the resistance was not to be in the sphere of long-term planning, but of continuous pragmatic activism, which made him the most significant intermediary for the 20 July 1944 resistance movement. The characteristic vagueness of the intellectual constructs which he adopted, and attempted to implement in practical terms, is certainly remedied to some extent by his succinct and expressive use of language. However this does not lessen the inherent contradictions in his programme. The philosophical assumption that an attitudinal consensus between rulers and ruled could be arrived at, is the one common element in the multifarious invocations of a specifically 'German way', which might ensure an organic resolution between capitalism and socialism. With Schulenburg this took the form of the notion, borrowed from the military, that the example set by the ruling class would naturally be followed by their subordinates. That had been his personal experience in dealing with people from all walks of life. The claim to exert authority was based not on rank and institutional power but simply on personal authority in dealing with others.

Schulenburg's highly subjective view was part of the Prussian tradition, which he repeatedly invoked in this context. It can be shown that much of his thinking was based on an uncritical and general extrapolation from the quite exceptional circumstances of Prussia's reform period, while of course disregarding its constitutional and proto-liberal elements. Schulenburg really did not understand the break that the reformers had made with the Frederician tradition. The influence of Oswald Spengler was decisive in all this. The 'Prussian heritage' that Schulenburg believed he was drawing on, served as a 'historical' utopia. However, this did not mean a return to the archetypal, reactionary Prussia. Schulenburg never considered a restoration of the Hohenzollern monarchy. On the other hand, he thought entirely in 'old Prussian' terms, and this led him to view Bismarck's constitutional policy and his 'compromise with capital and Jewry' as a denial of Prussia's *raison d'état*. It was precisely this 'alternative utopia' in the Prussian tradition that led Schulenburg logically into the anti-Hitler camp. By his own account, Schulenburg made his break with the regime as a result of the Fritsch affair and the unlawful dismissal of the army commander-in-chief in February 1938.[19] How deeply this event affected him is shown by something he wrote after visiting Fritsch's grave on 24 May 1941. Schulenburg considered Fritsch the embodiment of the Prussian tradition at its best:

> He was the man who used discipline to make the army what it is, and it is him we should thank for such Prussian features as it still possesses. This morning I saw his face before me, with his determined eyes, reminding us that, beyond his death, Prussia's moral challenge to the Reich still stands.

By deciding to join the resistance, Schulenburg was not abandoning his earlier convictions, but rather he clung to his belief in the 'coming Reich'. He did not believe that the corrupting influence of the Party 'fat-cats' had seriously jeopardized the army and the civil service, although in the later war years he was forced to admit that even in public administration Prussian principles were being jettisoned one by one. The characteristic energy with which he plotted to replace the Nazi leadership did not therefore negate the fact that, simultaneously in his official capacity, he promoted the reforms he considered necessary and unhesitatingly supported the war-effort by making administrative economies. It was not the Third Reich's expansionist policies as such that provoked his merciless criticism, but the methods by which they were carried through. German hegemony on the continent of Europe seemed to him to be a historical necessity. This was tied up with the *bündisch* concept of the Reich,[20] which with little modification, he had espoused since the late 1920s, later to be joined by supranational ideas.

In the minds of the great majority of members of the military opposition, Hitler and his Party satraps were a threat to the foundations and continuity, as they saw it, of the great and powerful Prusso-German state, whose representatives they felt themselves to be. This was also true of Schulenburg, initially fighting on the terrain of the existing state, whose legal governance, despite all the Nazis' breaches of the law, appeared intact and susceptible to reform. He therefore adhered to his fundamental objectives, which concerned the reshaping of the constitutional and administrative structure according to the views laid out in his 1934 memorandum on the reform of the Reich. It was the impact of the war, especially the Allied bombing, that strengthened his interest in fundamental administrative reform. He saw that the role of the Nazi Party was disappearing, and this meant that he devoted greater attention than before to organizational structures based on neighbourhoods and professions.

It was typical of his way of thinking that his chief concern was to prepare the necessary personnel for the overdue restructuring. He therefore built up the extensive personal network on which his plans for the 20 July coup relied. This applied particularly to the area of general government administration. Since Schulenburg avoided committing to paper the wide-ranging contacts he made, their extent has generally been underestimated. That is precisely why Schulenburg was so crucial and indispensable a figure in the resistance. By contrast, his contribution to the conceptual plans of the 20 July resistance movement has often been exaggerated. The 'great' reform memorandum, known to have been lost, can probably be largely reconstructed from fragments found after his death. It is possible that the plans of the Kreisau Circle had a certain influence on him. However, in matters of principle we find significant differences.

It is obvious why Helmuth James von Moltke had some difficulty in convincing Schulenburg of the practicability of the Kreisau plans for constitutional and administrative reforms. In November 1942 he noted that there was a certain 'gulf that would never be bridged' between himself and Schulenburg. True, Schulenburg also emphasized the need for 'decentralization' and an 'organic' structure; but his *étatisme* based on strong personal leadership differed profoundly from Moltke's rejection of the modern Moloch-like state, with which he contrasted his idea of 'small communities'. Kreisau's ideas displayed strong elements of federalism, but Schulenburg, for all his stress on rural autonomy, remained wedded to unitary government. This did not stop him from dwelling at the same time on *bündisch* notions of a Greater Reich. However, his logic did not force him to abandon the nation-state, as Moltke had. Similarly, the constitutional ideas developed by Carl Goerdeler were a long way from Schulenburg's political concepts. In many respects Schulenburg was closer to the ideas of Adam von Trott and Claus Schenk von Stauffenberg. This is particularly true of the strong note of paternalism in Schulenburg's social thinking, which admittedly could veer into an exaggerated emphasis on the principle of 'self-help'.

Yet these differences in concept did not prevent Schulenburg from looking for collaboration in the coup wherever it was offered. He agreed without hesitation to contact being made with the communists, though such a move was very controversial within the 20 July movement. He had originally expected that the struggle over a new order would not begin until the war had ended. Once it had finally become clear to him that the Nazi policy of brutish aggression would hurl the Reich into the abyss, both militarily and politically, he was typically determined, from the end of 1941 onward, to serve the cause of the coup that he now openly envisaged. He was one of those who had never succumbed to Hitler's mesmeric power. The oath of allegiance was not a serious problem for him. He was aware of the risk and he did not hesitate to act; his deep religious conviction helped him to believe in a positive outcome. 'Beyond the raging whirlwind of our age,' he was sure he could see 'the forces of good combining, and despite storm and peril, despite all the human and material losses that we will suffer, a true order coming into being, both deep in ourselves and in the way we are governed.' He went on to say that he was indifferent to whether 'destiny chooses me for a role in this or demands my life as a sacrifice. All that matters to me is that I follow my conscience, through which God speaks to me'. The extreme challenges of the war strengthened him in the conviction that they had to succeed in pushing forward to the desired new governmental order.

Looking back from this distance in time, it is all too easy to show how far Schulenburg overestimated the opportunities open to Germany in foreign policy, as late as 1943. We still do not really know much about how his views changed in the light of the looming military defeat. In an extraordinary situation, such as that created by the last years of Nazi rule, what counts is not merely insight but the internal consistency of people's actions. There is much to suggest that the resolve to commit high treason against the Nazi regime could only have been inspired by the vision of an alternative utopia. The so-called pragmatists and political realists were largely absent from the anti-Hitler resistance.

During their climb to power the Nazis had promoted themselves as guardians of the Prussian heritage. In fact, the Prussian tradition, however one understands that, was never more systematically violated than during the Third Reich. Fritz-Dietlof von der Schulenburg took up the challenge this presented. When he was appointed vice-president of the Berlin police, he told August Winnig that he would be Hitler's Fouché.[21] He was certain of the justness of his cause, even when it led him to his death. The interrogations in the Gestapo headquarters in Prinz-Albrecht-Strasse and his composure during his trial betray no hint of weakness. His assessment of the regime was devastating, because it was the truth, and even his captors were impressed. He was too strong even for Roland Freisler, the feared president of the People's Court. Of all the plotters of 20 July, Schulenburg was the most robust. It is significant that he never strove for personal power; in the preparations for the coup he willingly allowed the post of Reich Minister of the Interior to go to Julius Leber. 'To each his own' was the maxim for which he gave his life. Without his tireless activity, without his uncompromising rejection of the internal basis of the regime, there probably would have been no 20 July. Yet its failure only showed that the Prussian alternative Schulenburg was striving for, no longer existed.

6

German anti-Hitler resistance and the ending of Europe's division into nation states

In writing the history of the German resistance it has become customary to describe the participants in the 20 July Plot as 'German patriots'. There is no doubt that originally the principal motives for their action were nationalistic. The plotters saw themselves as champions of the 'true Germany' and, as Schlabrendorff[1] has so memorably written about Henning von Tresckow, they donned the 'Robe of Nessus' as 'traitors to the nation', in order to regain respect for the nation besmirched by the appalling crimes of the Nazi regime. Under a hail of bullets from the hastily assembled firing squad in the war ministry courtyard, Claus von Stauffenberg and his closest associates died with the cry *Es lebe das heilige Deutschland!* ('Long live sacred Germany') on their lips.

It is true of the great majority of the 20th July movement that behind their decision to resist the regime was the concern to avert the imminent destruction of the German nation, brought about by the hubris of Hitler's war policy. Many believed that the regime was threatening to gamble away the early nationalistic policy successes which had won the support of the majority of the German people, namely settling the question of Germany's eastern frontier, and bringing Alsace-Lorraine, Austria and the Memel region[2] back into the Reich.

Concern for national interests was a central motive for the formation of the opposition movement in 1938, which attempted to prevent Hitler from provoking another world war through his resolution of the Sudeten question by military means. It was the older group of anti-Hitlerites, centred on Goerdeler, Hassell, Beck and Popitz, who held the traditional belief in a state based on military might. In their minds there was no question but that German hegemony must be restored and the Treaty of Versailles reversed. Their only difference with Hitler was over method, not objectives.

When, against all expectations, Hitler's foreign adventurism proved successful, the opposition hoped that the territorial gains of the Reich could be secured, even if the regime was brought down. This took the form of unrealistic expectations that the Western Powers could be persuaded to be generous in accommodating German demands in the east. Despite all their protestations of faith in a future European peace settlement, Goerdeler and Hassell in particular remained trapped in a dream world of nationalist aspirations. Adam von Trott himself realized this, although his views on frontier questions were considerably more flexible and, strong though his emotional objections to Anglo-American policy were, he cannot be accused of the Wilhelmine imperialism of Goerdeler, Hassell and some of the senior military officers.[3]

By contrast, only a few of the later plotters, such as Moltke and Yorck von Wartenburg were aware, as early as 1933, that it was a mistake to cling to traditional nationalist concepts of military power. Moltke had always known that Germany could not win the war, though up to 1942 he hoped that hostilities would cease through the exhaustion of both sides, before the total collapse of the Axis Powers. He came to the reluctant conclusion that the survival of Europe depended entirely on Germany being defeated. He realized early on that his own homeland of Upper Silesia would be sacrificed to the Nazis' vainglorious ambitions.

In both domestic and foreign policy matters, the men and women of the 20 July movement had to go through a long and exhausting learning process. The most painful thing, for some of the plotters at least, was the gradual realization, only becoming a certainty in the weeks before the attempted coup, that there was absolutely no chance of securing even those of Hitler's territorial gains that had been achieved within the national borders revised under the Treaty of Versailles.

Contacts which the opposition made with the British government from 1938 onwards all had the purpose of persuading Britain to take a firm stand against Hitler's intended aggression. At the same time, however, they wanted Britain to recognize the *Anschluss* of Austria and the cession of the Sudeten region by Czechoslovakia and even to agree to a revision of Poland's border with Germany. In the latter case their demands ranged from a restoration of the 1918 frontiers to a creation of ethnographic zones and a removal of the 'intolerable' Polish corridor separating East Prussia from the rest of the Reich. The opposition did not understand that such demands were bound to meet with suspicion in London, and that the emissaries of the resistance, even such respected figures as Goerdeler and Trott, were ultimately considered to be tools of the German General Staff. In 1943 even Moltke was suspected of being a double agent. The opposition failed to appreciate that Britain had entered the war with international objectives – among them the guarantee to Poland – and was unwilling and unable to modify its war aims in order to facilitate a change of leadership within Germany.

Thus it was the tragic fate of the opposition's peace-feelers to the west, that although carefully noted by the Allied secret services, only rarely and then by devious routes did they come to the attention of leading politicians in London and Washington. Nevertheless, we can only admire the tenacity with which Goerdeler and later Trott, who had been promoted to unofficial 'foreign minister' of the resistance, clung to the illusion that the Allies could be persuaded to make concessions to a non-Nazi government in Germany.

As late as 1943 Goerdeler believed that, through the mediation of the Swedish bankers, Marcus and Jacob Wallenberg, he could persuade the British government to agree to relieve a post-Hitler German government of the burden of unconditional surrender. Goerdeler also hoped to reach an accommodation over the Polish border question, even though the Wallenbergs had warned him that the new government first had to be formed before any thought could be given to diplomatic moves. However, Goerdeler felt caught in a difficult predicament. He had been bombarding the generals with messages urging them to intervene against Hitler's reckless policy of aggression, whereas *they* were putting pressure on *him* to come up with assurances that the Allies would not take military advantage of a toppling of the Nazi regime. What is more, he found it hard to free himself from the idea of restoring the German nation-state that had been so painfully truncated by the Treaty of Versailles.

On the other hand, the inner circle of conspirators centred on Stauffenberg recognized that such territorial demands must be abandoned, and that at best the 1937 frontiers might be secured. Hopes of perpetuating the *Anschluss* of Austria evaporated, when the rightwing resistance established contact with their Austrian counterparts, who made it very clear to the Germans that Austria's future lay only in independent nationhood, as agreed in the 1943 negotiations in Moscow.[4] Even Julius Leber seems, like Goerdeler, to have cherished hopes of retaining Alsace-Lorraine in the Reich, possibly by means of a plebiscite. All this was illusory, as was the hope, still alive in 1944, that at least the Russian front could be held over the long term.

The failure of their direct contacts with the British and Americans made Moltke, even more than Goerdeler, devote the greatest attention to winning over the rest of Europe. Here he believed he could perceive signs that a common European attitude of mind was forming, a resistance to the suppression of the European character by the USA and the Soviet Union. On the other hand, the majority of the conservative-nationalist opposition were espousing the policy of global expansion, which made Germany's previous objectives as a nation-state look outmoded. In the run-up to the German invasion of the Soviet Union, Beck, Hassell and Oster raised a complaint that opportunities for the Reich in eastern and south-eastern Europe were being wantonly put at risk and Germany's leading role threatened. Popitz, Beck and the still influential Carl Schmitt raised ideas of this kind for discussion in the semi-opposition forum known as the 'Wednesday

Club'. At the same time the creation of a united Europe was also debated by the generally pro-Nazi top management of industry and the related government departments. Germany's swift victories in Western Europe prompted a good deal of euphoria in this regard, and in turn had a considerable impact on the resistance's foreign policy thinking.

Goerdeler was equally open to plans for the creation of a united Europe. Since he had begun acting as an economic adviser to Göring and Schacht he had tirelessly advocated the return to a deregulated economy on the continent of Europe, and believed that this could only be achieved through a regional structure. Hence, it was no great step from this to his numerous memoranda, in which he dealt both with the problem of a single European economy and that of a future political structure for Europe. To begin with he believed that European co-operation could be achieved without any diminution of Germany's national sovereignty. He, along with Beck, Hassell and Popitz, made the assumption that in a future Europe Germany's leading role must be assured. Thus Hassell dreamed of an 'occident under German leadership' and, like Goerdeler, hoped that the peoples of Europe could be united in their defence against Bolshevism. Adam von Trott, who was known for his socialist leanings, expressed himself somewhat differently when he hoped to bring about a 'fraternal bonding of the ordinary people of Europe' against the capitalist powers and the threat from the USSR.

The emergence of pan-European policies, which the conservative foreign policy-makers of the Weimar Republic had rejected out of hand, has a lot to do with the complete alteration of the foreign policy landscape since 1939, which now favoured the formation of regional spheres of influence. But it was also a reflection of the enforced economic isolation of continental Europe under Nazi rule or ascendancy. In many respects resistance thinking filled the vacuum in official policy on Europe. In his memorandum 'The Goal', written in late 1941, Goerdeler made a plea for Germany to proceed with discretion in Europe. Germany ought not to humiliate the smaller nations, and should give all European nation-states the freedom 'to create internal conditions that best suit their character and needs'. This was the only way to succeed in forming the much-needed 'European bloc' under German leadership. He was principally addressing the generals when he wrote: 'Provided timely action is taken, i.e. breaking off the war in favour of a sensible political system, within ten to 20 years the federation of European states will be a fact.' At that point in time Goerdeler did not want to abandon the normal attributes of a nation-state and considered it absolutely necessary to preserve the independence of the Wehrmacht 'as an indispensable tool of domestic policy and a school for educating the nation.' It well illustrates the learning process Goerdeler was going through, that barely a year later he was warming to the idea of a European army. But he found it difficult to free himself from the idea of a leading role for Germany in a united Europe. To that extent he retained a certain proximity to ideas such as those put forward by the historian, Karl Richard Ganzer, in his 1941 book *Das Reich als europäische Führungsmacht* ('The Reich as the leading power in Europe'). Support for the idea that Germany could retain its mission to lead came from other quarters too. Thus Fr Alfred Delp, whose background was the distinctly nationalistic Catholic youth league called *Neudeutschland* (New Germany), declared that 'a Europe without Germany, indeed without Germany as one of its leaders' was unthinkable. Behind this lies a specifically occidental perception that viewed with anxiety the intervention of 'alien [i.e. non-European] powers' like Russia and the USA. Delp feared the dissolution of Europe's unique blend of classical antiquity, Christendom and 'Germanity'. Considerations of this kind also inspired the ecumenical dialogue which, since 1941, had been influenced by the anti-Hitler movement. The churches were particularly concerned with 'safeguarding the integrity of European life', to quote an essay by Willem Visser't Hooft, the Dutch clergyman who provided an important link between the opposition in Germany and churches abroad.

Those anti-Hitler plotters who belonged to the German nationalist camp looked upon Europe chiefly from the standpoint of German hegemony or, as in the case of Hassell, of domination by *Mitteleuropa*. On the other hand, the more neo-conservative wing of the opposition, principally represented by the Kreisau Circle, was more wedded to the idea of a European state, which had a strongly federalist component, and thus accommodated the domestic policy ideas of Moltke and Yorck.

In this context, mention should be made of Georg Angermaier (1913–1945), a lawyer who advised Augustin Rösch and Alfred Delp in connection with the Committee for Religious Orders, and who was responsible for a number of documents contributed by the Jesuits. Angermaier emphasized the need for a valid model for European man, one which 'could only be derived from Christ'; he also postulated the 'European nation' as the 'only form possible for a future European order'. He hoped that the war would bring an end to nationalism in Europe and lead to the restoration of 'unity of the occident'. The state, Angermaier insisted, was 'not the ultimate form of community in the life of nations'.

These ideas were principally directed against the communist threat from the east, but at the same time stressed the obligation of western civilization to give an example to the world. Angermaier agreed with Delp that a 'pan-European' order could more easily be achieved by means of the *Reich* form, which he considered the most appropriate for 'governmental organisation in the German region'. Moltke and Yorck were ready to go further and to sacrifice the governmental integrity of the Reich. However, the consensus that emerged on this point was in favour of maintaining the unity of the German Reich.

Nevertheless, there was a general belief that Europe must eventually be unified. The way forward was shown by the 'White Rose' resistance group,[5] which was in turn influenced by the publishers of the Catholic journal *Hochland* and had close ties with Kreisau. In their fifth leaflet, distributed in 1942, the 'White Rose' strongly advocated a new European order: 'Only generous cooperation between the peoples of Europe can create the ground on which it will be possible to build a new edifice.' Moltke and Yorck also saw the defeat of Nazism as a European challenge, and were among the first to call for a federal European state with undivided sovereignty and the power to issue directives to the self-governing territories, into which they proposed to split up the traditional nation-states, especially Germany and France.

Moltke saw the course towards European unification already being laid in the fascist war economy. It certainly appeared that a single European economy was perforce being created by the Nazis' economic plundering, particular as the Nazi regime, faced with the Allies' European propaganda, had no choice but to offer the nations of Western Europe a bright future, if only on paper. The economic interdependence of the countries under German domination was bound to affect the situation that would emerge at the end of the war. The men of Kreisau could see that the collapse of the Nazi regime would do serious economic damage to the whole of Europe, and that this could only be overcome by pan-European co-operation.

As early as 1941, Moltke, in his memorandum 'Starting-point, Goals and Tasks', expressed the expectation that 'a great economic community would emerge from the demobilization of armed forces in Europe', and that it would be 'managed by an internal European economic bureaucracy'. Combined with this he hoped to see Europe divided up into self-governing territories of comparable size, which had their 'origins in history' and which would break away from the principle of the nation-state. Although their domestic constitutions would be quite different from each other, he was sure that, thanks to his deliberate encouragement of 'small communities' that would assume public duties, a broadly uniform political attitude would prevail throughout the elites bearing moral responsibility for the new order in each of the self-governing territories. In an analogy with the domestic constitutions his concept was of a European community built up from below. This was what lay behind his now famous remark to Lionel Curtis: 'For us, post-war Europe is less a question of borders and armies, of complex organizations and great schemes, and more one of re-establishing the image of humanity in the hearts of our fellow-citizens.' At the same time he believed this would ultimately lead to the creation of a common European consciousness.

Moltke devoted enormous energy to establishing contact with resistance organizations throughout Europe, and Visser't Hooft believed he could bring about a unification of all European resistance, with the shared objective of a Christian renewal of Europe. Indeed, the Kreisau Circle was distinguished by its far-sighted vision of Europe, and Trott dreamed of achieving a synthesis between the two Europes, the 'democratic pre-mass Europe' and the 'democratic post-mass Europe'. [These are Trott's own English terms *Tr.*]. Trott expected that European federalism would 'finally overcome European nationalism, especially in its military manifestation' and saw it as 'the practical application of the Christian-European tradition'.

As early as the winter of 1939–1940 Adam von Trott had given thought to a European tariff and currency union, the setting up of a European Supreme Court and single European citizenship, as the basis for a further administrative unification of Europe. A little later, Moltke called for the setting up of a 'supreme European legislature', which would be answerable, not to the (national) self-governing bodies, but to the individual citizens, by whom it would be elected. This was a far-sighted anticipation of the directly elected European Parliament of today. A memorandum that has only recently come to light, on 'The Problem of a European Constitution', is written in Theodor Steltzer's hand, but was passed to friends in Sweden in October 1942 with the agreement of the Kreisau Circle. It shows us what importance this question had for the inner group within Kreisau. In conjunction with the earlier memoranda, the paper called for the 'formation of a European federation'. This was intended to rule out any kind of national hegemony, but would provide for a government empowered to negotiate on behalf of member-states.

Originally, Moltke had in mind a division of the world into two: an Anglo-Saxon union centred on the USA and including Britain, and a unified continental Europe, to which parts of Africa would be added. Hassell and Goerdeler cherished similar ideas. Uncertainty remained as to the future of Russia, which Moltke, in his early paper, 'Starting-point, Goals and Tasks', still wanted to regard as the 'responsibility' of the European zone. Now, however, there was a clear ambition to bring both Britain and Russia into the European Union. Typically, there was an emphasis on Christendom as the foundation of the European ethos that was to be created.

At the instigation of Moltke and Yorck, the third Kreisau conference in June 1943 dealt in detail with questions of the European economy, a division of labour in Europe, and a settlement over agricultural markets to deal with possible overproduction. The conference called for common policies on taxation, credit and transport, as a precondition for the merging of national economies in Europe. By now, not only the Kreisau Circle but also Goerdeler and his followers took for granted the creation of a single European currency, a fact which admittedly reflected the fictive status of non-German currencies within the German bloc.

Initially Goerdeler and his group had strong reservations about Kreisau's radical programme for Europe, but from 1942 onward their positions became ever closer. Thus, in 1943, Goerdeler, too, was calling for the dismantling of tariff barriers, 'equality of economic rights' and standardized transport arrangements; he also advocated the setting up of European ministries of economics and foreign affairs. Later he gave concrete form to these aims and now spoke of 'a European federation of states', upon which significant sovereign rights, including that of maintaining an army, were to be conferred. In his August 1944 memorandum, 'Tasks for a German Future', he stressed that the world war 'must lead to a close union of the nations of Europe, if the sacrifices are to have any purpose'.

It would be misleading to assume that this faith in a single Europe simply arose from a situation in which Germany no longer had any chance of pursuing a nationalist foreign policy and the opportunities for a German hegemony had been gambled away for any foreseeable future. Even though considerations of this kind had an influence on the conservative wing, the path had consciously been taken from self-interested nationalism to the overcoming of nationalist attitudes. Moreover, as Goedeler stated in his memorandum of early 1944, 'Practical Measures for Reshaping Europe', the development of a 'living, internal unity in Europe' was the only prospect that remained for meaningful political action.

From the outset, Europe meant more to Kreisau than a receptacle for Germany's failed nationalist state and more than a means of preventing future wars, which, as the anti-Nazi plotters recognized, would inevitably lead to the final destruction of the continent. In this respect the Kreisau concept rid itself of the 'German way' syndrome and bore markedly pan-European characteristics. It was concerned with regenerating the culture of Western Europe with its roots in Christendom and Humanism, a culture that had been retreating in the face of modernization since the age of absolutism and the Enlightenment.

Moltke and those of like mind originally hoped that, with its end, the war's opponents would come to power in every European country and jointly press for a 'truly European peace settlement'. From 1943 onward the outlook became dramatically bleaker. The demand for unconditional surrender, formulated at the Casablanca meeting between Churchill and Roosevelt, ruled out a German initiative – which in many respects would also have been a European one – following the collapse of the Nazi regime that could now be anticipated with certainty. Moltke, who otherwise had such utopian inclinations, proved in this matter to be coolly realistic. Nonetheless, the Kreisau Circle continued to cling to the hope that the victors would also be carried along by the growing impulse for a new order, which they would see as genuinely European and, when the war ended, would not stand in the way of the necessary fundamental reconstruction of Europe.

In the spring of 1943 the future scenario was transformed by the rapprochement between the Western Allies and the Soviet Union, and their increasing military successes, from which Moltke concluded that 'Germany's contribution to the establishing of order in Europe' would be made within the 'triangle of tension between Russia, Britain and America'. Even so, he glimpsed opportunities for directly and indirectly preventing the feared 'organizational violation of European life' – a way of thinking that shared Alfred Delp's views about the 'non-European powers' of the USA and USSR. In this context he stated unambiguously that 'Germany's right of codetermination in European affairs' was the 'indispensable condition' for bringing peace to Europe.

The vision of transforming European nation-states into large self-governing bodies, which in many respects anticipated a 'Europe of Regions', was linked with the hope of being able to claim a 'right of European codetermination' for Germany and thus a degree of autonomy equal to that granted to the other member-states. It was clear to Moltke that, in return for this, he would have to accept the dissolution of the Reich. Looking to the post-war era he wrote: 'The success of our work will probably bring about the total collapse of our national unity.' Yet he and Yorck were prepared, he said, 'to look this in the face'.

However, there was a slender hope that by putting in motion the Kreisau programme even before the final surrender and by equipping the provincial governors (*Landesverweser*) with all the attributes of sovereignty in case the Reich lost its power to nego-tiate, it would be possible to avoid complete subjugation by the Allied Powers. The Allies might then be persuaded to accept a spontaneous reconstruction of Germany taking place from the bottom up. In the words of a Kreisau document from the spring of 1943: 'However far the suppression of German initiative may go under foreign domination, it will still be necessary for small and medium-sized self-governing bodies and technical organiza-tions to go on functioning spontaneously'. Combined with this was the hope that 'the real internal reform of Germany will have the effect of building trust in the rest of Europe'. Consequently, it was important that Germany's very defeat should have an active impact on the regeneration of Europe as a whole.

The 'notion of personal socialism given reality through sound forms of local self-government', which had been developed by Kreisau as a palliative against mass- and class-based society, was at the same time presented by them as a 'generally applicable solution to Europe's social and economic problems'. This was to be Germany's 'constructive contribution' to the efforts to bring peace to Europe. Conversely, the road to Europe also represented an attempt to guarantee 'the peaceful flowering of national culture' for Germany as well, and to prevent the intrusion of 'inappropriate political arrangements' [i.e. parliamentary democracy as seen by the German conservatives *Tr.*].

The vision of a federal Europe growing from the nucleus of German federalism may be regarded as the product of utopian thinking. Nevertheless, the underlying concept of a dualism between the European super-state and the regions below the level of the nation-states represents a model for a federal Europe, which to this day has not been superseded. However, equally bold designs for a future Europe came from other quarters of the anti-Hitler resistance. Among them was the resistance group built up by Hans Robinsohn[6] and Ernst Strassmann,[7] which can be seen as a liberal-democratic variation on the conservative-nationalist opposition, with which it merged after Strassmann's arrest in 1942. In a memorandum written in autumn 1941 Robinsohn made the assumption that after the war there would have to be a federation of European states with binding membership. The principle of national sovereignty was, he said, outmoded and Europe would not allow itself to be forced into the mould of nation-states. Robinsohn went on to point out that the only way to a united Europe was through a Franco-German reconciliation – which is precisely the path that Konrad Adenauer followed as Germany's first post-war Chancellor.

The transition of the conservative-nationalist opposition to Hitler from having a strong commitment to the nation-state to accepting the idea of a single Europe did not take place without ruptures and obstacles, and only a certain number of the plotters were prepared to draw the obvious conclusions from the excesses of nationalism in the Third Reich. Nevertheless, it did entail a crucial political learning process, which after 1945 facilitated Germany's integration into the institutions of Europe. The Christian character of the European idea – Steltzer expressly spoke of Europe under the Cross – and the ecumenical contribution to the rebuilding of Europe were, however, just one factor among many which have made European integration possible in the second half of the twentieth century.

Julius Leber
and the German resistance to Hitler

Julius Leber (1891–1945) occupies a unique place in the history of German resistance to Hitler. Leader of the Social-Democratic party (SPD) in the north German city of Lübeck, editor of its newspaper, the *Lübecker Volksbote* ('People's Messenger'), and an SPD deputy in the Reichstag from 1924, he was dubbed by the notorious president of the People's Court, Roland Freisler, 'the Lenin of the German workers' movement'. This was a misnomer since he was not a professional revolutionary; he did not propound any specific programme and always advocated a pragmatic, reality-driven policy for the German Social-Democratic Party. What is undeniable is Leber's unyielding steadfastness, his determination and willpower which, during his imprisonment, no amount of maltreatment and humiliation by the Gestapo was able to break. It was these qualities which made Leber, of all the plotters of 20 July 1944, the most dangerous opponent of the Nazi system. His Gestapo interrogators quickly realized that Leber did not fit into the category of superannuated party hack, but was a man of the people, whose voice was listened to by the ordinary workers, and that he was one of the very few plotters who had what it took to win the confidence of the masses.

In his trial before the People's Court in October 1944 Leber, though repeatedly prevented by Freisler from making a coherent statement, took upon himself full responsibility for the attempted coup. In succinct words he outlined the political future, had the putsch been successful. Paramount was the removal of the Nazi regime of terror, and Leber made no secret of his willingness to make an alliance with the Devil himself, in order to overthrow the regime. In his view, the profound crisis that had culminated in the Nazi tyranny, dated from the outbreak of war on 4 August 1914. Its real causes were perceived by Leber as continuing social injustice, the preservation of outdated social privilege and the failure of an economic system which, in time of crisis, threw the entire burden on to the shoulders of the working and jobless masses. A future social order would, if it were to achieve stability, have to be based on the precedence of labour over ownership. Leber had therefore made up his mind that, once the regime was overthrown, he would not support a political compromise between the different groupings in the resistance, but would pursue a consciously socialist policy, which would bring the idea of 'social democracy' to full fruition. This meant at the same time abandoning 'class socialism', thereby removing the SPD from the stricture of being exclusively a party of the proletariat – which he had accused the party leadership of clinging to under Weimar.

Like many of his generation Leber believed he was living through a period of profound historical change, which was forcing society to progress to new forms. As a staunch republican he had consistently advocated extending the democratic foundations of the Weimar Republic. In contrast to the typical social-democrat party officials, Leber was not worried by the traumatic tension between the assumption of governmental responsibility and holding on to the party's customary role in opposition. He moved with greater ease within the complex power-spheres of the republic and was bitterly critical of the irresponsible manner in which the party leadership sacrificed positions of power for the sake of ideological purity and a false devotion to their supporters. With good reason he rejected a politics that lost sight of the overall direction in a tangle of tactical manoeuvres. Like Carlo Mierendorff and Theodor Haubach, he felt that democracy conducted in small public meetings (*Versammlungsdemokratie*) had outlived its usefulness and instead strove towards new political forms, which took account of the need for 'emotional faith within the mass-movement' and did not leave the field of emblematic propaganda open to the Nazis alone.

Leber's bitter settling of accounts with Weimar social democracy, which at the same time represented despairing self-criticism, must be viewed against this background. The document he wrote while in prison in 1933,[1] on 'The Causes of the Death of German Social Democracy', contained a hard-hitting rebuke to the Social Democrat leadership for its lack of initiative, lack of ambition to achieve power and above all lack of a vision capable of inspiring the masses. In retrospect he regretted that the German revolution of 1918 had run out of steam and complained of insufficient determination in imposing socialist principles in the economic sphere. He rightly pointed out that the party machine was decrepit and the senior SPD officials lacking in political flexibility; but most of all he highlighted the absence of any forceful personalities in the party leadership. Justified as this criticism may have been in detail, it caused a problem in that it suggested illusory alternatives specifically in the area of foreign policy. It only becomes comprehensible when seen in the context of Leber's scepticism towards the Weimar parliamentary system, which in essence he had ceased to consider viable from the late 1920s.

During his arrest and interrogation in 1933 Leber, cut off from reliable sources of information, was for a time under the impression that the Nazis might succeed in finding a long-term solution to the problems of society. But he quickly realized that the Nazi regime was, in almost every respect, turning the vision of a 'national socialism' into its opposite. From immediately prior to the convening of the Reichstag on 23 March 1933, Leber was continuously imprisoned and thus deprived of any opportunity to influence political events. His years in prison and concentration camp brought him to a profound crisis of political faith. Only after his release, when he got in touch with Gustav Dahrendorf,[2] Ernst von Harnack[3] and Ludwig Schwamb,[4] did his old political convictions return. Apart from informal links with Leuschner, his circle of acquaintances was initially restricted to the re-establishing of former connections: at this point he was not thinking in terms of a conspiracy.

His experiences in prison had taught Leber that there was virtually no prospect of building a plot against Hitler from the previous organization of the workers' movement. The overwhelming majority of social-democratic resistance groups had failed to survive the first half of the 1930s. The clandestine German Communist Party (KPD) had to suffer repeated assaults by the Gestapo. In practice it never managed to do more than secure or rebuild its network of conspirators. Though Mierendorff, Leuschner, Leber and a number of like-minded people hoped to build a united front in 1938–9, which would embrace all political tendencies, this proved to be quite simply unfeasible. Despite his early contacts with Leuschner and Mierendorff, it was not until 1943 that Leber came upon the 20 July group of plotters.

Leber's contact with Goerdeler in the autumn of that year was limited to an exchange of information. Leber deliberately refrained from taking a view on Goerdeler's plans for a new order. It was only later that the considerable difference between the political opinions of the two men became apparent. At the same time, Helmuth James von Moltke tried hard to persuade Leber to contribute to the plans of the Kreisau Circle, especially after the death of Carlo Mierendorff in an air raid in 1943. Moltke was anxious to give a greater voice to representatives of the working class in the Kreisau discussions. However, Moltke's feelings toward Leber – to whom he gave the significant cover-name of 'Neumann' ('new man') – never really warmed, since Leber was hesitant to give any views on the Kreisau concepts for a new order and maintained a circumspect distance from them. As much as Leber agreed with the fundamental motives of Moltke, Trott and Delp – to bring about a socially just and humane order – he could make nothing of the idea of 'small communities' on which the Kreisau plans were founded. He might have shared the basic principle of mobilizing the willingness of individuals to take on responsibilities; however, he was too much of a pragmatist to see this as a component of social policy, or to abandon the centralization of politically responsible forces. Whereas the middle-class conspirators, faced with the Nazi mobilization of the masses, were anxious to create political units of a manageable size, in which the individual personality would carry some weight, Leber had no fear of centrally-led mass organizations.

Leber was no political theorist. As a consistent opponent of Nazism he did not share with the conservative-nationalist resisters their characteristic desire for legitimacy, which led them to offer a comprehensive social and constitutional alternative to the Nazi system. Nonetheless, he agreed with them that there could be no return to the discredited parliamentarism of Weimar. He was less concerned with alternative concepts than with creating the practical conditions for a successful coup d'état. In this he was in agreement with Fritz-Dietlof von der Schulenburg, who had been the tireless driving-force behind the planning of the coup. Schulenburg had spent some of his schooldays at Lübeck's famous Catharineum high school and was still in touch with its former headmaster, Georg Rosenthal, who was Julius Leber's father-in-law. This indirect personal relationship made it easier for Leber to engage in an exchange of ideas with the Prussian aristocrat Schulenburg, who then seized the opportunity to introduce the still hesitant Leber to Claus Schenk von Stauffenberg.

It is a remarkable sidelight on the history of the 20th July conspiracy, that a close relationship developed spontaneously between Leber and Stauffenberg and rapidly turned into friendship. As regards social origins and political background, it is hard to imagine a greater contrast than that between the blue-blooded Swabian on the one hand and the social-democrat republican from Alsace on the other. A bridge was provided by Leber's military career,[5] which significantly came to an end in 1920 because, as an officer, Leber had actively spoken in favour of the republican constitution. He had strongly supported a realistic and positive defence policy for the republic, both as a member of the Reichtag's defence committee and at the party congresses in Kiel and Magdeburg. He also shared Stauffenberg's basic position of staunch nationalism.

There is much to suggest that Stauffenberg and Leber saw qualities in each other that they themselves were lacking. Leber was fascinated by the succinct and direct manner, sometimes frank and sarcastic, of this senior officer in the General Staff, who had learnt soberly to accept military and political realities. This was no less true of Leber himself, who had freed himself both from hopes of a Greater Germany and from his love of Alsace-Lorraine,[6] given the hopeless diplomatic position of the Reich. Like Stauffenberg, he was critical of Goerdeler's illusions regarding foreign policy. Stauffenberg dispensed with formalities in his dealings with others and tended to come straight to the point; in this he did not fit Leber's mental image of the typical aristocratic Prussian officer in the German army. This, combined with his implacable determination to act, met with Leber's unalloyed admiration. Even at the outset, we find in Leber none of the suspicion felt by Leuschner's close collaborator, Hermann Maass, which led him to fear that Stauffenberg was merely interested in securing the privileges of an elite that had outlived its usefulness.

For his part, Stauffenberg showed the greatest respect for Leber, the workers' leader. Apart from their common commitment to action, this was more than a little due to Stauffenberg's awareness that, in the event of the Nazi regime being overthrown, everything would depend on the attitude of the workers. In Leber he believed he had found a popular leader who would be able to bridge the historic – and to him tragic – gulf between the army and the workers. Stauffenberg stated that the army, being at once the most conservative institution and the one most closely linked to the people, must not be allowed to repeat the mistake of 1918, when it came out openly against the workers. This shows how deeply marked he was by the experience of 1918–19, and it was precisely on this point that Leber and Stauffenberg could agree.

Stauffenberg wanted at all costs to avoid a re-run of the purely military coup staged by Kapp and Lüttwitz in 1920.[7] He was convinced that Leber would be able to bring about the necessary political integration after the coup, something he doubted, with some justification, that Goerdeler could achieve. Stauffenberg therefore had in mind appointing Leber as Reich Chancellor; however Leber declined. The thought that the forces of the labour movement ought not to be exhausted too soon through taking full responsibility for the transitional government was probably at the back of his mind.

Both Stauffenberg and Leber recalled the German uprising of 1813[8] as an example of unleashing a popular rebellion, whereas the older plotters, like Goerdeler and Beck, looked to the Prussian reforms as their historical model. This difference also posed the question of their relationship with the communist resistance movement. We can be sure that Leber and Stauffenberg never considered making a separate peace with the Soviet Union as a way out of the dilemma posed for the German resistance by the western Allies' demand for unconditional surrender. There was no basis whatever for the suspicion, voiced by Gisevius[9] to the US intelligence chief in Zürich, Allen Dulles, that Stauffenberg had ambitions for a Soviet-style government of workers and peasants. It is likely, however, that Stauffenberg and Leber both saw the need to reach an understanding with the communist resistance movement and possibly to get them to agree to a moratorium. With Adolf Reichwein, Leber decided to arrange a meeting with the Saefkow group, which led to his arrest on 5 July 1944. This initiative had been a matter of controversy in the resistance camp; it was welcomed by those closest to Stauffenberg, whereas Goerdeler objected to it.

Although Leber did not directly participate in the Kreisau and Goerdeler plans for a coup d'état, he did achieve a key position through his links with Schulenburg and Stauffenberg. This was because they thought Leber would be able to bring with him the social-democrat sympathizers in the working class. Of all the socialists active in the 20 July resistance movement – Leuschner, Maass, Mierendorff, Haubach, Reichwein – there is no doubt that Leber was the most gifted politically. Leuschner, who for a long time considered himself to be the leading representative of the former socialist camp, principally provided the element of organized labour in the plans of the Goerdeler circle. The Kreisau Circle then reluctantly accepted the model of the 'German Labour Union', which was closely based on the Nazi DAF (German Labour Front). This led logically to the idea of a unitary labour union, which had been decided on as early as 1933 by the Council of Labour Union Leaders. This made the separate political representation of workers' interests – in other words the creation of a socialist party – seem largely superfluous.

Leber was highly sceptical of the corporatist concepts of the Goerdeler group, particularly since Leuschner had made considerable concessions in his programme to the Christian and nationalist labour leaders including Jakob Kaiser, Theordor Brauer and Max Habermann. Moreover he doubted, probably rightly, whether former officials selected to run Leuschner's proposed union executive were still available to be deployed in a revolutionary situation. Admittedly, his criticism of this superannuated cadre overlooked the fact that there was no alternative but to resort to trusted political personnel from the late Weimar period. His antagonism toward Leuschner, which was frequently mollified by calls for socialist solidarity, lay not least in Leber's distrust of purely bureaucratic political solutions, and indeed the labour union plans suffered from just that fault.

It was no accident that the figure of Julius Leber took centre stage in the preparatory discussions of the various groupings associated with 20 July. This was just at the moment when the (communist-inspired) National Committee for a Free Germany was launched, and the conservative-nationalist conspirators began to realize that alongside the military planning of the coup and the compiling of government lists, there also had to be a democratic underpinning of the transitional government. Whereas it had originally been thought that the transfer of power would take place in an authoritarian framework, in other words without the involvement of political forces, it now dawned on people that they would have to create a popular democratic movement, which would at the same time act as a counterpoise to communism. The idea of founding an all-party popular movement can chiefly be traced back to Carlo Mierendorff, who before his death had formulated a provisional programme called 'Socialist Action'. This was largely a revival of Christian traditions but also contained clear socialistic objectives. In the months leading up to the coup, there were some – often acrimonious – disputes between Leber and the labour union group about the political programme of the proposed popular movement. It proved impossible to reach an understanding before the attempted coup of 20 July 1944 took place.

Leber spoke out against abandoning social-democratic traditions, but his reaction against excessive emphasis on Christian elements was more one of pragmatism than of principle. If the popular movement was to fulfil both the function of neutralizing the remnants of the Nazi Party, and that of creating a counterweight to the strong communist movement that was anticipated, then it must distance itself from a specifically Christian and confessional programme. The need was all the greater if, as anticipated, the communists came forward with a popular front and a strongly nationalist programme. Furthermore, Leber recognized that in view of the impending collapse of the Third Reich, they would have to expect influence to be exerted by the exiled leadership of the German Social-Democratic Party (SPD) in London.[10] Planning on the assumption of a political vacuum, as the conspirators had done in the early years, proved to be completely unfeasible.

Within the circle of the 20 July resisters, there was a consensus that Julius Leber should be offered the Ministry of the Interior. Originally this post had been earmarked for Schulenburg, but the Count himself made the suggestion that he should serve as Leber's Permanent Secretary in the ministry. Leber and Schulenburg worked together on detailed preparations for the provisional government's takeover of broadcasting and the press. Leber agreed with the nomination of Goerdeler as Chancellor and Beck as Reich President. On the other hand Leuschner, for all his loyalty to Goerdeler, was sceptical as to whether he was a realistic choice as Chancellor in view of the changed political situation in Europe as a whole – in both Italy and France the influence of communism was growing strongly. However, the strongest objections came from members of the Kreisau Circle, who were opposed to Goerdeler's economic programme of free-market capitalism. Yorck von Wartenburg talked in plain terms about a 'Kerenski' solution, which went counter to the expectations that Kreisau had of its new political order, and which would not be able to withstand the pressure from the left.

In the final months before the attempt on Hitler's life, after many false starts, finally took place, Leber was one of the inner group of plotters around Stauffenberg. The latter decided to press ahead with the coup immediately, among other things in the belief that he could not manage without Leber.[11] It was Leber's analysis of possible domestic coalitions that most influenced Stauffenberg. Unlike Goerdeler, the Stauffenberg group now had no illusions about their scope for diplomatic manoeuvre. Leber approved the names selected for the cabinet, but only on condition that it be put in place before the impending military defeat of Germany. Otherwise he saw no alternative but to put forward an unambiguously socialist programme, since therein lay the only chance of resisting communist pressure, now reinforced by the approaching Red Army.

All of this helps to explain the virtually hopeless situation of the 20th July plotters. Nevertheless, to have made the attempt to bring down the Nazi regime from within remains a crucial contribution, and one in which Leber played a major part. As regards his political views in this late phase of the resistance, we generally have no more than indirect evidence, often only from the record of Gestapo interrogations. Leber avoided taking up a position on constitutional questions. He favoured a democratic form of personal leadership, with plebiscitary features. His socialist republicanism was aimed at producing universal social justice and breaking down class barriers. In many ways his political philosophy had a Jacobin streak, and indeed the French republican tradition in general played an important part in his thinking. However, his staunch patriotism did not prevent him from accepting the realities of the diplomatic situation. He was a pioneering campaigner for social justice, yet at the same time he never failed to understand the imperative of state power.

Even under the harshest conditions of imprisonment after 20 July, Leber always remembered the workers of Lübeck who, when he was already behind bars, unanimously elected him their president. After years of humiliation in the concentration camps and prisons of the Third Reich, he took the path of active resistance, not to fulfil political pipe-dreams, but because he felt a commitment of solidarity with the workers who had voted for him. He sent a message to the workers of Lübeck to say that he had done what was in his power to do. He felt a bond, far stronger than before, with Lübeck, which he considered his true home, even though he had not once been back there since 1933.

Julius Leber was a man of few words, reserved and wary of false praise. But his powerful frame concealed a sensitive character. When the time came to protest, his conduct was prompted not by reckless heroics, but by a sense of duty and a determination to preserve his own identity. He was fully aware of the risks entailed in the attempted coup. He knew how dangerous it was to make contact with the outlawed KPD. He himself had always been firmly opposed to communism. But in the extreme situation of the impending coup every effort had to be made to save Germany from civil war. Leber noted with some scepticism the apparently moderate political demands of his communist interlocutors. Their aim was clearly to prevent the development of an independent SPD policy. This was why Leber was dubious about continuing the talks, but in fact the Gestapo stepped in before things could go any further.

As a patriot Leber subordinated his own life to the cause. If this German republican is remembered today, it is because he stands for the many nameless people who fought to preserve and win back freedom and human dignity in that darkest period of German history. The quiet pride that made him immune to Freisler's tirades and enabled him to survive repeated torture, isolation and despair, may in part have been due to his indissoluble links with the Hanseatic city of Lübeck, whose mercantile tradition blended with his social republicanism.

8

Wilhelm Leuschner and the resistance movement of 20 July 1944

The union leader and Social Democrat, Wilhelm Leuschner (b.1890)[1] was executed on 20 September 1944 in Plötzensee gaol, with the cry of 'unity!' on his lips. In remembering him it is relevant to examine the part played by labour unions in the 20 July uprising. We usually think of union resistance in connection with the anti-Nazi activities of the International Federation of Transport Workers. In addition, unionists were involved in the underground activities of socialist resistance groups, some of which were independent, others connected with the exiled leadership of the German Social-Democratic Party (SPD) in Prague. Similarly, unions were represented in the clandestine German Communist Party (KPD). Less attention is paid to the fact that representatives of various politically orientated labour unions not only played a leading part in the 20 July movement but were also indispensable in integrating the various groups within the conservative-nationalist opposition to Nazism.

In 1931, when the so-called Boxheim Papers came to light,[2] Wilhelm Leuschner, together with Carlo Mierendorff, warned of the dangers of Nazi tyranny and in July 1932 showed solidarity with the activist groups in the *Reichsbanner*.[3] It did not take the long years of maltreatment in the prisons and concentration camps of the Third Reich to make Leuschner decide on active resistance. However, while the communists and leftwing socialists were still flirting with the idea of mass action, he did not share their hope that the Nazi Party would rapidly run out of steam, thus leaving the field open for a socialist revolution. However, he did see himself as the champion of the Free Labour Unions, of their institutions and the commitments they made to their officials and members. Furthermore, despite the 'Enabling Law' of 24 March 1933 and the 14 July ban on founding new political parties, developments in Germany did not seem entirely set in stone. He felt there should at least be an attempt to defend the interests of organized labour under the Third Reich.

Leuschner's effectiveness and political prudence are beyond question, but he was not a man to make radical decisions, at any rate not until he had explored all the political avenues. He did share the national euphoria that was to be found in many union leaders; but within the General German Federation of Labour Unions (ADGB) Leuschner advocated the policy which, late in 1932, led to negotiations with Reich Chancellor von Schleicher about creating a 'union axis', with the aim of providing stability to the 'presidential' system.[4] In addition to encountering resistance from industry and the agricultural lobby, this attempt foundered on Gregor Strasser's indecision about making a complete break with Hitler[5] and also on the ADGB's mistrust of Chancellor von Schleicher. As late as April 1933 Leuschner took part in other negotiations with officials of the NSBO, a Nazi organization of party cells in factories and businesses, about the future of the labour unions. Parallel with this he was instrumental in bringing about a merger of the party-affiliated unions and the formation of a 'United Unions Executive' which, at the end of April 1933, made an offer to the Nazi rulers of 'positive cooperation' in their new state. At the same time the executive emphasized both the independence of the labour unions from any political party, and their essential role in the shaping of social policy.

The *Gleichschaltung* (which amounted to Nazification) of the ADGB on 2 May 1933 and the arrest of its top officials pulled the rug from under any arrangement of that kind. The Christian labour unions, which had been given a temporary reprieve until the conclusion of the Concordat with Rome, suffered the same fate a few weeks later. The policy of accommodation with Nazism had reached its dubious culmination in the extraordinary appeal by the ADGB for union members to join in the hijacked May Day festivities. But this did not arise merely from short-term tactical considerations; the idea of unifying the labour unions had been energetically promoted during the Depression and had been put into practice at plant level in the election of works councillors opposed to the NSBO. Among the Christian and liberal union associations, in particular, the idea of unification was linked with that of a corporatist reshaping of the Weimar constitution, a solution which, in view of the discredited state of the parliamentary system seemed to represent a constructive alternative. The union executive committed itself to a programme likely to find some support among sections of the National Socialist movement, who initially toyed with *berufständisch* ideas. The strategy of 'hibernation' under the protection of outward legality, which was at first adopted by that part of the SPD leadership that had not emigrated, could not be applied to the unions. But Leuschner equally rejected the alternative suggestion of voluntary dissolution of the unions.[6]

However, Robert Ley, the head of the Nazi 'German Labour Front' (DAF), then went on the rampage, confiscating union assets and meting out brutal treatment to the union leaders. But he lacked any clear social policy and the conflicts with the left wing of the NSBO were in no way resolved. At the beginning of June 1933 Leuschner seized the opportunity, when called on to do so by Robert Ley, to attend the International Labour Conference in Geneva. While there he prevented the German Labour Front from gaining the higher international status that Ley was seeking, and for this Ley took a bitter revenge. At that time Leuschner still hoped it would be possible to sideline the leader of the DAF and to extract tolerable conditions under which the unions might survive in the Third Reich. This was certainly an illusion. Yet the loss of power, which the DAF suffered through the institution of the Trustees of Labour[7] was a pointer in that direction.

After the arrest of Schlimme[8] in 1937, Leuschner of necessity grew into the role of leader of the outlawed national union executive, which now existed only on an informal basis. Its activities were predominantly defensive and aimed at pressing the material claims of former union members, which remained valid despite their transfer into the DAF. In this, an especially important function was fulfilled by Ernst Fraenkel,[9] before he emigrated to the USA in 1938.

After being released from the Börgermoor concentration camp in 1934, Leuschner intensified his contacts with former unionists, especially Jakob Kaiser and Max Habermann.[10] This activity was financed by a metallurgical company, which Leuschner ran in conjunction with Hermann Maass. This provided not only a secure income but also the opportunity to get close to the Gestapo under the guise of business dealings. In doing so, Leuschner was pursuing the line adopted by the united unions executive in April 1933. However, the informal contacts maintained between officials, chiefly at the level of industry associations, especially the German Metalworkers' Association, were gradually broken off due to Gestapo investigations, and any chance of contact with émigré groups was destroyed. Leuschner's network therefore became more of a recruitment organization, which could have gone into action after a change of regime. However Leuschner had few illusions about the possibility of political effectiveness, as is shown by his statement in August 1939 that Germany was one vast prison in which rebellion was tantamount to suicide.

Leuschner participated in the plans of the group around Jakob Kaiser and Max Habermann, which was also joined by Theodor Brauer and a number of Christian labour leaders, who were still following the line of April 1933. Leuschner himself remained fairly passive on matters of principle, while devoting particular attention to organizational questions. Leuschner's marginal involvement in conspiracy did not entirely escape the notice of the Gestapo; however, in the pre-war years the regime tended to be lenient towards the moderate wing of the former Social Democrats, as long as they did not campaign publicly or cultivate contacts abroad. At this time even Leuschner had no realistic prospect of taking action, though he considered a change of political system possible, and in Berlin labour circles his name was mentioned as a future Reich Chancellor. Despite the miserable results achieved by the

DAF in the elections for works councillors – elections which, for that reason, were banned from 1936 onwards – he recognized that the majority of workers were tending to resign themselves to the new circumstances and could not be directly mobilized against the regime.

Leuschner's links with Christian labour leaders brought him into contact with anti-Hitler personalities within the Nazi government hierarchy. It was no coincidence that his acquaintance with Carl Goerdeler was made through General Hammerstein.[11] Under the Third Reich, a repeat of the Schleicher experiment[12] offered the best chance of bringing the forces of the labour movement back into play. After some initial reticence, which was increased by the very different political backgrounds they came from, Leuschner's relationship with Carl Goerdeler became deeper. For his part, Goerdeler sought support in labour union circles, after the concepts he had set out in his memorandum, 'The Goal', met with sharp criticism from Popitz and Hassell. Goerdeler's two co-conspirators rejected his economic liberalism and were much keener than he was to retain the authoritarian structures created by Nazi policy.

With the introduction of Leuschner and the group of Christian labour leaders, the social and political spectrum of the Goerdeler circle changed fundamentally. From 1942 on, Leuschner brought his trusted associate, Hermann Maass, into the circle's discussions. But he hesitated to reveal to Goerdeler the full extent of his contacts with a large number of free labour unionists and social democrats. He was now thoroughly involved in underground activities with the intention of immediately activating a cadre of leaders for the planned 'German Labour Union', in the event of a successful overthrow of the Nazi regime. Goerdeler, who was keen to forge stronger links with the social democrats, was not always happy about this, and in fact Leuschner put a brake on his activities when it became important to win over Julius Leber.[13] Conversely, Goerdeler reacted with some annoyance when Leuschner made direct contact with Claus von Stauffenberg. Although the proposals of the Goerdeler circle for a new political order bore the imprint of its founder, there is no doubt that Leuschner, Kaiser and

Habermann, who intended to lead the new unified labour union, exercised a power of veto. Under pressure from them, Goerdeler found himself forced to move further away from Popitz, who rejected Leuschner's union plans, seeing them as creating a 'state within a state'. In fact Goerdeler no longer saw a part for Popitz in the provisional government.

It was typical of Leuschner's political temperament that in planning the new order he essentially concentrated on pushing through his programme for the labour unions. Originally Goerdeler had intended, in full agreement with the conservative wing, to take over the DAF essentially unchanged. By reason of his experience in local government and his basically liberal economic views, Goerdeler showed more understanding than his colleagues of the need for labour union organization. By contrast, those on the political right, including its neo-conservative wing, had since the 1920s attempted to replace free collective bargaining by structures based on professions or W*erkgemeinschaften*.[14] The animosity towards the labour unions that had built up during the Weimar period was something which military officers like *Generaloberst* Beck and Claus von Stauffenberg also had difficulty in overcoming. This took its most extreme form in the plans of the Freiburg Circle of academic economists, and most of all in the views of Constantin von Dietze, with whom Goerdeler was in contact. Goerdeler himself originally proposed a general ban on strikes and lockouts and an expansion of the system of labour trustees (*Treuhänder der Arbeit*). Ever since Oswald Spengler's concept of 'Prussian Socialism', the notion had been widespread that it must be possible to allay the conflict between capital and labour through a state-imposed social compromise. This coincided with Christian 'solidarist' thinking,[15] which, in the late 1920s, was exerting increased influence in the Centre Party.

Leuschner was in agreement with his Christian union colleagues, and also with Max Habermann of the DHV (German clerical employees association), that a relapse into 'Marxist class-based labour unions' must be avoided. Hence, the involvement of clerical staff and public servants in the employee organization was something they decided on from the outset. There were differences on the question of whether there should be a return to trade and professional associations, or whether preference should be given to industry-wide bodies. The key point was that what must emerge was a single, politically neutral, centrally organized union, embracing all employed people, other than the self-employed. Here the idea gained acceptance that compulsory membership, which was already a fact in the DAF, should be retained. This made sense since wide-ranging autonomous powers were to be granted to the 'German Labour Union'. In addition to co-determination at plant and industry level, Goerdeler insisted that unemployment insurance and recruitment services should also become union responsibilities. Similarly the union was to be represented in the proposed self-governing bodies of the economy and in the *Reichständekammer* (Reich Chamber of Estates, Goerdeler's notional second chamber of parliament). Leuschner added to this programme the nationalization of key industries, the building up of an extensive union education system, and the right of the union to own and run its own businesses.

This was the result of a multilateral compromise. On the one hand was Goerdeler's principle of keeping the state out of industrial relations as far as possible and not allowing free market forces to be hindered by excessive intervention through social policies. Then there were the corporatist ideas, brought to the table mainly by Christian labour leaders. All this in turn blended with Leuschner's revival of ideas that harked back to the 1914–1918 war economy and the Wissell-Moellendorff plans for government intervention to deal with large numbers of demobilized troops coming into the labour market. It is not surprising that this model came up against rooted criticism, not only from the right wing under Popitz, but even from the Kreisau Circle with whom, despite the close friendship between Leuschner and Mierendorff, considerable differences arose. The concept of plant- or company-based unions, developed by the Kreisau Circle, was utopian in character, not so much because of the rights it granted to employees' representatives, but rather because of its orientation towards skill-based small and medium-sized businesses, which in practice imposed a severe restriction on the free movement of labour.

It says much for Leuschner's tactical adroitness that he was able to persuade the Kreisau Circle to accept the 'German Labour Union' as a transitional solution, even though it was in clear contradiction with Moltke's concept of 'small communities', in other words the wide application of the principle of subsidiarity to governmental responsibility. Quite apart from this specific position, the programme for a 'German Labour Union' exuded the spirit of a 'top-down' organization, which was not merely due to the clandestine conditions under which it was drafted. In the last analysis this concept was equally born out of the expectation that it would be possible, through administrative measures, to achieve a peaceful resolution of social conflicts and to make labour disputes largely unnecessary.

In this Leuschner did not differ from the strongly centralist tradition of the Free Labour Unions, which favoured state involvement and the imposition of standard working conditions, and which was a product of the conditions prevailing in the Kaiser's Germany. Only now – in deference to Goerdeler – it was necessary to accept a considerable degree of disengagement of the state from social policy. On this question a fundamental dispute arose with Leber, who was in any case very sceptical as to whether the cadre of leaders proposed by Leuschner would, if the regime were overthrown, be sufficiently effective or even available at all. The ironic comments by the Gestapo's interrogating officers about this overage union team was in many respects justified. But this was a general problem for the resistance, since it was largely dependent on those groups and links that had existed before the Nazis seized power, and which could not rely on spontaneous support from the younger generation.

It seems that Leuschner only involved himself in Goerdeler's constitutional plans to a limited extent, and then only when they impinged on the interests of organized labour. He himself regularly called upon the advice of Ludwig Bergsträsser, who in turn maintained contact with historians and former parliamentarians and was much more deeply concerned with parliamentary matters than were the other groups within the conservative-nationalist resistance. However, he recognized that in the period of transitional government the unions and the churches would both have a central role in the political reconstruction.

It must remain an open question as to how Leuschner visualized the regeneration of the party system, and whether he shared the neo-conservatives' grudging concession that parties could be formed, if at all, on the basis of selecting rather than electing their politically active members. The concept of the 'German Labour Union', finalized in 1942, appears not to have allowed for the reestablishment of a multi-party system. In fact, given the direct political influence of the major interest groups in society and the authoritarian elements in the form of government envisaged by Goerdeler, political parties would have been largely unnecessary. For Leuschner this question was not of primary interest. He could work happily with many political refugees from Weimar's extreme right, and saw no problem in collaborating with the white-collar DHV union. Equally, we can conclude that he did not anticipate serious resistance from the socialist camp.

In the factional disputes from 1943 onwards, Leuschner took up a position alongside Goerdeler and the Christian labour leaders. When they demanded that the proposed non-party popular movement should adopt a Christian programme, Leuschner – unlike Leber – did not oppose them. This incidentally shows how little consideration he gave to questions of ideology. On the other hand, his judgement of Goerdeler was certainly not without reservations, however much he took Goerdeler's side and was influenced by him, for example in criticizing the inaction of the military. Yet, out of a feeling of solidarity and loyalty he dropped the idea of possibly replacing Goerdeler as Chancellor in a post-Nazi cabinet, while not entirely ruling out independent action at a later point in time.

On the question of how the Nazis might be overthrown, Leuschner agreed with Goerdeler that this must be the job of the military. Leuschner saw no advantage in dragging the mass of workers into a bloody conflict that might turn into a civil war, nor did he even think it a possibility. Similarly he firmly opposed efforts by Leber and Adolf Reichwein to establish contact with the outlawed KPD; in this he was clearly expressing the strongly anti-communist attitude of the German labour unions since 1919. The union concept that he developed was not envisaged as a weapon with which to overthrow Nazism. However, Leuschner played an active part in building a network of contacts for the conservative-nationalist resistance, and in planning its recruitment and selection. He made an impressive attempt to persuade the Austrian socialists to join the resistance, though this met with a clear refusal from Adolf Schärf.[16]

Leuschner, Kaiser and Habermann shared with the conservative plotters the handicap of being unable to predict the reaction of the masses to a coup d'état. Perhaps unwisely they hoped that their former membership would respond to the calls of their erstwhile officials. Mierendorff, Leber and Theodor Haubach shed doubt on Leuschner's claim to have the organization behind him. However, there was scarcely any alternative to reactivating the old union cadre, if they were to avoid the risk of virtual civil war – as Leuschner was determined to do. Leuschner rejected the idea of backing the coup with a call for a general strike. Unlike Leber and Mierendorff, he placed less importance on the need to mobilize the population to give their support to a new government, although he strongly advocated the founding of the 'non-party popular movement'.

The austere realism of Leuschner's political calculation sets him as much apart from Goerdeler's paternalistic sentimentality as from the euphoric visions of Mierendorff and Haubach and equally from the thinking of Leber and Stauffenberg, who dreamed of a mixture of military putsch and popular uprising, modelled on that of 1813. Leuschner's position was closer to that of those conservative-nationalists who cherished the hope that they could defeat the Nazi regime essentially by institutional reform and putting new people in to run it. On the other hand Leuschner was staunchly opposed to the restoration of former privileges. What mattered to him was that the workers should have an equal say in defining public policy and managing the economy.

Leuschner's work as an opponent of Nazism was guided by the conviction that the labour union structure could be successfully revived and deployed in the cause of political stability. He thought it certain that the former union officials, for whom he had earmarked senior posts in the 'German Labour Union' or as Political Commissioners (in the provisional military districts to be set up after the 1944 coup), would not shirk their tasks. This was despite the fact that, for security reasons or due to communication problems, they had not been informed, or at best had only been given hints about the conspiracy and the functions that had been allotted to them. Leuschner was right, to the extent that the power of union solidarity survived the Nazi reign of terror, a fact that he discovered from countless meetings with former union members. It is also remarkable that in the rebuilding of the unions in 1945 the older generation of labour leaders played a key role, and the trust shown to them by the membership had not been lost.

Leuschner made no secret of what he wanted to achieve: On the one hand the former labour leaders could not refuse to contribute actively to the ending of a war that was taking Germany to disaster, nor to help in the removal of a criminal regime. Nonetheless, as Leuschner saw it, the prime responsibility for these events did not lie with the workers, and hence they should not have to bear the main burden of overthrowing the regime. On the other hand, such a step must in his view be accompanied by a permanent guarantee of union organization for the working population, an organization which could only have the strength to achieve a fair balance between labour and capital and to impose a just social order if it was united.

The ideas of Goerdeler and the Kreisau Circle for a new political order showed a deep distrust of any restoration of a Weimar-type parliamentary democracy. A similar distrust is displayed in their highly *dirigiste* plans for organized labour. In a way Leuschner, too, harked back like the conservative-nationalists to Hindeburg's rule by presidential cabinet, in the last phase of the Weimar republic. But we may assume that Leuschner was thinking more in terms of transitional arrangements.

The anti-pluralist flavour of these plans is similarly reflected in Jakob Kaiser's revival of the programme, first announced by Stegerwald[1] in Essen in 1920, of a Christian-Socialist and simultaneously nationalist party of integration, which had the potential objective of creating a 'permanent' majority party. All this shows how far German political culture – even among convinced opponents of Nazism – had moved away from the traditions of liberalism and democratic socialism and was showing certain affinities with fascist structures.

At the same time we must not forget that Leuschner, the labour leader, managed to persuade the conservative-nationalist opposition to give far greater prominence to social justice in their concepts for a new order in Germany. He also contributed largely to refocusing the originally arch-conservative plans away from a predominantly agrarian and middle-class model of society, towards one based on the social and economic realities of an advanced industrial economy. Since labour leaders and social democrats would have to be given a crucial position after the overthrow of Nazism, if the transitional government was to have internal political stability, their role was also to be that of bringing about a merger between the Kreisau and Goerdeler circles and the inner core of plotters around Stauffenberg.

If, from today's perspective, we fail to find a stronger democratic impulse in the intellectual contribution of the labour leaders, which may be one reason for their relative failure under Weimar, we must still not overlook the motives that drove them to join the resistance. For men like Wilhelm Leuschner who, with his usual restraint remarked during his Gestapo interrogation that he was 'unable to relate personally to National Socialism', the motive came from a belief in the historical necessity to create a just society. In a very deep sense their actions sprang from a feeling of solidarity with the union membership, oppressed, condemned to silence, maltreated or sacrificed in a senseless war.

In their interrogations the Gestapo found it hard to understand why a man like Leuschner, who was managing a successful business, important to the war effort, took the path of resistance, as did Carlo Mierendorff, Julius Leber and many others. They were certainly not concerned with defending a social hierarchy or, as the Gestapo tried to insinuate about Leuschner, with satisfying a personal ambition, but with fulfilling an obligation that they had assumed as elected representatives of the workers. The reticent Leuschner has left us hardly a word that reveals his inner motives. In his letter of August 1939, mentioned earlier, he wrote: 'Tell our friends that we still are what we have always been.' Adolf Grimme, who knew Leuschner well, called him 'a hero without a uniform', who toughly and tenaciously, without sentimentality, carried forward the daily struggle for peace and liberation in the service of the labour union movement, and who went to his death in the knowledge that he had always remained true to his own principles.

Carlo Mierendorff's
'Socialist Action' programme

Among the papers of the Kreisau Circle kept by Count Helmuth James von Moltke was a document that diverges from the general thrust of the other texts. Under the heading 'Mierendorff's Call to Arms', it purports to be an 'action programme' for 'Socialist Action'. Carlo Mierendorff[1] drafted it in Berlin in late May and early June 1943 and dated it 14 June of that year, the same day as the Kreisau Circle's third midsummer conference. However, Mierendorff – like Theodor Haubach – was absent, possibly for reasons of secrecy, and so the document was handed to Moltke by Eugen Gerstenmaier, who took part in the conference. In the event the paper was not dealt with in the group's deliberations; nonetheless, Moltke retained the programme among the other Kreisau texts. This leads us to conclude that he saw it as an embodiment of Kreisau's ideas.

'Socialist Action' emerged from an action committee that was to meet for the first time on Whit Monday 1943. The committee was to consist of representatives of various opposition groups including the German Communist Party (KPD) and was to be given the task of launching a comprehensive popular movement that would transcend party politics. Mierendorff probably did not yet have any clear idea about how to set about constituting the action committee, and it is possible that he briefly considered converting the Kreisau gathering into just such a committee. But the Kreisau Circle did not even include liberals, let alone communists. Similarly, we can only speculate about which individuals he had in mind as 'signatories' of the manifesto, mentioned in its preamble. This cannot even be deduced from parallel sources and so the question has remained unanswered.

Carlo Mierendorff's call for the formation of 'Socialist Action' was the beginning of an 'independence movement' among the socialists who had thrown in their lot with the Kreisau and Goerdeler groups, and who began to hold separate meetings attended by Emil Henk[2] and Ludwig Schwamb, among others. From the late summer of 1943 Mierendorff, Haubach, Reichwein and Leber were urging swift action, and tried to involve themselves in Claus von Stauffenberg's preparations for a coup d'état. In this context there was a cross-connection with Wilhelm Leuschner in spite of the persisting differences between them concerning the dominant role that Leuschner assigned to the labour unions in relation to social democracy. This *rapprochement* may in part have been due to 'Socialist Action' also recognizing that a continuation of the war would lead to a collapse of Germany's social and economic structures and that waiting in the wings was no longer an option.

Independent action by the socialists within the 20th July movement was bound to meet with the disapproval of Moltke, who saw it as the formation of an unwelcome splinter group. This conflict concealed a fundamental disagreement on the strategic assessment of how the anti-Nazi opposition should proceed. Moltke firmly rejected the plans for a coup in the summer of 1943, which were chiefly being forced through by Goerdeler and was scathing about the activities of 'their Excellencies', who did not want a genuine revolution, but merely to overthrow the Nazi regime. As Moltke saw it the Reich was not yet in a sufficiently receptive state, politically or morally: 'In truth, much more [of Germany] must lie in rubble and ashes before the time is ripe.' For a time, he was perhaps able to win Mierendorff over to his point of view, though not in the longer term. It was not until the late autumn that the quarrel with Mierendorff and Leber could once more be laid to rest.

It is against this background that the call for 'Socialist Action' must be read. There can be no doubt that it reflects Mierendorff's personal style; there is little to suggest any corrections by his normally cautious friend, Emil Henk, whereas many of Haubach's Christian-Socialist ideas did find their way into it. The rousing language of the appeal did not quite compensate for the lack of precision in its political concepts. Nonetheless, we may assume that this proclamation did actually represent the programme of the government that was to replace the Nazi regime. Hence, Mierendorff's manifesto provided the basis for the drafts of a government declaration and the structure of the popular movement, which, in the final weeks of planning before the attempted coup, led to heated debates among the plotters.

The language of the appeal differs considerably from that of the Kreisau texts, with its use of terms like 'action', 'Hitler's dictatorship', 'Nazism' and 'united front', which belonged to the discourse of the political left. And yet we find in it many thought-processes that directly echo those of Kreisau. The text reflects Mierendorff's characteristic ambivalence, which arose from his declaration of faith in socialist aims and his deep roots in German idealism. It is certain that the syncretic character of the document shows his desire to reconcile diverging political tendencies. This ambition of Mierendorff's emerges most clearly in the symbol of a cross within a circle, which he uses to evoke the new mass-movement.

Analogously with this, 'Socialist Action' sought to combine Christian and socialist values and create a united front in the battle against Hitler's dictatorship, which could embrace all streams of anti-Nazi opinion. This might be dismissed as utopian, and yet it was in every respect a sensible and necessary attempt to unite the various strands of the resistance. Looked at in this way, the programme met the demands of the moment, even if there was no real chance of gaining the active support of the communists.

The programme contained classic socialist aims such as the introduction of a 'socialist economic order', the guarantee of 'a secure livelihood for those employed in industry and agriculture and for the farmer on his soil', the expropriation of 'key companies in heavy industry', the abolition of 'the pernicious abuse of political power by large-scale capital', and autonomy for business with 'equal rights of participation' for the workers. This was a clear catalogue of socialist demands, which largely matched the aims of Kreisau, albeit couched in rather less esoteric language.

However, the emphasis was certainly not on material objectives. These were placed alongside the demand for 'the restoration of justice and the rule of law' and thus derived from values, which in turn had their roots in Christianity. In consensus with Kreisau, the programme demanded the 'abolition of constraints on conscience' and the creation of 'social justice'. This is reminiscent of Fr Alfred Delp's famous call for 'the opportunity to create a renewed, dependable human environment', which he flung in the face of Roland Freisler and his People's Court. It also recalls Delp's conviction that the desired 'reform of mentality' presupposed a fundamental 'reform of physical conditions'.

Similarly, Mierendorff called for 'unconditional tolerance as regards religion, race and nationality' and 'respect for the foundations of our culture', which were 'unthinkable without Christianity'. This set of demands would later lead to lively controversy and to attempts to find an acceptable formula that would express the need to maintain the Christian faith as the basis of western culture, without frightening off those who advocated a radical secularization of the state. Furthermore, the manifesto spoke out for the restoration of 'human dignity and political freedom' and of the 'honour trampled on by the crimes of Nazism' and for returning to the nation its self-respect. With these phrases the programme sought to address not only the working class but also the armed forces.

The attempt, through 'Socialist Action', to join forces with Christian groups, the social-democratic and communist movements as well as liberal groupings was to have culminated in the creation of 'non-party popular movement for the salvation of Germany'. It remains unclear whether this was to become active immediately or not until after the collapse of the regime. According to the text the action-committee was to be set up without delay. In practice the objective, as Julius Leber summed it up, was to form 'a new kind of popular front based on all surviving and viable social and democratic forces'.

The constitutional aims of the appeal, with its demand for the dismantling of 'bureaucratic centralism' and for a 'state built up organically from its provinces', followed the federative model propounded by the conservative-nationalist resistance. The phrase that recurs in this context is 'the need to overcome party conflict'. This was principally aimed at reconciling the two hostile wings of the German labour movement but it also reflected the then prevailing antipathy to the parliamentary system. The vision of a 'resourceful nation' coming together among ruins and graves and 'ordering its life in a spirit of true liberty' mirrored Mierendorff's own radically democratic self-image.

The text contained a note of independence in its ringing declaration of faith in a freely constituted nation, which 'must prove itself before the judgement of history' to be stronger 'than the destiny' which had been intended for it by the regime. Among all the papers on constitutional policy, both from the Kreisau and Goerdeler circles, Mierendorff's is the only one that expressly refers to the need for a popular organization and thus for a democratic foundation for the overthrow of Nazism. The manifesto summoned 'all upright Germans to honourable collaboration' and thus was far removed from traditional elitist notions.

There is much to suggest that with his 'Socialist Action' Mierendorff was picking up an idea originally developed by Hans Robinsohn. Before his enforced emigration to Denmark Robinsohn had built up a relatively large resistance group which, unlike the 20th July movement, had a strongly liberal orientation. As early as the mid-1930s Robinsohn's memoranda raised the question of the democratic legitimation of a revolutionary government, whereas this was not seriously considered by the conservative-nationalist resistance until the founding of the National Committee for Free Germany in the spring of 1943.

The idea of creating an all-party alliance to defeat fascism was already firmly implanted in Robinsohn's mind. He was also convinced that it was necessary to neutralize the influence of the Nazi Party through a popular organization with its own branch offices right down to district level; and to provide a plebiscitary basis for the revolutionary government, which it would need if events slid towards civil war.

Hans Robinsohn's resistance organization, which continued under the leadership of Ernst Strassmann, broke up after Strassmann's arrest in 1942. A number of its members joined the conservative-nationalist resistance. There is evidence that Theodor Haubach was closely acquainted with this group and that from 1939 onwards the relationship was a personal one. This strongly suggests that the concept of a non-party popular movement came through Haubach to Mierendorff, who took it up at a moment when it was very much in the air and was being put into practice in various popular-front movements in countries beyond the Reich. It spread into what was later to become the communist bloc, and in the French resistance it took the form of Gaullism.

In calling for the launch of a 'non-party popular movement for the salvation of Germany', Mierendorff's action programme exposed the most serious weakness in the 20th July movement's plans for a coup d'état. It is true that both the Goerdeler and Kreisau circles had put forward relatively comprehensive and in some ways unusually detailed proposals for Germany's social, political and constitutional future, and these were certainly not intended simply as transitional arrangements. On the other hand it remains unclear how the revolutionary government would secure the consent of the population. Ideas about when elections would be called were at best vague, and the plotters tended to prefer indirect elections from the districts, rather than a national ballot.

While reform of electoral law had a prominent place in both Goerdeler's and the Kreisau Circle's constitutional model, the involvement of political parties, originally accepted as necessary, was viewed with growing scepticism. Their thinking in this regard was unclear. Jakob Kaiser had considered bringing in an all-embracing 'Labour Party' (he specifically used the English name) to replace the two workers' parties. In doing so he was referring back to Adam Stegerwald's Essen speech in 1920, which proposed a kind of Christian umbrella-party. Goerdeler hoped initially to be able to dispense with parties altogether, although, wedded as he was to the National-Liberal tradition,[3] he believed they were unavoidable for good reasons.

Leuschner's concept of a 'German Labour Union' basically allowed no room for a powerful Social-Democratic party. For this reason he was extremely cautious about voicing an opinion. Of the situation as it stood in 1942 Hermann Maass has said: 'The question of whether, in addition to the Labour Union, a specific political organization was to be formed, had not been settled.' At all events, no one wanted to bring back 'the former multi-party system' and, at best, considered creating 'a party selected from a narrow group of politically aware elements'. In the Kreisau Circle, as we see from Fr König's dossier, earlier references to political parties became less frequent in later drafts and finally disappeared altogether.

In this set of circumstances Mierendorff's proposal, however problematic it appeared on closer examination, nonetheless had a liberating effect. The idea of forming a 'non-political popular movement' was eagerly taken up by all sides, although with differing interpretations from the outset. Goerdeler thought of putting this movement in to replace the Nazi Party, which would have to be abolished. During his later interrogation by the Gestapo he said: 'Like you, we no longer wanted a state run by political parties. The popular movement was intended to unite all social and occupational classes, in all parts of Germany.' What he had in mind was an organization controlled by the government, which might provide the foundation for the later formation of political parties.

On the other hand, it is not clear what ideas the men of Kreisau brought to this debate. There is considerable evidence that Moltke was attempting to combine the concept of a non-party popular movement with his aim of creating a new democratic elite from all social classes and even a 'party of the like-minded', extending beyond the borders of nation-states. Theodor Haubach, who shared Mierendorff's views and who tirelessly championed them after Mierendorff's death, supported the strongly Christian tone of the call to action, and affirmed its obvious democratic conclusions with great emphasis. But he did flatly reject the involvement of communists that Mierendorff had hoped for.

In the differing tactical and organizational interpretations of the concept of a popular movement, the latent divergent tendencies within the 20th July movement began to emerge. When it came to settling on a programme for the popular movement, these differences came fully into the open. Goerdeler sided with the Christian labour leaders in advocating a Christianity-based programme, and in this he gained the support of Leuschner, who was presumably anxious above all to achieve some kind of unity. In the compromise that was under discussion in early 1944, Mierendorff's original wording had only been slightly altered and now read: 'The popular movement declares its belief in German culture and in the Christian past of the German people'.

Julius Leber, flanked by other socialists, protested strongly against this formulation, having already objected to the 'Christian portrayal of the state' as proposed by Jakob Kaiser. Leber said he refused to allow 'the longstanding principles of social democracy simply to be thrown overboard for the sake of desired unity'. In view of the preparations for the attempt on Hitler's life, which were rapidly taking concrete shape, it was no longer possible to reach 'final agreement on a proclamation of the "popular movement" and its political content'.

It would be wrong to play down this fundamental conflict and to assess it as no more than the result of increasing nervousness – although that did have its effect. However, such an interpretation is regularly found in the older literature that draws on statements by Eugen Gerstenmaier. Mierendorff's original aim of bringing in the communists was not pursued further, particularly after the failed attempt by Leber and Adolf Reichwein to get in touch with the outlawed national executive of the KPD under Franz Jacob and Anton Saefkow, an attempt that ended in tragedy.[4] On the other hand the plotters agreed to establish the non-party popular movement at the latest by the time the coup took place. This was a reaction to the changed political situation since the founding of the National Committee for a Free Germany and the intensification of communist activity. Opposition in Germany could now be expected both from the left and the right.

It was precisely with an eye to the outlawed communist party that Leber wanted to avoid a Christian programme. This coincided with the intention of Stauffenberg's inner circle of plotters, to provide the revolutionary government with as strong a left wing as possible. Leber agreed with the ideas that Mierendorff had set in train with his 'Socialist Action'. He envisaged a revolutionary reshaping of the nation on the lines of the German Uprising of 1813, and he was at one with Claus von Stauffenberg in this. It was difficult to reconcile this with giving the popular movement a Christian slant, which tended to look back to *berufsständisch* ideas and probably also overestimated the unifying power of Christian ideals.

Regardless of conceptual differences, these discussions represented a remarkable step forward in the education of the conservative-national resistance, towards a democratic underpinning for the revolutionary government and a democratic mobilization of the population. At the same time it was an expression of a re-politicisation that was observable in European politics generally, which even within the Nazi Party led to a revival of hostilities between rival factions, and which ultimately brought to an end the period that had been marked by a complete ossification of Europe's domestic political scene. The outbreak of factionalism within the 20th July movement, notwithstanding their fundamental agreement about the inhumanity of Nazi tyranny, does not represent a relapse, but a shift towards the European norm. With his clarion call for 'Socialist Action' Carlo Mierendorff, the pioneering social democrat, must be credited for having given the first impetus to a movement which, tragically, he did not live to see become a reality.

10

Adolf Reichwein's road to resistance and the Kreisau Circle

Unlike the majority of conservative plotters, who only began to adopt an anti-Nazi position in the autumn of 1938, when Hitler brought Germany to the brink of war over the Sudetenland, Adolf Reichwein[1] had firmly distanced himself from the Third Reich right from the start. From 1930 onwards he had repeatedly warned against the Nazis seizing power and made an effort to mobilize the countervailing forces of social democracy. As a former adviser to Becker, the Prussian Minister of Education and Cultural Affairs, and as a contributor to *Neue Blätter für den Sozialismus* ('New Pages for Socialism'), he could expect disciplinary action and, on 24 April 1933, under Article 5 of the Law on Professional Civil Servants, he was dismissed from his professorship at the Pedagogical Academy in Halle.

Reichwein was presented with the choice either of emigrating to Turkey, where he could continue to practise as a university lecturer, or accepting a junior school-teaching post. He decided to stay in Germany and teach in a single-class rural school. With help from former ministry colleagues he succeeded in getting a posting to a village elementary school in Brandenburg.

This retreat to the depths of the country did not, however, lessen his commitment to public affairs; instead he concentrated more heavily than ever on the model of 'active learning' that he had earlier thought out and tested in practice himself. These plans for educational reform, to which he devoted most of his energies, have been called an attempt to preserve 'a secret model for ordered freedom'. He managed to insulate his activity from the direct impact of Nazi propaganda, and did not abandon his aim of 'flinging the village open to the world', in the face of the pseudo-romanticism and inward-looking peasant ideology of Nazism.

In fact he succeeded, through apparent concessions, in obtaining membership of the NSLB, the Nazi federation of teachers, and with the help of sympathizers in the Reich Ministry of Education he was able not only to build up his elementary school into a model establishment, but also to gain considerable public recognition for his reforming pedagogical work, not least through his highly acclaimed pamphlet, *Schaffendes Schulvolk* ('Creavity in the Classroom'), which was published in 1937. At the same time he forged links with the *Reichnährstand*[2] with a view to expanding his school, though the approach of the Second World War put an end to this.

In these professionally successful years Reichwein saw the opportunity to make something happen, and his career reminds us that the men and women of the resistance were committed to direct intervention and saw no point in speculating about the future while sitting on their hands. Hence, of necessity, they had to play a double game, making compromises with the system. Furthermore, as shown by the sympathetic support Reichwein received, in spite of everything, from people in the education ministry, this system was still by no means totally Nazified. In December 1938 Reichwein wrote to his friend Wilhelm Flitner: 'If my political credentials were more in line with today's requirements, greater things could probably be achieved. Still, I try through meetings here and there to move a few things forward.' Like most of his contemporaries, he no longer counted on a rapid change of regime. Early in 1938 he wrote from his country school to a friend, Rolf Gardiner, to say that he was not without hope 'that in ten years time or even longer, we will once again be allowed to make a stronger and more profound contribution'.

Reichwein's many and varied personal connections were largely responsible for the fact that in 1939 he was given the task of setting up the education department of the Museum of Ethnology in

Berlin. This work gave him a chance to re-establish or strengthen old contacts with people who shared his political views. At the same time it gave him an opportunity to bring his educational ideas to a wider audience. His personal antipathy to the Nazi Party was no less strong, but he was obliged to make a certain degree of accommodation with the regime in order to ensure the survival of his ideas. He told an artist friend in 1937 that one could not continue to 'live without casting a shadow': the only way out, he said, was 'to accept the inevitable and go one's own way'. As early as 1933 he had remarked to another friend, Robert Curtius, that his sense of personal orientation remained 'unshaken'.

Against this background, we have to ask how it was that Reichwein made the step from a partial accommodation with the regime, albeit clearly distanced from it, to active participation in the resistance. His move to Berlin has no direct connection with this, but did make it possible for him to establish many contacts with the anti-Hitler opposition, which he quickly did. There is indirect evidence that Reichwein renewed his links with Carlo Mierendorff in 1939, and through him, with Emil Henk; both were waiting for opportunities to remove the hated regime. For the moment, however, there was no more than an exchange of ideas, which led to the forming of an informal group of five, one of whom, Carl Dietrich von Trotha, was in contact with Moltke. The meetings were held in the winter of 1941–2.

Reichwein devoted characteristic energy to his educational work for the museum, which occupied him fully until his death. It provided him with a constant point of reference, to which was added, from the summer of 1940 onward, his growing commitment to the Kreisau Circle. Like Moltke, Einsiedel and other resisters, Reichwein had been an active supporter of the 'work-camp' movement in the late 1920s. Young intellectuals of the day saw this movement as a way of overcoming the mutual antipathy between the affluent middle classes on the one hand, and workers and peasant-farmers on the other.

In spite of his sympathy with socialism, Reichwein initially distanced himself from organized labour. During his student years in Marburg his position was close to that of the Guild Socialists,[3] and his aim was to be able, through establishing cells among the elite, to penetrate the capitalist system from below, as it were, and in the long term to change it. Reichwein was stimulated by Karl Marx but critical of his notion of the class struggle. His own thinking was towards a social structure that would combine the 'free self-development' of the individual with a strong awareness of social obligation. In this context he coined the formula of 'a way of life based on mutual service'.

The idea of a reconciliation between the working class and the bourgeoisie was derived from the debates of Marburg's 'Academic Association', at whose Whitsun conference in 1923 Reichwein made a plea for a new social synthesis and called for 'politics to be liberated from the economy'. In this context he promoted a plan for a 'Work-land Settlement' (*Werkland-Siedlung*), in which a group of people were to establish a cooperative, self-sufficient rural business community, as the nucleus of new structure within the capitalist system. He hoped that by bringing together work and the rest of life, he could liberate people from the 'selfish economy of the individual'.

This train of thought, though seemingly esoteric, took on a real shape in connection with Reichwein's work at the adult education centre in Jena between 1923 and 1929, in which great importance was given to workers' education. In the education programme that he devised, Reichwein tackled the central themes of Weimar social policy, including the problem of workers' representation in management at company and industry-wide level. He saw his call for a 'business democracy' as a 'watchword of future economic development'. He sought to overcome the conflict between capital and labour through a partnership model of 'small groups'.

There is no need to elaborate on how closely Reichwein's ideas for the future structure of society and the economy overlapped with those of Helmuth von Moltke. The ideas of 'partnership' and 'neighbourhood' and the emphasis on the role of small groups as the nuclei of large-scale communities closely approximated to Moltke's concept of 'small communities' and, just as Moltke championed the idea of a fundamental new beginning for western society, Reichwein thought about developing a totally 'new way of life', which would replace the outmoded social conditions of the bourgeois era.

In his time at Marburg, Reichwein had envisaged a way of resolving the conflict between capital and labour through the creation of guilds, in which entrepreneurs and employees joined forces: 'An essential element in the guild idea is that it removes the sharp division between the functions of entrepreneur and employee. These are then re-combined in a higher-level unit of joint and equal responsibility in the business.' In a nutshell, this was the concept of the plant- or company-based labour union, which later appeared in the programme of the Kreisau Circle. There is ample evidence that Reichwein was instrumental in working it out in detail.

While working in Thuringia, Reichwein's sympathies moved towards the Social Democratic party, which he joined in 1930, probably not least because he realized that the worker education he had so energetically promoted would not have sufficient credibility unless it had an organization to fall back on. But he much regretted having to do this, given the prevailing inactivity of the party. As a member of the 'New Pages for Socialism' group, he originally sat on its advisory board and it was through this magazine that he met Theodor Haubach, Harald Poelchau and Adam von Trott zu Solz. He urged the creation of a broad, defensive political front against Nazism, at the same time as Carlo Mierendorff was struggling to overcome the political stagnation and paralysis of the German Social-Democratic Party. It is significant that there was a proposal for 'New Pages' to be renamed 'Socialist Action', the title that was to reappear on Mierendorff's action programme in 1943.

Like Mierendorff, Reichwein believed there would be no return to the Weimar system and, therefore, no revival of the German Social-Democratic Party. He leaned very strongly towards corporatist ideas, such as those to which space was given in 'New Pages for Socialism', and after 1933 his position moved towards religious socialism. This brought him close to Theordor Haubach, who had trodden a similar path, from expressionist poets, via the active social democrats, to religious socialism.

Reichwein's views on social policy were especially close to those of Moltke and Yorck von Wartenburg, the latter being the undisputed spokesman for the Kreisau Circle. Reichwein's interest in the principle of the *Arbeitschule*,[4] his championing of a decentralized education system and his emphasis on manual skills overlapped with the ideas of Moltke and Yorck, which found their most precise expression in the concept of 'small communities' and in the principle of 'personal socialism'. On the other hand, Reichwein must have been greatly fascinated by Moltke's historical perspective, which envisaged a sweeping fresh start and a totally new social order replacing the Nazi tyranny that marked the end of centuries of aberration dating back to the Reformation. All this appealed not only to Reichwein's own intellectual preconceptions, but also to his genuinely reformist temperament and his eagerness to shape events.

Moltke's interest in Reichwein was twofold: firstly, he was sympathetic with Reichwein's initiatives in educational reform and intended to bring them into the planning of the resistance group that he was about to form, the more so since Reichwein's political and social ideas matched those of Kreisau. Secondly, Moltke began at an early stage to seek out individuals who were able to forge links with the working class. Reichwein had important contacts among the leaders of organized labour. He introduced Moltke to Carlo Mierendorff, who quickly rose to become the leading workers' representative in the Kreisau Circle, and after his premature death (in an air raid) in December 1943, Moltke was unable to replace him.

Contacts with labour intensified from August 1940, as Moltke sought to gather likeminded people around him, to help in planning a political and social structure to replace the burnt-out Nazi regime on Day X. From the beginning, Reichwein's connections played an important part. Unfortunately, Moltke's letters to his wife, Freya, tell us nothing about the content of their many discussions, but it emerges that Moltke and Reichwein met fairly regularly. At the same time a friendship developed between their two families, and when the Reichweins were bombed out of their Berlin apartment, they moved to Kreisau.

At the same time Moltke found in Reichwein a reliable political ally who, like himself, felt he was a socialist at heart. Moltke involved Reichwein in the initial steps towards building up what later became the Kreisau Circle. After the first Kreisau conference Reichwein acted as the linkman with the former social democrats, especially Wilhelm Leuschner and Hermann Maass, whom he tried to convince of the advantages of the Kreisau plans. As Moltke wrote to Freya in January 1941, Reichwein 'made it possible to get quite a considerable group pulling together'.

The central position that Reichwein occupied in the Kreisau Circle has not been sufficiently recognized hitherto. Reichwein took part in the first and third Kreisau conferences and submitted a paper on educational reform to the second one. After the Whitsun meeting of the Kreisau Circle in 1942, Reichwein acted as a go-between, bringing the first declaration of principle to the attention of the socialists and labour unions. He then played a major part in the negotiations leading to the final agreed text of 18 October 1942. Along the way there were serious arguments with Leuschner and his emissaries over the question of labour unions. Leuschner's 'profound distrust' was rooted in his doubt that the collapse of the Nazi regime would bring about a political situation so completely new that any revival of former organizations such as the labour unions would be superfluous. Leuschner had particular difficulty in accepting the Kreisau concept of the company- or plant-based union, which was intended to bring together owners and workforce. He felt this was scarcely feasible in the real world of large-scale modern industrial companies.

This 'major battle with "Uncle"' (the code-name for Leuschner) led to the dispatch of Hermann Maass to the Kreisau Circle. With Mierendorff beside him, Reichwein presented the Kreisau position to Leuschner and Maass. Since Reichwein had been temporarily posted to the Warthegau (the region of western Poland annexed by Germany in 1939) and was then briefly absent after being bombed out of Berlin, Mierendorff hoped he could handle the final negotiations with Leuschner and Maass on his own. However, it became necessary to call him in again to prevent 'backsliding'. Thus Reichwein was at the heart of the interminable negotiations that led to the relevant resolutions of the Kreisau Circle in December 1942.

Reichwein also shared Kreisau's fundamental position in the sharp conflict between Moltke and the Goerdeler group, whose plans for a coup d'état Moltke rejected as premature. It seems that Reichwein agreed with Moltke on this; in his statement to the Gestapo he said that all Kreisau's plans were aimed at 'making a fresh start on the broadest possible basis, the moment the war was lost and the Reich occupied'. This chimes with his opposition to killing Hitler: 'The treatment is terrible, but it must take its full course, otherwise Germany will learn nothing.' Moltke was of exactly the same mind, believing that Nazism had to burn itself out before the construction of a new society could begin. However, as far as we can make out, Reichwein had changed his attitude by the spring of 1944, if not sooner. In January 1944 Moltke was arrested by the Gestapo,[5] and Reichwein, like other members of the Kreisau Circle, dedicated himself unreservedly to Stauffenberg's plan to assassinate Hitler and take over the country.

It is less easy to answer the question of what position Reichwein took in the quarrel between Moltke and Mierendorff, which began in November 1943 and was only superficially patched up. It arose when Mierendorff advocated the more pragmatic approach called for by Stauffenberg and Julius Leber, who approved of an attempt on Hitler's life. At the same time Mierendorff was associated with the imminent formation of a socialist splinter group.

In common with the socialist group, Reichwein backed Mierendorff's 'Socialist Action' programme. The strongly Christian emphasis of the action programme, which was expressly resisted by Julius Leber, had a counterpart in Reichwein and Harald Poelchau's programme for the 'establishment of a German *Christenschaft* (union or community of Christians against communism).

It is true that in the end no agreement was reached on a programme for a 'non-party popular movement for the salvation of Germany', that was to include communists 'not beholden to Moscow'. The different wings of Kreisau all had their own ideas on this. However, Kreisau made the crucial step from the previous revolutionary strategy, which involved wiping the political slate clean, to a more realistic assessment of internal political circumstances at the time of the planned coup. To this extent the plotters had gone through a remarkable learning-process.

In conjunction with this political about-turn came the realization that it would be necessary at least to reach an understanding with the outlawed German Communist Party (KPD) if the coup was not to end in political anarchy. It was recognized that after a successful putsch they would have to deal with the KPD, particularly since, with the creation of the National Committee for a Free Germany (NKFD), a programme had been formulated that abandoned the more abstruse aspects of communism and threatened to outflank the conservative-nationalist plotters.

From as early as 1943, Reichwein had regular access to the KPD through a former colleague at the Jena adult education college, Fritz Bernt. He also kept in touch with the KPD leaders in Thuringia, Theodor Neubauer, Magnus Poser and Walter Schmidt. It seems that the initiative for establishing formal contact came from these men and from the Saefkow-Jacob group in Berlin. Reichwein and Leber finally decided, despite opposition from all their fellow-plotters except Yorck von Wartenburg, to attend the ill-fated meeting on 22 June 1944 with Jacob, Saefkow and Thomas. It was as a result of that meeting that the Gestapo struck on 4 July, when Reichwein was on his way to a second meeting that had been arranged. The arrest of the communist officials, as well as Leber, followed in quick succession. This prompted Stauffenberg to bring forward the date of the planned coup, despite the unfavourable circumstances, since he believed that once the regime was overthrown, Leber would be indispensable.[6]

Even in retrospect historians argue vehemently about this contact with the communists. It was doubtless an illusion to hope that the outlawed communist cadre could make any move independently of Moscow and the programme of the NKFD. The promise of cooperation given to Leber and Reichwein by their communist interlocutors was no doubt made in good faith, even though, once the attempted coup had failed, the KPD ruthlessly condemned the conspiracy. Nonetheless, the attempt to achieve limited support, or at least a truce, on the communists' part might have had some prospect of success. On the other hand the wider hope of resisting the bolshevisation of Germany, controlled from Moscow, was extremely unrealistic and displayed an insufficient knowledge of the inner workings of the communist resistance.

As far as the role of Adolf Reichwein is concerned, the personal courage he showed in making these highly dangerous contacts is further proof of his total commitment to the overthrow of Hitler and the Nazi regime. He was one of the most dedicated partisans of the Kreisau Circle and when it in effect broke up he was an uncompromising supporter of Stauffenberg, who pressed ahead with plans for a coup. Reichwein was a staunch champion of involving the left wing in a future revolutionary government, and objected to the isolation of the communists, though he had no illusions about political conditions in the Soviet Union.

Reichwein played a major part in recruiting for the Kreisau Circle and his impressive contribution to the reform of schools and education found their place in Kreisau memoranda, even though his ideas remained controversial. His abandoning of the principal of faith-based schools met with strong resistance from the Catholic wing. Understandably, he was Moltke's choice for the post of Minister of Education in the revolutionary cabinet, and was also proposed by Wilhelm Leuschner for this job.

Adolf Reichwein embodied that intermediate generation, which did not simply want to return to the circumstances of Weimar or imperial Germany, but on the other hand was no longer able to believe in the potential of liberal parliamentary government. He therefore seized on Kreisau's federalist concepts, including the creation of a unified Europe with a regional structure. His was one of the most prolific minds in Germany's anti-Hitler resistance. Except for the Freiburg Circle, he was its only representative from the university community, the rest of whom maintained a stubbornly low profile.

Reichwein was, at the same time, an advocate of formulating an innovative democratic socialist programme; one which gave precedence to the personal responsibility of the independent individual and insisted that culture should have pride of place in the shaping of modern society. Thus his legacy embraces far more than the moral dimension but stands to this day as a challenge and a standard for the development of a democratic education system and a social order based on social justice.

11

The position of the military opposition to Hitler in the German resistance movement

The military resistance to Hitler has long been a favourite subject for modern historians. Among others, Klaus-Jürgen Müller, Peter Hoffmann, Gerd R. Ueberschär, Count Detlev von Schwerin and Bodo Scheurig have all described in detail the part played by senior military officers in the movement of 20 July 1944. In addition there have been numerous monographs dealing chiefly with the careers of individual officers. They make it possible to distinguish the different motives and objectives that led them into the resistance. At the same time the relevance of the rapidly changing overall military situation emerges more clearly than before. Intensive research into the history of the Second World War has made a crucial contribution to this.

Nevertheless, we have lacked until now a *comprehensive* account of the military opposition to Hitler. This seems to have become more urgent in the light of recent research into the German occupation of the Soviet Union, principally Christian Gerlach's account of the German occupation of Byelorussia (Belarus), in which he is critical of leading representatives of 20th July including Henning von Tresckow, Baron Rudolf-Christoph von Gersdorff and Count Peter Yorck von Wartenburg.

Quite apart from the revised research picture it is desirable to look at the military opposition to the Nazi regime as an independent movement and not primarily as an appendage to the group of conspirators centred around Ludwig Beck, Carl Goerdeler and Ulrich von Hassell. To be more precise, the early literature on the resistance nurtured the impression that the military officers acted essentially as the executive arm of the civil opposition, and that they came forward with a largely predetermined government list, believing that, once the Nazi regime was overthrown, they would be able to have a decisive influence on policy.

Contrary to this view it must be observed that the military opposition initially came from the Army Group Centre[1] and sprang from independent roots. This is where the problem of drawing a dividing-line between 'civil' and military opposition arises. We should not here take the term 'military opposition' to mean the entirety of all resistance within the armed forces. It is certainly legitimate to define it quantitatively, as Wolfgang Schieder has attempted to do. He assumes a total of 185 military conspirators, but at the same time concedes that the boundary between active conspiracy and passive approval of the coup is a fluid one.

It is nonetheless helpful to differentiate between the older and younger age groups in the military who, as Schieder shows, were each shaped by a different political upbringing. Some were already active as officers in the First World War, while others began their military careers between the wars, a fact reflected in their respective ranks. Those in the former category were predominantly generals, while the latter were mostly staff officers. Accordingly he talks in terms of a senior and a junior line.

This kind of systematic approach does, however, have the disadvantage that it conceals the discontinuity of military opposition between 1938 and 1942. The move to remove the Nazis in 1938, planned in close cooperation with Carl Goerdeler and Ludwig Beck, and Franz Halder's initiative, following the Polish campaign, to prevent an attack on France, are recognized as having been isolated episodes. The surviving core in the military thus lost the support of the fighting troops, especially since a number of senior officers, who had previously been identified with the intention to topple Hitler, now parted company with the opposition.

This was certainly true of *Generaloberst* Franz Halder and the commander-in-chief of the army, *Generalfeldmarschall* Walter von

Brauchitsch, who regarded any action against the regime as impossible in view of its military successes, fearing a split in the ranks of the Wehrmacht. Their principal motivation had been to avoid the expansion of the war and this now appeared to be a lost cause. The units commanded by remaining sympathizers of the conspirators were transferred to new locations and with them receded any prospect of an anti-Nazi coup. With the exception of the resistance circle formed within the Abwehr around *Oberst* Hans Oster, the group led by Ludwig Beck had no very close links with officers on active service. Halder and Brauchitsch had withdrawn from the group; *Generalfeldmarschall* Witzleben had been posted to Paris, and *Generalleutnant* Alexander von Falkenhausen to Brussels, and were thus on the periphery. The others had retired from the armed forces. It is therefore more appropriate to count Beck among the civilian opposition, who were chiefly represented in the initial phase by Carl Goerdeler, Ulrich von Hassell and Johannes Popitz. The struggle to persuade the army commanders to make themselves available for an overthrow of the regime was what characterized resistance activity until well into 1943. As Goerdeler and his followers saw it, the Wehrmacht should act as the crucial lever of political power in the insurrection, but once power had been won, it should immediately be ceded to the civil government. However, this arrangement was blurred by the intention to appoint Ludwig Beck both as head of state and commander-in-chief of the Wehrmacht, rather as things were done in the late Weimar period.[2]

Early research into the resistance generally accepted this viewpoint and scarcely inquired into the independent political objectives of the military. Furthermore, the close links between Beck and Goerdeler gave rise to the impression that the two men largely agreed on their constitutional policy (in fact Beck had no direct input into Goerdeler's programme-defining memorandum, *Das Ziel* ['The Goal'], even though it was based on a lengthy exchange of views between the two men).

As regards Beck's successor as Chief of the General Staff, *Generaloberst* Franz Halder, the few available sources of evidence indicate that, while he mistrusted the extremist tendencies within the Nazi Party and the SA (and proposed to use the army to hold them in check), he supported the authoritarian form of government and, like many of his contemporaries, excluded Hitler from his strictures of Nazism. With few exceptions, the officers who had been involved in the 1938–1939 plans for an insurrection, withdrew, just as Halder did, from the civilian opposition group around Goerdeler and, apart from Hans Oster, there were only isolated cross-connections with the Wehrmacht.

From the autumn of 1941 a new opposition took shape among a group of younger staff-officers, who at first only maintained informal contact with Beck and Oster. The driving-force behind this movement was Henning von Tresckow who, in October 1941, dispatched Fabian von Schlabrendorff to Berlin to make contact with the civilian opposition. We know this from Ulrich von Hassell's diaries. At the beginning of 1940 Tresckow was still in sympathy with the offensive against France that was being planned by von Manstein. However, if we accept Bodo Scheurig's judgement, after the French campaign Tresckow's former scepticism returned. He realised that the Reich was a long way from concluding a general peace; instead, Hitler was making preparations to continue the war with an assault on the Soviet Union.

From 10 December 1940 Tresckow held the post of senior operations officer in Army Group B, which in April 1941 was renamed Army Group Centre. At first it seems that he was poised between confidence in the campaign-plan assigned to his army-group and doubts as to whether it could be carried through. Even before receiving the order to attack he certainly feared that their Russian opponents had been underestimated, and declared that everything depended 'on the swift and unrelenting triumph of Army Group Centre' before the onset of winter.

Tresckow's scepticism and inner mood of protest were provoked by the methods called for by Hitler in the 'war of racial extermination', as well as his absurdly over-ambitious strategic objectives. He noted with growing bitterness that his warnings and reservations found no support in the OKH (army high command), which in turn was unable to get its opinions heard by the Hitler-dominated OKW (combined forces high command). His first steps were limited to preserving his own military identity and the respect of his troops. However, he failed in his attempt to persuade the commander-in-chief of Army Group Centre, *Generalfeldmarschall* von Bock, to withdraw the military jurisdiction decree, even though it was in clear contravention of international law. On the contrary, the *Kommissarbefehl*[3] was accepted from the very beginning and no restraint was placed on it.

After Tresckow had failed in his attempt to mobilize first von Bock and then von Kluge[4] against Hitler's methods, he decided to act on his own initiative and win the support of people who felt as he did. These men, whom he had placed in commands within the Army Group, included Baron Rudof-Christoph von Gersdorff, Fabian von Schlabrendorff, Count Hans von Hardenberg and Berndt von Kleist. His recruitment policy laid the foundations for a widely ramified resistance group, which revived the plans for an attempted military takeover.

The rise of this second opposition movement, which unlike its civilian counterpart did not shrink from employing clandestine methods, inherited its political philosophy from the military command-structure that Hitler had wantonly destroyed. After Hitler had assumed supreme command of the Wehrmacht (combined armed forces) in February 1938, the army continued for a while to maintain its autonomy, but this had now almost completely been forfeited. In many respects the very existence of the army was threatened by the increasing insignificance of the General Staff, the rapid changes in high-ranking personnel and the fact that, in December 1941, the Führer himself took over supreme command of the armies fighting on the Russian front.

Tresckow, as a trained staff-officer, could see that the constant overstretching of military resources through Hitler's all-or-nothing strategy was bound to have dangerous consequences in the medium term. At the same time, the progressive undermining of the professional foundations of operational leadership led to increasing bitterness among those officers who were not hypnotized by Nazi propaganda slogans and were able to maintain a critical view of the overall situation. At first there was a hope that by influencing the

OKW, OKH and individual army commanders, the necessary adjustments could be made to the plan of campaign. However, this proved illusory since the army commanders lacked the will and the moral courage to confront Keitel and Jodl (respectively chief-of-staff and chief of operations of the OKW), let alone Hitler himself.

Early in 1942 Tresckow decided to take matters into his own hands. His decision to find a way of removing Hitler was made under the shadow of a serious military crisis caused by the army being brought to a standstill outside Moscow late in 1941. Admittedly the intention to get rid of Hitler alternated with efforts to bring about a reform of the command structure which would in effect remove Hitler from supreme command of the army. The exact dates are uncertain since the statements of contemporaries, on which we rely in this matter, tend to project backward events that took place later.

In July 1943 Tresckow tried to arrange the arrest of Hitler in Vinnitsa, the eastern military headquarters in Russia. He subsequently attempted to stage a coup and had the brilliant idea of developing a scenario, codenamed 'Valkyrie', ostensibly to prevent a possible uprising by foreign slave-workers in the Berlin area, but in fact designed to seize all key buildings following Hitler's arrest or assassination. All this was done largely independently of the civilian opposition, though there were some sporadic contacts through the mediation of Hans Oster. Tresckow's plan was to set up a military dictatorship with the help of General Olbricht, chief-of-staff to the commander of the reserve army. When Tresckow was posted to Russia, he entrusted the execution of the coup d'état to Count Claus Schenk von Stauffenberg.

Tresckow's coolness, determination and brilliance in exploiting existing military institutions in furtherance of insurrection pointed the way. It was through him that the military opposition became the real driving force of the conspiracy. The plans for the coup were based on the 1856 law on the declaration of a state of emergency, to which Johannes Popitz had added guidelines, which were referred to in later appeals by the 20th July movement.

On the other hand, what political objectives were being pursued by the circle that was forming around Stauffenberg is an open question. His statement directed at Goerdeler, to the effect that 'the conditions of Weimar should not be revived by any group', indicates a considerable distance between the concepts of the civilian opposition under Goerdeler and Beck and those of the labour unionists Wilhelm Leuschner and Jakob Kaiser, who had by now joined the movement. The rather vague ideas Stauffenberg expressed, socially romantic and with a *berufsständisch* slant, show that he was keen to take an independent line.

Goerdeler's demand that the generals must be prevented 'from doing anything political' illustrates the growing tension between the older and younger groups of conspirators. It is almost impossible to determine whether anything more than a superficial exchange of ideas took place between Tresckow and Goerdeler on questions of constitutional and social policy. It is, to say the least, doubtful whether the 'close affinity' was sealed by 'a great meeting of minds', to quote Bodo Scheurig.

The links with Goerdeler and Beck had existed since the late summer of 1942 and were established by Fabian von Schlabrendorff, on whose evidence we are heavily reliant. Late in 1942 Goerdeler visited Army Group Centre in Smolensk and tried to get Kluge to support joint action by the generals around Hitler. Later, too, he backed Tresckow's efforts to persuade Kluge to act. However, his letter to Kluge dated 25 July 1943 was never sent.

Without giving precise dates, Schlabrendorff reports a meeting in Berlin between Goerdeler, Tresckow and Olbricht, at which Olbricht agreed to carry out the coup d'état with the help of the reserve army. In the late summer of 1943 these contacts intensified, but it must be assumed that closer links with the civilian group only took place when it was necessary to push ahead with the staffing of Operation Valkyrie. This applied mainly to drawing up lists of proposed political commissioners within the military organization, which began in the late autumn of 1943. These were to be subordinate to the relevant military authorities and obliged to take instructions from them, unlike the arrangements established by Otto Braun in the Weimar period.[5]

To begin with, Tresckow acted largely independently of Stauffenberg who, after returning from military hospital, took up the post of Chief-of-Staff of the Reserve Army. However, they shared the intention of removing Hitler and reached this decision through motives which distinguished them from the civilian opposition groups. It is true that there was a wide measure of agreement between the civilian and military conspirators, both in their fundamentally conservative-nationalist stance and in their disgust at the crimes of the regime. Yet only a minority saw these crimes as a direct consequence of the Nazi system. For Tresckow and Stauffenberg, not surprisingly, military considerations were what weighed most heavily.

This difference in emphasis is still just visible in the appeals to the people and the army for a coup d'état, drafted jointly with Beck and Goerdeler. In the texts written by Goerdeler the moral criticism of Hitler predominates, stressing his 'lust for glory' and 'power-mad arrogance', to which he had sacrificed 'entire armies without a pang of conscience'. By contrast, the words of an undated note by Stauffenberg, which he had with him on the day of the putsch, were far more sober: 'If the present course is pursued, the inevitable result will be defeat and the destruction of [Germany's] hereditary human reserves (*blutsmäßiger Substanz*). The fate that hangs over us can only be averted by removal of the present leadership.' Stauffenberg went on to condemn the pervasive corruption and jobbery, but stressed above all that the regime had no right to 'drag the whole German people down with it.' In this context he presented the task of the revolutionary government:

> After a change of government let the most important objective be that Germany should still be a power-factor that can be deployed in the interplay of forces, and that the Wehrmacht in particular should remain a viable instrument in the hands of its commanders.

For men like Tresckow and Stauffenberg, maintaining the army intact and avoiding a devastating military defeat were the prime considerations. If the same method of conducting the war continued to be used on the Russian front, a catastrophe was inevitable. Without hesitation they rejected Hitler's aim of crushing not only the Soviet system but the Russian state and of robbing Russia of its vital strength. The war, they declared, should

not be directed against the Russian people but only against the
Soviet system. As Stauffenberg put it, he had 'the instinctive
feeling that the Soviet Union could only be beaten with the help
of the Russians and the many other ethnic peoples living there'.
Similarly Tresckow, as Gersdorff remembered, had 'from the
outset' held the view that Russian nationalism had to be
mobilized against communism.

Hence Tresckow and Stauffenberg made consistent efforts to
establish Russian volunteer units, and later the Vlasov army, and
in doing so deliberately tried to bypass instructions to the contrary
coming from the Führer's headquarters. Originally, both officers
hoped to achieve military stability on the Russian front, even after
the regime had been overthrown. The motive of saving the army,
which gained ever greater importance for them, is understandable
when seen against the background of enormous losses, which could
be laid at the door of Hitler's string of wrong decisions and his
overestimation of German strength. The sombre mood and the
sense of crisis triggered by the battle outside Moscow were
expressed openly in letters from Helmuth Stieff. They were
combined with a growing revulsion at the brutal treatment of
prisoners-of-war, Jews and other civilians, which led to a
strengthening of the will to resist in the Russian opposition.

This aspect was expressly addressed in Stauffenberg's note:

> The treatment of occupied lands represents a significant factor
> in the grave overall situation. The Russian campaign began with
> the order to kill all commissars, and went on by allowing
> prisoners-of-war to starve to death and carrying out manhunts
> with the aim of rounding up forced labour. This represents the
> beginning of the end of the whole war.

This note seems to reflect the fact that the annihilation of the
Jews and the war against partisans were less in the forefront of
Stauffenberg's mind. Nonetheless, there is no mistaking the fact
that it was not mere tactical considerations that deterred him from
putting the *Kommissarbefehl* into effect and taking measures against
the civilian population; he also found Hitler's policy of violence
morally repugnant.

This view is supported by an account from a fellow-officer, Alexander Stahlberg, of a conversation with Tresckow on 17 November 1942, in which the latter stated openly that the activities of the SS in the rear of the front line were not a matter of 'isolated excesses' but 'systematic extermination of human beings'. Army Group Centre possessed reliable information about the exterminations, the extent of which defied 'all imagination'. He saw them as 'dishonouring the self-sacrifice of the soldiers at the front'. When Tresckow tried to put *Generalfeldmarschall* von Manstein[6] in the picture, the field marshal refused, in the face of good evidence, to give any credence to reports of the systematic liquidation of Jews.

The motives governing the actions of the military resistance were certainly varied. But we can be sure that an important one was their concern for the units under their command, indeed their responsibility for keeping the army intact, and not driving it into a hopeless and murderous war that was bound to end on German soil and would, as in 1918, trigger a revolutionary uprising. To this was added their criticism of the irresponsible way Hitler interfered with operational decisions right down to battalion and company level, something which showed his contempt for professional officers and which needlessly cost lives.

For the members of this younger generation of officers, on whom the German revolution of 1918–1920 had left a strong impression, an ingrained anti-communism went without saying. Tresckow and Stauffenberg were no exception. Indeed, Stauffenberg had originally stated that the Nazi regime could only be dealt with when Bolshevism was out of the way. The anti-Soviet stereotype operating here nourished the illusion that it would be possible simply to put the ruling Soviet *apparat* out of action and thus obtain the support of the ethnic Russian population. This attitude suggested that, like Hitler and the Nazi propagandists, they equated Bolshevism with the Jews.

Opinions of this kind were to be found among many leading members of the military resistance. In their operational orders army commanders like *Generaloberst* Erich Hoepner or Carl-Heinrich von Stülpnagel even surpassed the OKW in the use of anti-Semitic language. Thus, in the battle-orders for Operation Barbarossa, issued by Hoepner to his Panzer Group IV on 2 May 1941, we read that the impending battle 'to ward off Jewish Bolshevism' must be fought with 'unprecedented harshness' and 'directed with an iron will towards the complete and merciless destruction of the enemy'. In particular there must be 'no sparing of those who uphold the present Russian-Bolshevist system'. This from a man who, since the mid-1930s, had been a convinced opponent of Nazism and in whom Stauffenberg placed great hopes.

The strongly anti-Bolshevist attitude among men critical of Hitler helps to explain why, even within Army Group Centre, there was no resistance worth mentioning to the methods used in combating the partisans, even though these quickly changed into a systematic extermination of the Jewish population in the occupied territories. It is difficult, to say the least, to understand why the senior officers of the Army Group were ready to assume the presence of a widespread partisan movement and to give uncritical credence to reports to this effect from the *Einsatzgruppen*.[7] These reports went through the hands of Gersdorff and Tresckow, and it is a fact that, in the summer of 1941, Soviet partisan activity was only just beginning to get under way and did not play a serious part until 1942. Christian Gerlach has pointed out that Gersdorff, as security officer for the Army Group, had direct involvement in the anti-partisan actions, while Tresckow was also personally concerned with these on numerous occasions; it was not only the line officers who had responsibility for what went on in the rearward areas. Between June 1941 and May 1942, the rear of Army Group Centre reported the shooting of 80,000 partisans and suspected partisans.

There is abundant evidence not only that, in the anti-partisan activities of Army Group Centre, were large numbers of innocent civilians liquidated, but also that these were for the most part local Jewish communities. There needs to be an examination of the degree of direct involvement in this by members of the resistance, especially Henning von Tresckow, Baron Rudolf-Christoph von Gersdorff, Baron Georg von Boeselager and others. It is true that Gersdorff, in an appendix to the war-diary of Army

Group Centre, recorded the opposition expressed by officers to 'the shooting of Jews, prisoners and commissars'. This was considered 'a violation of the honour of the German army'. Similarly, in his 'assessment of the enemy' dated 10 March 1942, he pointed out that it was particularly 'the rapid spread of information about the plight of Russian prisoners-of-war' that was giving a lasting boost to Russian resistance, and that a 'sharp change of attitude to the treatment of prisoners and to propaganda' was necessary. This view was circulated among the most senior Reich officials by the Reich Minister for Occupied Territories, but it was an illusion to expect any intervention from the top.

As far as Henning von Tresckow and his fellow conspirators are concerned, we cannot escape the impression that from the winter of 1941 a growing disillusionment took over and that they were becoming aware of the criminal operations of the *Einsatzgruppen* and SS brigades. We may perhaps allow that Tresckow was not sufficiently aware that the pretext of anti-partisan operations, which in many cases were carried out by units of the regular army, often concealed the systematic liquidation of the Jewish population. However, his personal contacts with Arthur Nebe[8] and closeness to Gersdorff, who was responsible for these measures, make this difficult to accept. There is, however, little purpose in narrowing down this question to the involvement of specific individuals.

Following the extremely pessimistic assessment of the military situation in the wake of Stalingrad, the objections of senior army officers to the policy of genocide which was in fact being carried through, came to the fore more strongly, yet humanitarian considerations were still apparently taking second place to the that of preserving the moral integrity of the army. At the same time we must not overlook the fact that prominent members of the military resistance, including General von Stülpnagel and the Quartermaster-General, Eduard Wagner, actively supported the extermination of the Jews or took part in drawing up the 'criminal orders' for this programme. Equally, Tresckow's collaboration with Arthur Nebe, who commanded *Einsatzgruppe* B, cannot be dressed up as an attempt to stem the brutal measures, since Nebe must be regarded as one of the most blatant exponents of the policy of annihilation.

Hence, we have no alternative but to admit that a considerable number of those who played an active part in the July Plot, and in many cases lost their lives as a result, had previously participated in the war of racial extermination, or had at least approved of it for quite a time and in some cases had actively promoted it. As a rule this happened under the cloak of fighting the partisans, yet those who were directly or indirectly involved could scarcely fail to see that the SS brigades and *Einsatzgruppen* were carrying out a comprehensive 'ethnic cleansing', to which the Wehrmacht, if only by condemning large numbers of Russians to starvation, were giving active support.

In reaching a verdict on individuals, we should not place too much importance on the question of how they reconciled guilty involvement with their concern to extricate themselves from this and ultimately to accept the consequences of active resistance. What is more significant is that one of the roots of the conspirators' action was their intimate knowledge of the criminal policies of the Nazi regime and not least of the Wehrmacht itself. And even though political and military interests predominated, these were increasingly matched by moral motives.

Among the military opposition, and in the 20th July movement generally, we can discern an ambivalence in their attitude to the Jewish question. This had a lot to do with the persistence of the conservative anti-Semitism of imperial times among the German upper classes. The number of people who, from the outset and from personal conviction, rejected the Nazi persecution of the Jews, was very limited, and even opponents of the regime, such as Hoepner or Werner von Fritsch, welcomed Hitler's anti-Jewish measures. However, the majority of civilian conspirators, who did not become aware of the systematic liquidation of European Jewry until the latter half of 1942, went through a rapid learning process in this respect. The military opposition, meanwhile, apparently went through the same process, even though the criminal actions of the regime had been taking place in front of their eyes.

In the preparations for the attempt on Hitler's life, the independent action of the military opposition played a prominent part. It is no coincidence that a meeting prior to 20 July 1944 of the people destined for office in the new government failed to take place, nor was Goerdeler informed of the impending assassination, though in this case fears about security may have been the decisive factor. There was no question but that Beck was to hold the position of *Generalstatthalter*, or head of state, while Stauffenberg was apparently thinking of replacing Goerdeler with Julius Leber as Chancellor, either immediately or after a transitional period.

Stauffenberg famously said, 'the Wehrmacht is the most conservative institution in our state that is at the same time rooted in the people'. He also said that the officer corps 'must not fail again and let the initiative be taken out of their hands' as they had done in 1918. These words indicate that Stauffenberg would in no way have been satisfied with acting as a lever of power in the hands of the civilian opposition. It is impossible to be more precise about this, since the relevant papers have nearly all been destroyed. Nonetheless, it seems doubtful that, had 'Valkyrie' been successful, any use would have been made of the political appeals that Goerdeler had prepared, as a government statement and for a speech to be broadcast to the nation.

The history of the military resistance represents a unique example of the conflict between politics and warfare. Tresckow and Stauffenberg took the action they did, because they recognized the pointlessness of continuing the war on Hitler's terms, and they feared involvement of the Wehrmacht in the escalation of Nazi crimes. Without the willingness of the Wehrmacht to submit to a great extent to Hitler's demand for a war of racial extermination, those crimes would have been impossible, notwithstanding isolated attempts to free the army from the odium of this criminal policy. After the defeat on the outskirts of Moscow in the winter of 1941, this gradually began to change, but the decision to take a genuinely opposing stand was made by only a few, a fact which rules out military opposition as an alibi for the Wehrmacht as a whole.[9]

It is significant that the decision to act to save Germany came from senior army officers who made no secret of the fact that, unless the dictator was put out of action, Germany was heading for catastrophe. This knowledge was combined with a growing feeling of remoteness from the military and political style of the regime, which was trampling on the Prussian tradition, while at the same time trying to exploit it. The position of the predominantly conservative group of officers who had originally – and with very few exceptions – welcomed the 'National-Socialist rising', was summed up most cogently by Fritz-Dietlof von der Schulenburg, when he said that 'the Prussian challenge to the Reich' stood as firmly as ever.

CHAPTER 12

Anti-Hitler resistance and the Nazi persecution of the Jews

The attitude of the German anti-Hitler resistance to anti-Semitism and to the Nazi persecution of the Jews has remained controversial to this day and is a problem that for a long time was largely suppressed. From the German side, it was Christof Dipper, in 1983, who first took up the subject. Detailed research since then into the history of the resistance and of the Second World War suggests that it may now be possible to draw some general conclusions. As is to be expected, attention has to be focussed on the conservative-nationalist resistance, since for socialist resistance groups and for the outlawed German Communist Party (KPD), the Jewish question was of fairly minor importance.

From the outset, the political left was forced into opposition and illegality by the Nazi regime. It kept up the struggle against Nazism primarily in order to assert its own continued existence. After the smashing of most of the socialist resistance groups by the mid-1930s, and the repeated assaults by the Gestapo on the clandestine KPD structures, the emphasis of resistance shifted to the upper-middle class, who had initially welcomed the Nazis' seizure of power in January 1933 and for the most part lent it active support. The impetus to resist came from men who had belonged to the political class under the Weimar republic. It then spread to the upper ranks of the civil and the diplomatic services and beyond to the sidelined labour organizations and to individual members of the officer corps.

As members of the elite, they all occupied senior positions within the government hierarchy or were starting professional careers that would take them to the top in public life. An overwhelming proportion welcomed the *Machtergreifung* in 1933, hoping it would usher in a sweeping new start in political and social life, both at home and abroad. Even when being interrogated, much later, by the Gestapo, many plotters still expressed the view that the principles of National Socialism were basically sound, but had been shamefully betrayed by those in power.

Their rebellion against the regime was inspired in each case by individual motives, among which the national interest played an important part. It is perfectly clear that, as a general rule, the Nazi persecution of the Jews was a minor factor in their decision to commit high treason. This is true even of those on the political left, among whom anti-Semitic attitudes were only occasionally to be found. Furthermore, it was never the intention of the KPD or leftwing socialist resistance groups to involve Jews in their conspiracies and thus increase the risk of exposure by the Gestapo. Nevertheless, in communist underground propaganda, the importance of the persecution of the Jews should not be underestimated.

Hence it was no coincidence that the Baum resistance group, [1] which was made up of Berlin Jews, operated separately from the outlawed KPD. The *Neu Beginnen* ('Fresh Start') group, in which Jews played a key part, was equally unwilling to highlight the Jewish question in their programme. It should, on the other hand, be noted that in individual leaflets the KPD did tackle the persecution and extermination of the Jews, though without attracting much attention beyond their own ranks.

In contrast, the conservative-nationalist plotters were forced to undergo a painful process of admitting the truth, especially where the Jewish policy of the regime was concerned. Many of them had grown up in a segregationist tradition of anti-Semitism, which had set the tone among Germany's conservative elite ever since the Tivoli Programme of 1892.[2] Thus, they sympathized with the anti-Semitic agitation that had been rife in Germany since the revolution of November 1918. They also supported the banning of Jewish immigration from Eastern Europe, which had risen sharply for a while under the impact of the 1921 Option Treaties;[3] and they were keen to reduce the overrepresentation of Jews in certain professions, even though this was declining in any case for structural reasons.

The Nazi Party's programme did not really go beyond the objectives of conservative anti-Semitism. It demanded that the immigration of Jews from the east be stopped, that Jews be subject to the same laws as aliens and denied access to public service and the professions. Count Reventlow was someone who crossed over from the right wing of the DNVP (German National People's Party) to the Nazi Party and then joined the German National Freedom Party. In 1935 Reventlow still cherished the illusion that a kind of national autonomy could be established for German Jews. The mounting violence of the SA and the Nazi Party against Jews was a matter of regret for conservatives, but they portrayed this as mere teething-troubles that would soon fade.

There is not the space here to describe in detail the array of illusions shared by Hitler's middle-class coalition partners, illusions which included trivializing the unremitting violence suffered by Jews. These politicians consistently showed two different faces: they protected successful and well-assimilated Jews against acts of violence or expulsion from professions, yet they also supported measures against what was seen as an excessive presence of Jews in the German population.

Johannes Popitz, who retained his post as Prussian finance minister, even after Prussia had been completely absorbed into the Reich, declared his willingness to make certain concessions on the 'Jewish Question', in the expectation that anti-Semitic activities would be brought under control by legislation. A 'top-level' meeting was held in the Reich Ministry of Economics on 20 August 1935, to agree measures relating to the persecution of Jews. At the meeting Popitz stated: 'We should make a few concessions, then draw a line'. However, this acquiescence to Nazi pressures put the government bureaucracy on a slippery slope, which eventually led to full complicity in the criminal policies of the regime. The initial willingness to leave open the Jewish Question as a 'recreation-ground' in which the Nazi Party could work off its anger and hatred, culminated in the general undermining of the rule of law.

Deep-rooted anti-Semitism could even be found in people who dissociated themselves from the regime. A prime example of this is provided by *Generaloberst* Baron Werner von Fritsch who, though dismissed from his post as commander-in-chief of the army in a reprehensible way by the Nazis, was an example to many younger officers and later joined the resistance. Fritz-Dietlof von der Schulenburg was one of those who saw Fritsch as the incarnation of the Prussian tradition.

This was the same Fritsch who, even after being driven out of the army, could still talk of the 'massive and indisputable successes of the Führer'. After the end of the First World War, Fritsch said, he had reached the conclusion that, in order for Germany to 'become great again', it had to fight three battles: one against the workers, one against Rome's domination of the Catholic Church and one 'against the Jews'. Germany was, he claimed, still 'right in the middle' of the last of these.

It is, of course, difficult to draw general conclusions from this instance. However, it is equally hard to deny that numerous members of the 20th July movement shared these anti-Semitic attitudes to a certain extent. This is true of many senior officers who, influenced by the Russian revolution of October 1917 and Germany's in November 1918, built up a combined resentment against communists and Jews. This was a reflection of the anti-Semitism that was widespread in the senior ranks of the army even in 1917, which culminated in the so-called 'Jewish headcount'.[4] This led to deliberate discrimination against the Jewish section of the population and a mood of extreme anti-Semitism that was shared by most of the German upper class in the first two years after the war, especially in the light of Munich's short-lived 'soviet republic' of 1918–1919.[5]

This anti-Semitism surfaced with a vengeance in the war against the Soviet Union and explains why men who later became prominent in the military opposition did not consistently refuse Hitler's demand on 30 March 1941 for a war of racial extermination, and to a large extent accepted the whole package of criminally inspired orders. Anti-Semitism in varying forms can be found in people such as Hoepner, von Stülpnagel, Wagner and Beck; even in Wilhelm Canaris, the anti-Nazi head of the Abwehr, and probably in Claus von Stauffenberg and his two brothers. The only exceptions appear to have been Helmut Groscurth and Hans Oster.

Even in the ranks of the civilian opposition we find a thoroughly ambivalent attitude to the anti-Jewish policies embarked on by the Nazi regime. Most of the conspirators later had their eyes opened to Nazi crimes. While they had always distanced themselves from the violent methods of the regime, not least in the light of the *Kristallnacht* pogroms of November 1938, they came to the view that every form of racial discrimination was unacceptable. Yet even then they took a legalistic view of any out-and-out repudiation of anti-Semitism.

The position taken by Carl Goerdeler on this is of particular interest: it reflected the intellectual tradition of the German right, which had been shaped by a moderate anti-Semitism. As *Oberbürgermeister* (chief mayor) of Leipzig he had to face growing pressure on the Jewish community, from the moment the Nazis seized power. During the national boycott of Jewish businesses, on 1 and 2 April 1933, he personally tried to oppose the violence directed against Jewish furriers and publicly backed the Jewish businessmen who played a key part in the city's economic life. However, he was unable to prevent the removal of Jewish officeholders in the cultural life of Leipzig, though he managed to mitigate it. But in 1935 he was forced to accept the discriminatory Nuremberg Laws, which he personally condemned. On the other hand he did nothing to limit the effect on (Jewish) personnel of the law for the reconstruction of the professional civil service.

Goerdeler did try to avert the increasing extremism of anti-Jewish policies by speaking out clearly in favour of adherence to legal processes. That is why he accepted the civil service law and even applied it in his own city departments, typically under the illusion that in the long run the dismissals could be kept within judicial bounds. In all this, one of his principal motives was to avoid prejudicing the good name of his city, and indeed of the German nation, through the mistreatment of the Jews. In a memorandum to Hitler of August 1934, Goerdeler called for 'Germany's racial policy to be consolidated'. He justified this by pointing out the negative repercussions abroad, which would go beyond existing trade boycotts to the withdrawal of foreign loans, leading to a massive devaluation of the German currency. In a characteristically defensive manner, he pointed out that 'the provisions of the law could, of course, scarcely be objected to abroad as measures of self-protection, if from now on they were enforced with strict discipline and without violence or pettiness'.

In the years that followed, as far as he became involved at all in the question of Jewish marginalization, Goerdeler emphasized that Germany's economic interests required a legislative restriction on anti-Jewish measures. His rather dilatory approach, hoping for a compromise with the regime, was bound to fail, and pressure from the Party on his city administration intensified noticeably in Jewish matters. The conflict came to a head with the destruction of the memorial to the Jewish composer, Felix Mendelssohn. This act of vandalism was ordered during Goerdeler's absence from Leipzig by his deputy Rudolf Haake, who had long been a vocal opponent of Goerdeler's temporising policy towards the Jews.

However, the main reason for Goerdeler's resignation as *Oberbürgermeister* was the diminution of authority he had been forced to accept, due to the activities of the local Nazi leadership, who simply rode roughshod over him. Once he had forfeited the good will of the Reich government his position had anyway become untenable. It was this depressing experience that contributed largely to Goerdeler's personal antipathy to the Nazi regime, although the final break did not come until 1937.

The Party's attack on Mendelssohn, the great composer who was such an integral part of German culture, overstepped the limit which Goederler, like many conservatives, wanted to impose on the measures to exclude Jews from public life, by exempting assimilated Jewish groups from them. At all events, it is necessary to differentiate between nationalist racism and the segregationist anti-Semitism which – as already shown – was expressed in the Tivoli Programme of the German Conservative Party. However, even in the days of Wilhelm II, the difference between the two variants of anti-Semitism was frequently blurred.

In his 1941 memorandum 'The Goal', Goerdeler strikingly set out his fundamental position on the 'Jewish Question' by advocating the creation of a Jewish state in Canada or South America, thus associating himself with the ideas that had already been discussed at the international conference at Evian in the late summer of 1938. On this basis he wanted to treat all Jews living in Germany as registered aliens and to deprive them of citizenship, the right to vote and access to public office. However, economically he wanted to put them on an equal footing with the German population. It is true that he proposed exemption from these restrictions for Jews who had fought for Germany in the First World War, or who had been German citizens since 1871, as well as Jews baptized as Christians, who were Germans in August 1914. Even in his 'Thoughts of a man condemned to death', written in late 1944, Goerdeler returned to these ideas and recommended the formation of a Jewish national state somewhere overseas. Here, too, his original, underlying anti-Semitism surfaced when he wrote: 'We should not attempt to minimize what has been happening, but we should also emphasize the great guilt of the Jews, who had invaded our public life in ways that lacked all customary restraint.' It is against this background that we must stress Goerdeler's unambiguous rejection of the disenfranchising, deportation and murder of European Jews.

It is nonetheless surprising that Goerdeler, while hoping to render the Nuremberg Laws superfluous, at the same time regarded them as valid legislation, as he explained in 'The Goal'. By contrast, he called for the immediate repeal of the measures designed to disenfranchise, expropriate and socially segregate Germany's Jewish community. This repeal was essential, he said, not only in order to regain respect for Germany abroad, but also in the name of justice and to give the Germans back their self-respect. In the text of the 'Government Statement' prepared for the coup d'état, Goerdeler was clearer still. There we read: 'The persecution of the

Jews, which has been carried out in the most inhuman, deeply shaming and quite irreparable ways, is to cease.'

In memoranda produced by people in Goerdeler's circle some attention is also paid to the persecution of Jews. For example, in the 'programme' drawn up in early 1940 by Ulrich von Hassell he calls for the anti-Jewish legislation to be repealed and sharply censures the 'terrible atrocities committed with impunity against the Jews in the name of the Party'. On the other hand, the 'Provisional State Constitution' formulated by Popitz, only provided for a suspension of the anti-Jewish laws, 'pending a final dispensation'. To this extent the Jewish question was almost invariably brought up in the context of the restoration of law and decency. However, in practical terms, it continued to be presented as something that needed to be settled.

Nevertheless, these documents date from before the start of the deportations and the genocide, which came to the knowledge of the conspirators at a comparatively late stage. Among the leading members of the early civilian opposition, such as Popitz, von Hassell, Goerdeler and Schulenburg, the predominant attitude was one that had been handed on by the DNVP (German National People's Party), according to which the excessive influence of the Jews must be curtailed and a ban placed on Jewish immigration from Eastern Europe. This was true of Admiral Wilhelm Canaris who started from the assumption that only comprehensive racial segregation would solve the Jewish problem. In a similar way to Goerdeler, he considered resettling German Jews in the former German colonies in Africa and the Pacific, which would soon be handed back by France and Britain.

The anti-Semitism of Fritz-Dietlof von der Schulenburg was more pronounced, since he was in no doubt that Jews should be eliminated from public service and evinced unmistakably anti-Semitic prejudice. As late as 1938 he repeated his call for the removal Jews from government and the civil service. His biographer, Albert Krebs, attests that he 'was never able to rid himself of feelings of alienation toward the intellectual and material world of Jewry.' He was appalled to learn of the crimes perpetrated against the Jewish population in the occupied Soviet

Union, but this was not a major factor in his determination to see Hitler removed.

As for the inner circle of the conservative-nationalist resistance, they maintained extremely close ties with the Jewish members of the upper class and supported them when the persecution became more intense. For example, Goerdeler made contact with Leo Baeck[6] through the industrialist Robert Bosch, but there is good reason to doubt whether Baeck's clarion-call 'For the Day After' ever existed.

In contrast to the 'great and the good' whose anti-Semitic prejudices varied in their intensity, there were the declared opponents of the regime within the *Abwehr*, Hans Oster and his confidant, Hans von Dohnanyi, as well as Helmut Groscurth, all of whom opposed the racial policies of the regime in the strongest terms and are distinguished by their uncompromising repudiation of Jewish persecution. Groscurth's reaction to the *Kristallnacht* pogrom was strikingly unambiguous: 'We must be ashamed even to be German,' he noted in his diary.

For quite a number of conservative-nationalist conspirators their reaction to the events of *Kristallnacht* marks a mental turning point in their attitude to the regime. A typical example was Urich von Hassell, who as early as 1935 was sharply critical of the anti-Jewish legislation, in November 1938 confiding to his diary that he lamented this 'despicable persecution of the Jews' not so much for its damaging impact abroad but rather because it was morally undermining 'our domestic life'. There was a similar reaction from Hans-Bernd von Haeften, who expressed his bitter disappointment at the passive attitude of the Christian churches.

In December 1938 Goerdeler commented on the recent events in a letter to his British contacts: 'The persecution of the Jews will continue with even greater ferocity... Hitler desires the ultimate destruction of Jews, Christianity and capitalism.' From Goerdeler, a profound optimist, constantly concerned to achieve harmony and to reconcile opposing views, these were strong words indeed. But they were no more than a counterpoise to the hopes, which he nourished anew on his trips to the USA and Palestine, that it was possible to reach a mutual and 'positive solution to the

Jewish problem – Palestine does not meet the requirement – between all the states with an interest and involvement in it'. In fact his position was always in favour of marginalizing, not assimilating Jewry.

One clear exception can be found in Dietrich Bonhoeffer who, though otherwise a traditional German nationalist, was sensitive to anti-Semitism because of his family relationships and friendships with Jews, and who recognized the assassination of Walther Rathenau, back in 1922, as an alarm-signal.[7] His theological approach was an attempt to overcome the authoritarian notion that the state had a right to intervene in the secular life of the Jewish population. As late as 1933, in his essay 'The Church and the Jewish Question', he described this as 'one of the historic problems which our state must deal with'; the state was 'without doubt justified in following new paths'. At the same time, however, he confronted the state with the Church's demand for even-handed justice. It was only by gradual stages that he freed himself from the influence of Lutheran anti-Judaism, which saw the Jews as bearing the curse of being Christ's murderers. He then made it clear beyond doubt that the Church owed a duty to 'all the desolate and deserted, from whatever party or social class they come'. Bonhoeffer pointed out that it was the actions of the state itself that had become the source of injustice. It was necessary 'not just to tend to those crushed under the wheel, but to bring the wheel itself to a halt'.

It is true that in taking this position Bonhoeffer was an outsider. Of his fellow-churchmen, only Provost Bernhard Lichtenberg and, to some extent, Bishop Theophil Wurm[8] shared the consistency of his views. The latter, after sending many protests to the government to no avail, opted to issue repeated internal condemnations of 'the policy of annihilation against Jewry', without ever making them public. On the Catholic side Archbishop Josef Frings of Cologne condemned the liquidation of the Jews with much the same consistency and courage as Bonhoeffer, as did Cardinal Preysing, with whom Helmuth James von Moltke had frequent meetings. However, all these individuals spoke from a standpoint of segregationist anti-Semitism, a fact which robbed their protests of ultimate consistency.

A more consistent standpoint on the Jewish question was taken by a group of conservative-nationalists in the entourage of Goerdeler and Beck, who met separately as the so-called 'Counts Circle' and later the Kreisau Circle. The founder of the latter, Helmuth James von Moltke, was free from the anti-Semitic prejudice so common among his class. Similarly, the long historical view he took of the Nazi regime – as the culmination of centuries of pernicious development, starting with the Reformation and leading to the loss of personal Christianity – differed fundamentally from that taken by the 'great and the good', who looked to the age of Bismarck and the Kaisers for their models.

Unlike the supporters of Goerdeler or Stauffenberg, for Moltke and Yorck von Wartenburg nationalistic motives were only of secondary importance. Both men made their judgements from a Christian and universalist viewpoint, and regarded the defeat of Nazism not primarily as a German problem, but one which genuinely concerned the whole western world. Neither of them faced the problem of having to separate a supposedly beneficial policy of segregation from criminally violent treatment of the Jews. For them, Jewish persecution had become symptomatic of the long decline of the west.

The light-hearted manner in which Moltke, as he himself tells us, poured ridicule on the anti-Semitic indoctrination he received in the civil-service training-school, shows a degree of mental detachment which can only be explained by his abandonment of nationalist views and the Anglo-American influence he absorbed. It was largely due to these factors that Moltke observed the successive stages of Jewish persecution with far greater acumen than did the rest of the conservative-nationalist opposition, and was able to produce factual documentation of it. In his work with the *Abwehr* he was bombarded with evidence of German crimes in south-eastern Europe and in the occupied zone of the Soviet Union. He was deeply affected by this information, as he was by the deportation of Berlin Jews taking place before his eyes, and he asked himself whether this knowledge made him guilty as well; writing to his wife Freya on 21 October 1941, he told her he could not 'get rid of the ghastly feeling that I have let myself be corrupted, that I am no longer reacting fiercely enough to this sort of thing.' He knew well enough that the worst was still to come.

Thanks to his access to information in the *Abwehr*, Moltke acted very much as the opposition's seismograph for the intensifying assault on Jewry. Nevertheless, it was difficult, even for him, to get a reliable overall picture. He found out about the Wannsee Conference[9] early on but, like other civil servants, did not attribute prime importance to it. On 10 October he received an eyewitness report about the installations at the Treblinka extermination camp. It was clear that mass extermination was taking place there, something which up till then, as he admitted to Freya, he had been unable to believe.

Yet it was not until March 1943 that Moltke gained a more solid and detailed picture. While in Stockholm on 25 March 1943 he gave Lionel Curtis an accurate account of the typically German form of anti-Semitism: 'at least nine-tenths of the population are unaware that we have put to death hundreds of thousands of Jews. People still believe that the Jews have merely been taken away somewhere and are living the same kind of life as before, only further east, where they originally came from, perhaps in somewhat reduced circumstances, but safe from air raids.' At the same time Moltke gave an account of how Auschwitz was being developed into a death camp but added that the information available to him was 'only in a very vague, unclear and very imprecise form'. In March 1943 Adam von Trott reported on a concentration camp in Upper Silesia, apparently Auschwitz, with around 40–50,000 inmates and a killing rate of 3–4,000 people per month.

Moltke's efforts to establish contact with the 'White Rose' resistance group, which regrettably did not succeed before the group was rounded up, were at least partly motivated by a desire to find out more about the exterminations alluded to in the group's leaflets. They certainly referred to what was happening in Poland, rather than to the extermination policy in occupied Russia. At the same time, as he told Freya, Moltke was doing everything in his power 'at least to throw an impeding spoke in the wheel of Jewish persecution'. The information he passed on to the Danish

Foreign Minister about the imminent deportation of Danish Jews was nothing less than spectacular and, in combination with earlier disclosures, led to the rescue of nearly all the Jews in Denmark.[10]

The Jesuits in the Kreisau Circle also denounced with great firmness the deportation and murder of Jews. This emerges strikingly from a November 1941 statement by the Jesuit Provincial, Augustin Rösch, in which he spoke of 'the dreadful plight of the Jews, thousands of whom are now being dumped in the Polish ghettos'. Fr Alfred Delp also strove in many different ways to help stricken Jews and condemned the gassing of Jews as 'a loathsome capital crime', which made up his mind in favour of killing Hitler.

In the same period Popitz informed von Hassell, albeit only indirectly, about the mass gassings and the extent of the extermination measures. The Confessing Church was in possession of more precise knowledge, yet the protests of Bishop Wurm remained within that organization. Resolutions of the synod of the Old Prussian Union in Breslau on 17 October 1943 were limited to a passing mention of the genocide. Similarly, there was an absence of any public statements by the Catholic clergy, even though the Curia possessed full information through its links with bishops in south-eastern Europe.

It seems very likely that even in resistance circles the systematic nature of the extermination process was unknown and that they were inclined to believe it was an operation carried out by Himmler[11] on his own initiative. This reinforces the assumption that it would have been impossible for individuals to obtain adequate information, as the example of Karl Dürkefelden shows. [12] He did not get a complete picture until the summer of 1942 and only then by listening to BBC broadcasts. As greater knowledge of the mass crimes of the Nazi regime against the Jews of Europe filtered through to the resistance, so did their motives for protesting against them become moral as well as nationalist.

The reality of the mass murder provoked passionate opposition even among those who had previously sympathized with the regime on Jewish matters. It was the massacres he had seen in the Ukraine that persuaded Axel von dem Busche[13] to join the plot to assassinate

Hitler. In the notes written by Goerdeler while in prison in 1944 we read that Hitler had 'bestially annihilated millions of Jews'. He pointed out the crimes of the regime, but in the same breath stressed that the Bolshevik peril made it necessary, even at this late stage, to try to reach an understanding with Britain.

All this moved the Jewish question further up the agenda of individual factions within the resistance. In late 1941 Hans Robinsohn advocated, in a memorandum written from Swedish exile, a tactical treatment of the 'Jewish question' once the Nazis had been overthrown. He recommended the repeal of all discriminatory legislation and of the requirement to wear the yellow Star of David, with the suspension of all legal proceedings. However, once the Holocaust began, more fundamental steps were needed. In 'First Instructions to Provincial Governors', produced by the Kreisau Circle in August 1943, we read: 'All laws and regulations which discriminate against individuals on account of their membership of a specific nation, race or religion, will cease to have effect.'

Similarly Goerdeler stated in the newly drafted government statement that the 'Jewish persecution' must stop immediately and the concentration camps be closed down. The Schönfeld Memorandum, jointly issued by Goerdeler and Moltke in May 1942, gave the assurance that the Jewish population would be immediately transferred to a 'decent status' and that confiscated Jewish property would be handed back. In the same context we find an offer to work towards a comprehensive resolution of the Jewish problem, in concert with other nations. This memorandum was passed on to the British Foreign Secretary, Anthony Eden by the Bishop of Chichester, Dr George Bell, with the comment that the intention of the German opposition was to repeal the Nuremberg Laws immediately and to cooperate in finding an international solution. That may also explain why Adam von Trott stated categorically, in a memorandum to the British government: 'The New Germany would be willing to cooperate in any international solution to the Jewish problem.'

Trott himself was one of those conspirators who can hardly be accused of any anti-Semitic feelings. However, he wrote a letter that appeared in the *Manchester Guardian* on 21 February 1934, in which he attempted to play down the current anti-Jewish boycott in Hessen. In doing so he earned a reputation among his English friends as a defender of Nazism. In fact, it was a typical example of how conservative supporters of the Nazi regime were initially deluded into thinking that the anti-Jewish activities were only transitory.

An exceptional case is that of Constantin von Dietze and the appendix he wrote to the memorandum of the 'Freiburg Circle' on 'Political Arrangements for the Community'. This contained 'Proposals for a Solution to the Jewish Question in Germany', which represented a return to the old anti-Semitic clichés, and his simultaneous protest at the murder of hundreds of thousands of Jews does nothing to alter that fact. He favoured the idea of founding an international Jewish state; and he wanted to see the passing of a Jewish statute. This would automatically deprive Jews of German citizenship, but as compensation they would have their 'claim to economic activity and the opportunity for education' guaranteed under international law. It is extremely painful to read in the same document: 'The number of surviving Jews returning to Germany will not be so great as to be regarded as a threat to German national life'.

This distinctly *völkisch* variety of anti-Semitism was admittedly the exception to the rule, and it would be a mistake to try to discern the influence of Goerdeler on Dietze's proposals. We can also be sure that the memorandum did not meet with the approval of Bonhoeffer, who commissioned the work in the first place. On the other hand, as Christoph Dipper points out, the position it put forward was by no means isolated, as is shown by the statements on the Jewish question made by quite a number of conspirators when interrogated by the Gestapo, which should certainly not be interpreted as a tactic to obtain clemency from the Nazis.

When Count Nikolaus von Üxküll-Gyllenbrand stated 'We wanted to hold on to the racial idea, as far as was possible', he was not on his own, although the violent methods and above all 'the measures for exterminating Jewry' (Yorck) were rejected. The position of Popitz in many respects typified that of the conservative group among the conspirators. He admitted that he believed it right to 'remove Jews from government and economic life', but said he condemned 'the violence used, which led to the destruction of property and to arbitrary arrest and execution'. There was also sympathy for Jewish partners in mixed marriages and for assimilated Jews in general.

Among the motives behind the decision to embark on active resistance, the Jewish persecution generally played a fairly minor role, yet this changed in the light of the *Kristallnacht* violence and it took on a crucial importance when the facts of the 'Final Solution' became known, although the deportations as such received less attention from the German opposition. For the socialists and communists this question was certainly not a key concern. The representatives of the churches, as far as they had any direct contact with the resistance movement, almost always restricted their protests to defending christianised Jews, if one ignores Bonhoeffer's largely isolated stance.

Operations aimed at hampering the regime and getting round the anti-Jewish measures originated primarily in the highly motivated and extremely active group in the *Abwehr*, led by Oster, Dohnanyi and Bonhoeffer, and culminated in the famous U-7 operation.[14] Oster confessed to the SS court-martial in Flossenbürg that 'the persecution of the Jews and the extermination policy, but also the war itself' had made him realize 'that the removal of the SS and the Gestapo was not in itself enough to clean up Germany'. Oster had, of course, been a staunch opponent of the regime from the moment it came to power.

Hans von Dohnanyi worked against the regime with similar consistency, being dismissed from the Reich Ministry of Justice and joining the *Abwehr*. In his case, disgust at the persecution of the Jews was the central motive. Helmut Friedrichs, a section-head in the Office of the Deputy Führer, stressed in his 1938 report, which forced Dohnanyi to resign, that Dohnanyi 'showed no understanding of the racial legislation of the Third Reich' and was 'inherently opposed' to it.

In retrospect it is depressing to see how few of these rescue attempts, objections and interventions produced any result. It is hard to assess how far the experience of the Jewish persecution contributed to the gradually dawning realization among the conservative-nationalist plotters that partial correctives would not be enough, and that the regime had to be completely overthrown. The civilian opposition saw that for the moment it was politically isolated in Germany and did not have the mass of the population behind it. Not being in a position to take action independently, it placed its hopes in convincing the military that intervention was necessary. But after a military revolt failed to materialize in 1938–1939, this prospect rapidly faded, especially since Beck's successor, *Generaloberst* Franz Halder, pulled back from the idea of a coup d'état, once Hitler's position had been temporarily strengthened by the conquest of Poland and the unexpectedly swift defeat of France.

The assault on the Soviet Union launched on 22 June 1941 made the situation even more difficult, since the troops were now fully engaged in warfare and the officers were occupied with specific operational assignments. Anti-Bolshevism was particularly strong among the officer corps and was further heightened by the slogans of the war of racial extermination. As long as the campaign's prospects of success were good, there was much less willingness even to consider overthrowing the regime. This would change only – and rather abruptly – when the German advance was halted outside Moscow, and the officers realized they were facing a long and costly war, whose outcome could not be predicted.

There can certainly be no doubt that even those who sooner or later gave their support to the resistance, willingly accepted Hitler's slogans about the war of racial extermination. There were a number of plotters, among them General Georg Thomas, and the quartermaster-general of the army, Eduard Wagner, who took an active part in planning the war in the east with all its predicted consequences, while others helped to formulate the series of 'criminal orders'. Senior officers like Stieff, Hoepner and von Stülpnagel adopted Hitler's terminology of extermination in the military orders and instructions they issued and did not recoil from echoing the Führer's extreme anti-Semitism.

Carl-Heinrich von Stülpnagel, who commanded the German 17th Army, is a prime example of this active compliance in waging a war of racial extermination. When his troops marched into Galicia, the region of eastern Poland with proportionally one of the highest Jewish populations in Europe, he ordered that the anti-Jewish and anti-communist section of the inhabitants be encouraged to carry out their own 'ethnic cleansing'. This coincided with Heydrich's instructions to his *Einsatzgruppen*, 'covertly to set in motion and intensify' actions of this kind, 'and steer them in the right direction'. Heydrich was able to refer expressly to Stülpnagel's initiative when he gave instructions to spare those members of the Polish intelligentsia who might be useful as 'instigators of pogroms'. The advancing troops made no effort at all to prevent the massacre of Jews by the indigenous population. Instead the army gave approval for the mass execution of Jews and worked closely with the firing squads.

It has been shown by Christian Streit that Stülpnagel was not only formally responsible for these incidents, but backed them personally to such an extent that that it is impossible to overlook his anti-Semitic motives. In a letter he wrote on 12 August 1941 to Army Group South he called for a 'greater struggle against Bolshevism and against international Jewry, which mainly operates on its behalf', while at the same time proposing that 'a certain degree of economic prosperity' be maintained for the Russian people. He demanded 'clear resolve about the Jewish element of the population', in order to avert the danger 'that sooner or later the Jews will clandestinely regain influence'.

At the opposite extreme to Stülpnagel's conduct was that of *Oberstleutnant* Helmut Groscurth, who had taken part in the opposition's plans for a coup d'état in 1939–1940. It is true that, as a staff officer in the 295th Infantry Regiment, which was under Stülpnagel's command, Groscurth had not raised any objections to implementing the *Kommissarbefehl*. However, in early July 1941, he protested against 'the mass shootings and murder of Jews and Russians, including women and children, by Ukrainians on the open streets' that had been instigated by *Sonderkommando* (Special detachment) 4a. These protests, alas, fell on deaf ears. A few weeks later he raised another protest, about the murder of 90 Jewish children who had been locked up without food or water in the village of Byelaya-Tserkov, after their parents had already been liquidated by *Sonderkommando* 4a, working with Ukrainian militia. Groscurth reported this to Army Group South, who referred him to the 6th Army commanded by *Feldmarschall* von Reichenau. But again he came up against a blank wall. He was informed that von Reichenau 'recognized the need to have the children got rid of and wanted to hear that… these measures had been carried out in this instance'. The children were shot, and the field commander in Byelaya-Tserkov justified this by saying that 'those brats had to be eradicated'. Groscurth, on the other hand, was reprimanded.

His attempt to get a principled ruling on this, by informing the Army High Command, the *Abwehr*, and to get some action from Army Group South under *Feldmarschall* von Rundstedt, failed all down the line. This episode reveals how hopeless it was to try to make the senior military curb the activities of the *Einsatzgruppen* against the Jewish population.

The example of Stülpnagel demonstrates that the attitude of senior commanders, and their unquestioned equating of Bolshevism with Jewry, can be traced back to an ideology imprinted on them by the revolution of November 1918. Von Stülpnagel is quoted as saying in 1935 that 'the double-dealing conduct and activities of the largely Jewish commissars' were reminiscent of 'the worst period at the beginning of communist rule'. Similar views, moulded in the final phase of the First World War and the early post-war period, were held by the majority of officers on the general staff.

It is particularly interesting to examine the attitude of the younger group of staff officers who joined the 20th July movement, first under the leadership of Henning von Tresckow and then of Claus von Stauffenberg. However, it has proved extraordinarily difficult to assess their position on the Jewish question. This is no less true of Claus von Stauffenberg and his two brothers and close allies.

It was Henning von Tresckow who adhered most markedly to the Prussian tradition but perhaps through his experience as a businessman in the 1920s he gained a remarkable breadth of vision, which distinguished him from the 'simple military men'. Yet even he was probably shaped by the experience of the November revolution. Among the papers found after his death were some 'Political Thoughts', dating from 1922, in which he puts forward the notion that 'the Anglo-American (otherwise known as Jewish) concept of capitalist democracy does the dirty work for communism and/or Marxism… albeit with the best intentions'. This shows the influence of Oswald Spengler's 'Prussian socialism', but also echoes the anti-Semitic cliché about Bolshevism and capitalism working in the same direction.

As head of operations in Army Group Centre, Henning von Tresckow was directly confronted with the impact of Hitler's concept of the 'war of racial extermination'. Yet neither he nor those he later conspired with had yet reached a position of head-on opposition. There were certainly negotiations about modifying the martial law decree, in which Tresckow played a significant part. The 'supplements' developed by Army Group B attempted to limit violations of army discipline and to ban excessive violence against the civilian population. However, they did not dispute the suspension of the relevant provisions of the Hague Convention on land warfare.

Tresckow's first moves were aimed at reforming the command structure, whose authority was to be effectively removed by Hitler's assumption of supreme command of the armies in the east. When this failed, and in the light of the serious setbacks outside Moscow at the end of 1941, he decided to act on his own initiative and to pave the way for Hitler's removal in a coup d'état. Tresckow felt there was no longer any justification for continuing to use present methods in waging the eastern war and Stauffenberg agreed with him. Both men were convinced that the objective of completely crushing not only the Soviet system but also the Russian state, and depriving Russia of its ability to survive, could only end in disaster.

This criticism of the methods of warfare was combined with a growing revulsion towards the violence used against prisoners-of-war, Jews and other civilians, which was stiffening Russia's determination to fight back. These notes by Stauffenberg suggest that the destruction of the Jews and the war against the partisans were not central to his considerations. Indeed this was the negative side of his distinction between the Bolshevist system and the Russian people. The anti-Bolshevik syndrome he shared with Tresckow seems to have been influenced by the equating of Jews with partisans. This may explain why Tresckow himself backed the fight against the partisans in the operational area of Army Group Centre with such energy and determination. Only later did he begin to have scruples about the methods employed, even though at an early stage they had led to the systematic extermination of the indigenous Jewish population. The reports from *Einsatzgruppe B*, which crossed his desk and were signed off by him, do not appear to have raised any particular doubts in his mind.

The paucity of sources does not permit any definitive statement about how deeply Tresckow and those like him were implicated in the massacres and extermination operations against Jews, or what their attitude was to them. Nor do we know how they viewed the plan to depopulate entire tracts of territory completely. What we can be certain of is that, in the light of the documents that have survived, the sanitized accounts in the memoirs of Fabian von Schlabrendorff and Rudolf-Christoff von Gersdorff are in need of correction.

Gersdorff's duties concerned the security of the Army Group and, despite his protestations about the 'honour of the German army', he was very deeply involved in the anti-partisan operations that provided a cover for the systematic liquidation of the indigenous Jewish population, including women and children.

A question mark hangs over the relationship that Tresckow and Gersdorff had with Arthur Nebe who, as leader of *Einsatzgruppe B*, was responsible for the death of at least 136,000 people. Nebe was subsequently portrayed as a moderate SS officer, brought into Army Group Centre by Tresckow to impose limits on the violence; but this does not hold water. Nebe was one of the real instigators of genocide; before his posting to Belarus, he worked for the *Reichssicherheitshauptamt* (Central Office of Reich Security) and carried out the first experiments in the use of poison gas as a technique of liquidation.

As far as Henning von Tresckow and his co-plotters are concerned, we find that, as 1941 gave way to 1942, they became ever more sombrely aware of the criminal activities of the *Einsatzgruppen* and SS brigades. As their assessment of the military situation became more pessimistic, so did their protests against the policy of genocide become more vocal. Yet their humanitarian concerns still clearly took second place to the view that the moral integrity of the army had to be preserved.

The inner circle of conspirators did not hesitate to bring individuals who were involved in the criminal policies of the regime into the planning of the coup: people like Arthur Nebe, head of the Criminal Police, or Count Helldorff, Berlin's Chief of Police, who had been prominent in anti-Jewish activities as early as 1933. Helldorff was a typically ambitious Nazi careerist, but after he had fallen out with Himmler he threw in his lot with the conspirators. There is no disputing the fact that his cooperation in the Reich capital seemed essential if the coup was to succeed, and we can hardly object if the conspirators, where necessary, came to an accommodation with representatives of the regime. The line drawn between good and evil was far from being as clear-cut as it has been represented in retrospect. As for the senior military, they were in any case running with the fox and hunting with the hounds, but some played an indispensable role, as Stülpnagel did in Paris. The same is true of the quartermaster-general of the army, Eduard Wagner, who had been instrumental in deploying the *Einsatzgruppen*, and of General Thomas, though he did distance himself from the shooting of Jews.

The attitude of the 20th July movement to the Jewish question, the persecution of Jews and the Holocaust was predictably ambiguous. The great majority of the plotters only gradually broke free from the basically anti-Semitic sentiment that tainted the German upper class and governing elite, but which made an exception for assimilated groups of Jews. Among the younger men we sometimes find a clear break with the prevailing sentiment, though the majority only became fully aware of the Jewish problem as the Nazis pursued their policy of persecution and extermination. In this context the experience of the pogrom of 9–10 November

1938 marks a turning point. Alongside the negative repercussions of the persecution on Germany's international reputation and the economic penalties, awareness of internal corruption came ever more to the fore, combined with moral repugnance at the inhuman treatment of the Jewish victims. For some individuals, knowledge of the Holocaust shocked them into their decision to remove the Nazi regime and kill Hitler. Yet this was not the principal motive; it was more a matter of avoiding the abyss into which the prolonging of the war would drive Germany, both domestically and internationally. The conspirators came to agree that the annihilation of European Jewry, which they were relatively late in recognizing as a systematic and comprehensive process, went hand in hand with the progressive destruction of human political instincts and a lapse into amoral survivalism. They opposed this with the demand for the 'restoration of the inalienable divine and natural rights of the individual human being', which included the Jewish fellow-citizen, and the personal independence of humankind as a condition of the right to control its own destiny.

This was the outcome of a political and moral learning process that took different forms. What needs to be stressed here is not the fact that anti-Semitic influences of varying intensity had an impact on the political attitudes and objectives of the conspirators, but that in the central question of the policy of violence against Jews they reached a common position. Despite their being rooted in the German political tradition and its anti-Semitic elements, it would be a mistake to tar the entire 20th July movement with the same anti-Semitic brush and to ignore the ringing terms in which many of the conspirators, under Gestapo interrogation, condemned the persecution and genocide of the Jews on both moral and patriotic grounds.

It is necessary to judge this emotionally loaded set of problems from the standpoint of those times, when the full horror of the Holocaust had yet to be revealed, and people fatally underestimated the explosive and criminal energy of the Nazi hatred of the Jews. For the resistance itself, it was a chapter of failure. The efforts of Tresckow, Oster, Groscurth, Goerdeler and many others to prompt the field marshals to act, by pointing out the horrors of the

genocide, proved ineffective, whether they approached Kluge or
Manstein. This experience contributed to the decision to smash
the regime and to kill Hitler as its prime mover. Nonetheless, the
Holocaust, as far as members of the opposition were aware of it,
took second place as a motivation, to that of averting military
defeat and the triumph of the Soviet Union. However, we must
acknowledge with respect that for the inner circle of conspirators,
in the critical situation of 20 July 1944, it became more important
to contribute by their own martyrdom to the moral recovery of
the nation, which, largely due to the crimes committed against
the Jews, had been dragged through the dust.

Notes

Chapter 1: Carl von Ossietzky and the concept of a right to resist in Germany

1. Author of the controversial pacifist novel, *All Quiet on the Western Front* (1929), Remarque (1898–1970) emigrated to Italy in 1929 and then to the USA in 1939.
2. Gustav Stresemann (1878–1929) was briefly Chancellor of Germany in 1923, then Foreign Minister until his death, during which time he negotiated the Dawes Loan (1924), the Treaty of Locarno (1925) and Germany's admission to the League of Nations (1926).
3. Colonel Henning von Tresckow (1901–1944) was a staff officer in Army Group Centre during the invasion of Russia. Closely linked with the Stauffenberg Plot of July 1944; when the coup failed he committed suicide. (See Chapters 11 and 12). In classical mythology Hercules donned a tunic impregnated with poison from the centaur, Nessus. When he tried to tear it off, his flesh came off with it.
4. Cf. Larry E. Jones, *German Liberalism and the Dissolution of the Weimar Party System, 1918–1933* (Chapel Hill, 1988) pp.17ff.
5. Leonard Krieger, *The German Idea of Freedom: History of a Political Tradition* (Chicago, 1957, 1972) pp.4ff.
6. Dahlmann was Germany's leading constitutional thinker of the early nineteenth century. In 1815 he published *Ein Wort über Verfassung* ('A Word on Constitutions'); his major work was *Politik* ('Politics'). In 1833, as one of the 'Göttingen Seven' (q.v.), he challenged the right of the King of Hanover to revoke the country's parliamentary constitution. In 1848, as a deputy in the Frankfurt National Assembly, he tried unsuccessfully to assert the assembly's authority over Prussia in the matter of Schleswig and Holstein; surprisingly, Dahlmann did *not* want Prussia to compromise with Denmark.

7. Rotteck, a contemporary of Dahlmann, was also an academic and politician with proto-democratic leanings. Elected mayor of Freiburg, Rotteck's appointment was vetoed by the government of Baden, on the grounds that he was 'subversive'.

8. When Victoria came to the throne in Britain, the century-old personal union between the thrones of England and Hanover was broken and under the Salic Law the Hanoverian crown passed to Victoria's uncle, Ernst Augustus, Duke of Cumberland. The new monarch immediately revoked the constitution of 1833. In protest, seven faculty members from the University of Göttingen refused to swear an oath of allegiance to the new king. As well as Dahlmann, they included Jacob and Wilhelm Grimm, of 'fairy-tales' fame. All were dismissed from their posts and three were forced into exile.

9. Germany's first democratic constitution, drawn up by the first national parliament, which met in St Paul's church, Frankfurt, in 1848.

10. Carl Schmitt (1888–1985), jurist and political theorist. Member of the Nazi Party and the Nazi Academy of German Law, his political philosophy has been described as anti-bourgeois, anti-liberal and anti-democratic, but also penetrating and clear-sighted. His books include *Political Romanticism* (1919), *Dictatorships* (1921) and *Guardians of the Constitution* (1931).

11. Paul Althaus, Professor of Theology at Erlangen University. This quotation is from his *Obrigkeit und Führertum* ('Authority and the Nature of Leaders'), 1936.

12. Count Helmuth James von Moltke (1907–1945). Appointed in 1939 as legal counsel to the foreign section of the armed forces high command (OKW). Worked for better German treatment of prisoners-of-war and adherence to international law. In 1940 founded the Kreisau Circle with Yorck von Wartenburg and others. See Chapter 3 onward.

13. Hans von Dohnanyi (1902–1945). Lawyer, civil servant and dedicated anti-Nazi, he was the brother-in-law of Dietrich Bonhoeffer.

14. Carl Goerdeler (1884–1945). Mayor of Leipzig (1930–37) and leading figure in the civilian resistance to Hitler. Appointed in 1934 as Reich Commissioner for Prices and Foreign Exchange, he soon became disillusioned with Nazism. As overseas representative of the Bosch company he made contacts in Britain, France and the USA. (See especially Chapter 3).

15. Johannes Popitz (1884–1945). Despite his ministerial position in the Nazi regime, in 1938 he began plotting with senior military officers to remove Hitler. However, his political views remained on the extreme right. Due to his connection with the July 1944 plot he was arrested and executed in October of that year.

16. Codename for preparations for the July 1944 coup (see especially Chapter 11).

17. Field-Marshal Erwin von Witzleben (1881–1944), who had been poised to arrest Hitler in 1938. He was close to the 20 July conspirators and was their choice as commander-in-chief. When the plot failed, he was arrested and executed in August 1944.

18. In 1948 Nawiaski was a member of a drafting sub-committee for the constitution of the 1949 German Federal Republic, which was then submitted to the Parliamentary Council.

19. Carlo Schmid, leading Social-Democrat politician of the post-war years.

20. Ludwig Bergsträsser, a member of the German Democratic Party (DDP) before 1933, returned to politics after 1945 as a Social Democrat. As a resister during the war he worked closely with Wilhelm Leuschner (see Chapter 8).

21. Jürgen Habermas, distinguished contemporary German political theorist.

22. In October 1962 the offices of *Der Spiegel,* the news magazine, were raided and the editor, Rudolf Augstein, arrested for betraying defence secrets. The Defence Minister, Franz-Josef Strauss, was subsequently dismissed.

Chapter 2: German society and resistance to Hitler

1. In Gordon A. Craig's *Deutsche Geschichte 1866–1945* (third edition, Munich 1981) the Kreisau Circle is not mentioned at all.

2. The Christian Democratic Union and its Bavarian sister-party, the Christian Social Union.

3. The German Social Democratic Party.

4. Ewald von Kleist-Schmenzin (1890–1945). Lawyer, landowner, monarchist, Christian and conservative, he was a staunch opponent of Nazism and was twice arrested in May and June 1933. At the time of Munich, he was sent to London by the army chief-of-staff, Ludwig Beck, to request support for the proposed removal of Hitler. He was aware of and approved the July 1944 Plot and was assigned a role in the post-coup administration. He was arrested the day after the plot failed, then imprisoned, tried in February 1945 and executed six weeks later.

5. See Peter Ludlow, *Pope Pius XII, the British government and the German opposition in the winter of 1939/40* (article in German in *Vierteljahreshefte für Zeitgeschichte* 22, 1974).

6. Founded originally in 1929 as the 'Leninist Organization', this brought together disaffected Social Democrats and communists. In 1932, foreseeing the Nazi seizure of power, it went underground. In September 1933 it published a document entitled *Neu Beginnen,* which attracted a great deal of attention in Germany and abroad. Following numerous arrests from 1935 onwards, the group went into exile, first in Prague, then in London, where some 20 members remained throughout the war, eventually achieving a reconciliation with the Social Democrats.

7. Founded in 1932, the *Roter Stosstrupp* chiefly comprised social democrats

and those further to the left, students, young workers and the unemployed. They distributed numerous leaflets until discovered in November 1933, when 240 were arrested and the majority given severe sentences. However the group continued to function, providing political refugees and Jews with hiding-places and false papers.

8. See Ian Kershaw, *The Hitler Myth: Image and reality in the Third Reich* (Oxford, 2001).

9. Following the removal of Mussolini in July 1943, the Nazi regime feared an uprising of foreign workers in Germany. Consequently, under the codename 'Valkyrie', contingency planning for the suppression of such a revolt was put in hand. This provided the perfect cover for the Stauffenberg plotters to develop their own plans for an army coup d'état.

10. See Chapter 4 *passim*.

11. Further details on all the individuals named here can be found where they recur in later chapters. See also Chapters 7–10 on Julius Leber, Wilhelm Leuschner, Carlo Mierendorff and Adolf Reichwein respectively.

12. After the banning of all political parties, other than the NSDAP, in 1933, the KPD was the only one to maintain a structure, albeit a clandestine one, in Germany. Other parties dissolved themselves or, in the case of the Social Democrats (SPD), went into exile.

13. A group of anti-Nazis working in the German Foreign Office, who met regularly at the Berlin apartment of Johanna Solf (1887–1954). They remained undiscovered until January 1944, when a dozen were arrested. Solf herself and five others were to have been tried on 28 April 1945, but were released in May.

14. The German military intelligence organization, which harboured many anti-Nazis, such as Hans Oster and, to some extent, even its director, Admiral Canaris.

15. Prompted by false information from Himmler and Göring about a planned coup, Hitler ordered the liquidation of the senior SA commanders, including his old friend Ernst Röhm, together with Gregor Strasser, the leftwing Nazi, and Strasser's political ally, ex-Chancellor (General) Kurt von Schleicher.

16. Count Peter Yorck von Wartenburg (1904–1944). Studied law and public administration and, from 1936 to 1941, was adviser to the Reich Price Commission. His refusal to join the Nazi Party robbed him of promotion after 1938. From 1938 to 1940 he worked closely with Schulenburg on plans for a post-Nazi Germany. He was conscripted in 1939 and in 1942 joined the staff of the Army High Command in Berlin, where he made contact with the military opposition. As early as January 1940 he collaborated with Moltke in forming the Kreisau Circle, which met regularly at his Berlin flat. Yorck was one of the first to advocate a coup d'état and, after Moltke's arrest in January 1944, worked closely with Stauffenberg on the assassination plan. When the 20th July Plot failed, he was arrested, tried and executed in September 1944.

17. Adam von Trott zu Solz (1909–1944). Son of the Prussian Minister of Education, he studied law in Munich and Göttingen and in 1931 won a Rhodes Scholarship to Oxford. He returned to Germany in 1933, passed the civil service examination and spent a year in 1937–8 travelling on a government grant mainly in China and East Asia. Early in 1937 he met Helmuth von Moltke in England. In 1940 he joined the German Foreign Office, from where he had regular contact with anti-Nazi figures in the Abwehr and Army High Command. From 1941 to 1943 he made several trips abroad and was seen as the 'official' representative of the Kreisau Circle. He was arrested in the wake of the July 1944 plot, tried and condemned to death in Berlin on 15 August 1944.

18. Baron Ernst von Weizsäcker (1882–1951). Diplomat, leader of the German delegation to the League of Nations (1928), head of the political department and then State Secretary in the German Foreign Office (1936–45). In 1938–9 he tried to use secret channels to London to counteract the warmongering of Ribbentrop and Hitler. His son, Richard von Weizsäcker was President of the Federal German Republic from 1984 to 1994. Admiral Wilhelm Canaris (1887–1945), head of the *Abwehr*, the intelligence service of the Armed Forces High Command. A German patriot who opposed Nazism on moral grounds, he took great risks in undermining Hitler's regime. Though his links with the 20th July Plot were not proven, he was tried and executed for treason in April 1945.

19. Following the successful Allied landings in Normandy, Rommel wrote to Hitler on 15 July 1944, calling on him to end the war. This had nothing to do with the attempt on Hitler's life five days later. However, Hitler suspected Rommel of treachery, and in October of that year he forced him to choose between being put on trial and committing suicide. He took his own life.

20. Communist social philosopher, still active in the 1950s and 1960s.

21. Both the early drafts for a new order, by Popitz, Hassell, Jessen and Beck, as well as the plans of the Kreisau and Goerdeler circles represent long-term planning, and were certainly not concerned with the immediate securing of power in the event of a coup. This does not necessarily mean that many of the plotters would not have had a change of heart in a fundamental alteration to the overall political situation.

22. Adenauer and Heuss were respectively the first Chancellor and first President of the post-war German Federal Republic established in 1949. Neither had played any part in the anti-Nazi resistance.

23. Abs was an executive of the Deutsche Bank under the Nazis and after the war became its chairman.

24. A school of macro-economic thinkers who favoured free competition, modified by regulation of working conditions. Ludwig Erhard, the architect of Germany's post-war 'economic miracle', came from this tradition.

25. Hermann Rauschning (1887–1982). Son of a Prussian army officer, he joined the Nazi Party in 1932 and was elected chairman of the Danzig senate. Despite his initial devotion to Hitler, he quarrelled with the local Gauleiter and was forced to resign in 1934. In the 1935 election he stood unsuccessfully *against* the Nazis and soon afterwards emigrated to Switzerland. He became internationally famous for two books: *Germany's Revolution of Destruction* (Zürich 1938, London 1939) and *Conversations with Hitler* (1939), though the latter proved subsequently to have been largely invented. After the war he moved to the USA, where he took up farming.

26. After the fall of Stalingrad in 1943, the German commander, Field-Marshal von Paulus, was taken to Moscow. There, no doubt under great pressure from the Russians, he fronted a propaganda organization, the National Committee for Free Germany, aimed at persuading the German people to call for peace. Using patriotic slogans the communist-inspired committee threatened to outflank the conservative and social-democratic resistance. Paulus was released by the Soviets in 1953 and died in East Germany in 1957.

27. In the post-war East German state, this system was introduced and manipulated in such a way that the so-called Socialist Unity Party (SED), another name for the Communist Party, became the only party.

28. On 2 August 1944, his first appearance in the House of Commons after the events of 20 July, Winston Churchill gave a detailed account of the progress of the war in Europe and the Far East. Not until the end of his speech did he make an oblique reference to 'tremendous events' in Germany and went on: 'The highest personalities in the German Reich are murdering one another, or trying to...' Churchill made it very clear that this would not weaken the Allies' resolve to demand Germany's unconditional surrender: 'Potent as may be these manifestations of internal disease... it is not in them that we should put out trust, but in the justice of our cause... Let us... listen to no parley from the enemy...'

Chapter 3: The social vision and constitutional plans of the German resistance

I. The sociology of resistance

1. Count Helmuth von Moltke (1907–1945). Legal adviser to the Armed Forces High Command. An early opponent of Nazism, he founded the Kreisau Circle of mainly upper-class resisters, who planned a new order to replace Hitler's regime. Arrested by the Gestapo in January 1944, he was executed a year later.

2. Lionel Curtis (1872–1955) was a far-sighted, if idealistic, British political theorist and government adviser, whose work led to the creation of the Union of South Africa, the founding of the British Commonwealth and

independence for Ireland and India. His disciples included T.E. Lawrence ('Lawrence of Arabia') as well as Moltke. See *A German of the Resistance: The last letters of Count Helmuth James von Moltke* (second edition, London, 1948) p.28.

3. George K. Romoser, 'The Politics of Uncertainty: The German Resistance Movement', in Social Research, XXXI (1964) p.73.

4. Hannah Arendt, *Eichmann in Jersusalem: A report on the banality of evil* (London and New York, 1994).

5. Theodor Haubach (1896–1945). A socialist member of the Kreisau Circle; he had close ties with Carlo Mierendorff, with whom, in the 1920s, he published a magazine, *Die Dachstube* ('The Garret'). In the last years of Weimar he joined the militant republican *Reichsbanner* movement. In 1929 he was press adviser to the Reich Minister of the Interior, Carl Severing. From 1930 to 1933 he worked closely with Paul Tillich's Religious Socialist circle. After the Nazis came to power he was twice imprisoned for his political activities. In autumn 1942 he took part in the second major Kreisau conference. After the 20 July Plot he was arrested in Berlin, tried, condemned to death and executed in January 1945.

6. Hermann Maass (1897–1944). After studying philosophy and sociology, joined the new College of Politics, dedicated to strengthening Weimar democracy. Later went into youth work but lost his job in 1933. Became a close colleague of W. Leuschner in the state government of Hesse. Built up anti-Nazi cells among industrial workers. Arrested in August 1944, tried and executed.

7. Ernst Jünger (1895–1998). Highly decorated hero of the First World War, poet and novelist of the right, (*Storm of Steel*, 1920). Extremely pro-Nazi at first, he was quoted as saying: 'I hate democracy like the plague', and even suspected Hitler of being a closet bourgeois. However, he never joined the party and distanced himself from it after 1935. In later life he turned to humanism and finally Christianity.

8. Ralf Dahrendorf (b.1929) is one of Germany's leading sociologists, having held professorships at the universities of Hamburg, Tübingen and Konstanz. He was director of the London School of Economics 1974–84. His *Society and Democracy in Germany* was published in English in 1968.

II. Overcoming the mass mentality

1. R. Dahrendorf, *Gesellschaft und Demokratie in Deutschland*, published in English as *Society and Democracy in Germany* (London, 1968).

2. Hans Schlange-Schöningen (1886–1960). Reichstag deputy of the rightwing DNVP 1920–1928; after 1930 tried unsuccessfully to rally a centre grouping. Joined Brüning's cabinet in 1931 but his mildly progressive views were unpopular. 1945–1949 helped to organize food policy in Germany. Author of *Am Tage danach* ('The Day After'), Heidelberg, 1946.

3. Dietrich Bonhoeffer (1906–45). Evangelical Protestant theologian and staunch opponent of Nazism. He studied in the USA, 1930–33, and was a pastor in London, 1933–35. In 1939 he visited the USA and Britain on behalf of the resistance. Arrested in 1943 in connection with an early plot to kill Hitler. Sent to concentration camp and executed in April 1945. His brother Klaus, also in the resistance, was shot at the same time.

4. Horst von Einsiedel (1905–1948). Coming from a professional background, he studied law and administration in Breslau. After graduating in 1930 he joined the SPD. In 1934, under Nazism, he found a post in the Reich Office of Statistics but soon had to give it up for political reasons. From 1939 he was a member of Moltke's circle, where he contributed ideas mainly in economics and agriculture. After the 20th July Plot he was fortunate to survive to the end of the war in Berlin. However in October 1945 he was arrested by the Soviet secret police and died in 1948 in an internment camp, under mysterious circumstances.

5. Lothar König (1906–1946). A Roman-Catholic who became a Jesuit priest in 1939. Used his contacts to ward off Nazi attacks on Catholic institutions and monastic orders. From 1942 took part in Kreisau discussions. Following the 20th July Plot, went into hiding in the cellars of his seminary until rescued in May 1945. Died soon afterwards from an illness contracted while in hiding.

6. Theodor Steltzer (1885–1967). Coming from a middle-class family in Schleswig-Holstein he studied economics and before the First World War became involved in workers' education. In 1920 appointed *Landrat* (district prefect). Due to his vocal opposition to the Nazi Party he was dismissed from his post in 1933. He was later arrested for anti-Nazi activities but released in 1936. In 1939 he was drafted into the Wehrmacht and from 1940 served as Lt-Colonel on the general staff in occupied Norway. In the same year was introduced to Moltke's circle. Arrested after 20 July he was condemned to death in January 1945. But thanks to intercession by friends in Sweden and Norway, Himmler postponed the execution and he was released on 25 April 1945. In the same year he was a co-founder of the CDU and was subsequently elected minister-president of the *Land* of Schleswig-Holstein in the new Federal Republic.

7. Eugen Gerstenmaier (1906–1986). Studied theology and philosophy, then in 1933–1934 took part in the defence of the churches against the Nazi-inspired 'German Christians'. He was briefly arrested by the Gestapo. From 1936 he worked in the External Affairs office of the Evangelical Church. This gave him an opportunity to travel abroad and he was soon regarded as an important helper by anti-Nazi groups. He was introduced to the Kreisau Circle by Adam von Trott. Although actively involved in the 20th July Plot, he was only sentenced to 7 years imprisonment in January 1945 and was liberated by US troops in April of that year. Under

the Federal Republic he was a CDU politician and served 1954–1969 as President (Speaker) of the Bundestag.

8. Otto Müller (1870–1944). Ordained as a Roman-Catholic priest in 1894. In 1918 became president of the West German Chapter of the Catholic Workers' Movement. From 1919 to 1933 served as a centre-party councillor on the city councils of Mönchengladbach and Cologne. Appalled by the Nazi treatment of the Catholic Church, he was already in contact with military anti-Nazi groups before the Second World War. Later hosted anti-regime discussions in Cologne. After the 20th July Plot he was arrested along with the Cologne group of conspirators and died in a police hospital in Berlin.

9. When Yorck was on trial for treason in 1944 he criticized the 'state's total claim on the citizen, to the exclusion of his religious and moral obligations towards God', to which Judge Roland Freisler retorted that both Christianity and National Socialism had to lay claim to 'the entire man'.

10. Pierre-Joseph Proudhon (1809–65). French socialist and anarchist thinker. Developed the theory of Mutualism, in which small units work together for mutual benefit. One of the prime movers of the 1848 revolution in France.

11. Jakob Kaiser (1888–1961). A bookbinder by trade, he rose to be a leading figure in Catholic labour unions in the Weimar period. In 1933, when the unions were replaced by the German Labour Front, he became a dedicated opponent of Nazism. He was a close associate of W. Leuschner, working on plans for the labour movement after the overthrow of Nazism. After the 20th July Plot he succeeded in eluding the Gestapo and with the help of his political ally, Elfriede Nebgen, whom he later married, went underground. After the war he was a co-founder of the CDU and later served as the Federal Minister of All-German Affairs.

12. Ludwig Reichhold, German political and economic writer of the first half of the twentieth century. His works include *Die Europäische Arbeiterbewegung* ('The European Labour Movement'), 1953.

13. Julius Leber (1891–1945). Socialist Reichstag deputy from the earliest Weimar days. A constant opponent of Nazism he spent the years 1933–1937 in concentration camps. On his release he made contact with the Kreisau Circle, Goerdeler and Stauffenberg. Arrested shortly before the July Plot, he was tried and hanged in January 1945.

14. See Chapter 9. Mierendorff was killed in an Allied air raid on Leipzig, on 4 December 1943.

III. National Socialism and Bolshevism

1. Ludwig Beck (1880–1944). Chief of the General Staff 1935–1938. In 1938 he urged the Army commander-in-chief, Brauchitsch, to protest against Hitler's planned invasion of Czechoslovakia. Brauchitsch reported this to Hitler and Beck was forced to resign. He remained in touch with

the resistance and was titular head of the Bomb Plot. When it failed he got a soldier to shoot him.

2. The memorandum was entitled *The significance of the Russo-Finnish conflict for Germany's present situation* (December 1939). Following Germany's invasion of Poland, the USSR took steps to secure its western frontiers and tried to force Finland to provide it with a military base in the Baltic, at Hanko. When Finland refused, Russia invaded the country on 30 November 1939. The Finns put up staunch resistance but on 3 March 1940 were forced to sign a treaty making territorial concessions to the Soviet Union.

3. Hans Oster (1888–1945). Chief assistant to Admiral Canaris, head of the Abwehr. A strong opponent of Nazism, in 1938 he warned Britain of Hitler's intentions in Czechoslovakia and Poland. Arrested after the 1944 Bomb Plot, he was imprisoned in concentration camps and hanged, with Canaris, in April 1945, just before the arrival of the US Army.

4. Franz Halder (1884–1972). German general, appointed Chief of the General Staff in 1938. Responsible for planning the invasions of Poland, Western Europe and Russia. Dismissed in 1942 for disagreement with Hitler over strategy. In 1944 arrested in connection with the Bomb Plot and sent to Dachau concentration camp. Liberated by the US Army in 1945.

5. Erich Kordt (1903–1969). Diplomat who served in London under Ribbentrop, heading his office when he became Foreign Minister. Kordt joined the Nazi Party in 1937. However, in June 1939 he secretly warned the British government about the impending Nazi-Soviet Pact.

6. Hasso von Etzdorf (1900–1989). Career diplomat who joined the Nazi Party in 1933. Private Secretary to Foreign Minister von Neurath and to U. von Hassell, the anti-Nazi ambassador to Rome. The memorandum he wrote with Kordt, entitled *The Looming Disaster,* was an appeal to the military leadership to refuse to carry out Hitler's orders. Despite close opposition links, he was not associated with the July 1944 Plot and survived the war to continue his diplomatic career. He was ambassador to London 1961–1965.

7. A friend of Trott, who emigrated to the USA.

8. Gregor Strasser (1892–1934). A radical Nazi who headed the party organization before 1933 and had a more left-leaning agenda than the Munich leadership. Continually at loggerheads with Hitler, he resigned from the party in December 1932. He was shot in the Röhm Purge of June 1934.

IV. Agriculture, regional planning and policy for small businesses

1. The author is using a term from nineteenth-century science. 'Organicism' was the doctrine that organic structure is merely the result of an inherent property in matter to adapt itself to its environment.

2. Paulus van Husen (1891–1971). A strict Catholic, qualified in law, fought in the First World War and under Weimar became a leading Centre Party politician in Silesia. 1934–1940 was a senior member of Prussian civil service, but due to his refusal to join the Nazi Party was not further promoted. Joined Kreisau Circle in 1940 as an important link with the Catholic Church. Arrested after the July Plot, he narrowly escaped execution thanks to the arrival of the Red Army in Berlin. From 1949 to 1959 held senior judicial posts in North-Rhine-Westphalia.

3. The word *Volksgenosse*, meaning 'compatriot' or 'national comrade' was the standard Nazi term for the German citizen under the Third Reich.

4. Friedrich Naumann (1860–1919). Liberal champion of social reform and Reichstag deputy of the late imperial period, who founded a 'National Social Association' in 1896. He was a founder member of the German Democratic Party (DDP) in November 1918 and was elected its leader shortly before his death less than a year later.

5. Ruralist member of Stauffenberg's circle.

6. In 1932 President Hindenburg had received his ancestral estate, Neudeck in East Prussia, as a gift from his fellow Junker landowners. The estate was purchased with donations from industrialists.

7. This region, centred on Stuttgart, was and is still known for its precision engineering industries set in a largely rural environment.

8. Wilhelm Stuckart (1902–1953). Lawyer and senior civil servant under Nazism, he helped to draft the anti-Jewish Nuremberg Laws and took part in the notorious Wannsee Conference, which led to the Final Solution. He was tried at Nuremberg but given a light prison sentence due to a lack of evidence against him.

V. Economic and social policy

1. Schmölders was Professor of Economics at Munich University before the Second World War, and his writings were regarded as gospel by the Kreisau Circle. He continued teaching until the 1960s.

2. From 1937 onward Goerdeler was economic adviser to the Bosch electrical company. Although wooed by the Nazis, its chairman, Dr Robert Bosch (1861–1942), a pacifist and an enlightened employer, remained firmly aloof from them.

3. Karl Blessing (1900–1971). Economist and banker, joined Nazi Party in 1937, governor of the Reichsbank but dismissed from this post in 1939 after refusing to be jointly responsible for the highly inflationary armaments spending. 1939–1941, director of the German arm of Unilever; 1941–1945, director of Kontinental Oil AG. Valued by Goerdeler as an adviser, Blessing was pencilled in as economics minister in a post-Nazi government. Survived the war and was Chairman of the Bundesbank 1958–1969.

4. Carl Dietrich von Trotha (1907–1952). Cousin of Moltke, he too grew

up on the Kreisau estate. In 1933 joined the Reich economics ministry. Played a leading part in the Kreisau's economic planning, but did not attend its major conferences and thus escaped detection after the July Plot. From 1948 until his death in an accident in 1952, he lectured in politics in Berlin.

5. Written while he was in prison awaiting execution, between September 1944 and February 1945.

6. From Goerdeler's memorandum to President Hindenburg, April 1932.

7. Heinrich Brüning (1885–1970). German Chancellor 1930–1932, a Catholic Centre Party politician and an economic moderate. Unable to gain majority support for his programme he obtained President Hindeburg's permission to dissolve the Reichstag and rule by presidential decree. He was dismissed by Hindenburg in 1932. When the Nazis took power he fled to the USA, escaping Hitler's 1934 purge, in which he would almost certainly have been murdered. He became a professor at Harvard and died in Vermont.

VI. Community, leadership and a 'new' élite

1. Ferdinand Tönnies (1855–1936). German economist and sociologist who first posited the distinction between *Gesellschaft* and *Gemeinschaft*. His key book is published in English as *Community and Association* (London, 1974).

2. Karl, Freiherr (Baron) vom Stein (1757–1831). Imperial aristocrat and civil servant, Prussian Minister of Economics (1804–1807) and Chief Minister (1808). A liberal reformer, he was one of the architects of Prussia's highly efficient and in many ways progressive administration.

3. Edgar Julius Jung (1894–1934). Author of *Sinndeutung der Deutschen Revolution* ('Making Sense of the German Revolution'), 1933.

4. The *Mittwochs-Gesellschaft* (Wednesday Club) was an informal grouping of academics, politicians and senior civil servants, who met regularly from 1932 to 1944 for discussions at a theoretical level. Its members included Nazis and anti-Nazis, as well as some who took no part in politics. Resisters such as Beck, Popitz and Hassell used the forum to gauge support for their ideas.

5. Pastor Schönfeld, a leading Protestant member of the Kreisau Circle.

6. Harald Poelchau (1903–1972). A Protestant cleric with political affiliations, he worked in 1931–1932 with Paul Tillich, the chief proponent of Religious Socialism. In 1933 he was the first prison chaplain to be appointed under the Nazi regime. He gave moral support to the victims of Nazi violence and accompanied many condemned people to their execution. Joined the Kreisau Circle in 1941 but avoided arrest in 1944 and provided a link between those less fortunate and their families. After the war he continued to work as a prison chaplain until 1951.

7. The term *Reich*, 'empire' or 'realm', has a long history, dating back to the

medieval Holy Roman Empire of the German Nation. It was revived in 1871 for the German empire of Bismarck and the Hohenzollerns, and even the Weimar Republic was nominally a *Reich*, with its Reichstag, Reichsmark, Reichswehr etc. Only in 1949 was the term finally replaced by *Bund* (federal state).

8. The Russian word *soviet*, meaning both 'counsel' and 'council', has its German equivalent, *Rat*. In April 1919 there was a brief attempt by Gustav Landauer and the writer Ernst Toller, to establish a 'republic of soviets', the *Räterepublik*, in Bavaria. Within weeks it was hijacked by hard-line Bolshevists, then brutally crushed by rightwing forces.

9. Cardinal Michael von Faulhaber (1869–1952). Appointed Archbishop of Munich-Freising in 1917 and Cardinal in 1921. Though welcoming Hitler's 1933 Concordat with the Vatican, he soon protested against its violation. In the same year he preached on the Jewish origins of Christianity and condemned racial hatred as a 'poisonous weed'. Collaborated on the 1937 papal encyclical, 'In deep Concern'. However, he maintained a distance from the Resistance, although Goedeler solicited his support. Interrogated after the July Plot, he declared his allegiance to Hitler.

VII: From the National Socialist *Führer*-state to a fascist-authoritarian monarchy

1. Friedrich Heinz was a *Freikorps* commander and early member of the Nazi Party, which he built up in northern Germany. However, by 1938 he had moved to an anti-Hitler position and was a leader of a proposed coup in that year.

2. A reference to the Prussian monarchy, five of whom were named Friedrich Wilhelm.

3. Dr Hjalmar Schacht (1877–1970). Initially a Democrat, Schacht was president of the Reichsbank 1923–1929. He later joined the Nazi party for which he mustered support from industry and banking. In 1933 he was reappointed to the presidency of the Reichsbank and in 1934 made Minister of Economics. However, he resigned in 1937 and allied himself with the resistance. After the July 1944 bomb plot he was jailed and narrowly avoided execution. At Nuremberg he was acquitted of war crimes and resumed his banking career.

4. Under Nazism, the Minister of the Interior, Wilhelm Frick, deprived the *Länder* of their political autonomy and placed them under centrally appointed governors.

VIII. The constitutional plans of Carl Goerdeler and the Kreisau Circle

1. Josef Wirmer (1901–1944). A Catholic student leader who joined the Catholic Centre Party during the Weimar republic. He campaigned for Brüning in the 1932 and 1933 elections and in 1936 joined the group of

anti-Nazi labour leaders headed by Leuschner. From 1941 worked with Goerdeler. Arrested and executed after the July Plot.
2.   A reference to Alexander Kerensky, whose 'Menshevik' or moderate socialist government in Russia was rapidly ousted by Lenin and the hard-line Bolsheviks in October 1917.

IX: Parties, labour unions and a collective 'democratic' movement

1.   The Parliamentary Council was convened in Germany in 1948 to approve the constitution of the new Federal Republic, which came into force he following year.
2.   Field Marshal Günther von Kluge (1882–1944). An artillery and general staff officer, he led the 4th Army in Poland, France and Russia, until injured in a car-crash in 1943. In July 1944 he briefly replaced Rommel in the western command until, in August, he was relieved of his post for failing to uncover the July Bomb Plot. Though sympathetic to the plotters, he had refused to join them. He had, however, promised to help them if Hitler was killed, and committed suicide soon after the plot failed.
3.   Since the end of the First World War only two parties had been in government in Britain: Labour and Conservative. The Liberals had been reduced to a rump, and only re-emerged as a political force in the 1970s.
4.   Peters was a lawyer who belonged to the Kreisau Circle and survived the war.
5.   Hermann Kaiser (1885–1945) was an early member of the Nazi Party and an army staff officer in 1939–1940. He joined the Beck-Goerdeler opposition to Hitler. He was arrested and executed after the 20 July 1944 Plot.
6.   Andreas Hermes (1878–1964). Catholic Centre Party member of the Reichstag from 1928, and President of the Federation of Farmers' Societies. Accused by the Nazis of embezzlement and imprisoned briefly in 1934. In 1939, after several years in South America, joined Goerdeler and Leuschner and was to be Minister of Agriculture in a post-Nazi administration. Condemned to death in 1944, but released by Soviet troops. He was a co-founder of the CDU.
7.   Allen W. Dulles (1893–1969) was head of US intelligence in Switzerland from 1942 onwards. He had made contact with the anti-Hitler plotters around Hans Oster in the *Abwehr*. Adam von Trott managed to visit him in Switzerland in January 1943 and April 1944. After the war Dulles became head of the CIA.
8.   Otto John (1909–?). A lawyer who joined the resistance through his friendship with Dietrich Bonhoeffer's brother, Klaus. After the failure of the July Plot he managed to escape via Lisbon to Britain, where he worked for the BBC German Service. After the war he was employed by the

German federal government, but in 1954 he defected to East Germany. He appears to have been framed as a communist spy by former Nazis, and was put on trial for treason.

X. The military coup and a 'democratic' popular uprising

1. Count Claus Schenk von Stauffenberg (1907–1944). A much-decorated army officer, he fought under Rommel in North Africa and was severely wounded. In 1943 he joined the Kreisau Circle while still serving as chief-of-staff of the Reserve Army, but became impatient with Kreisau's lack of action. He realised that there was no choice but to assassinate Hitler. In 1944 he volunteered to plant the bomb in Hitler's conference-room at his Rastenburg headquarters in East Prussia. Believing Hitler to be dead, he returned to Berlin and began organizing the coup d'état. When news of the Führer's survival came through, Stauffenberg was arrested within hours and summarily executed.

2. In the closing days of the First World War, Friedrich Ebert, the Social Democrat leader, fearing a repeat of the Russian revolution in Germany, struck a bargain with General Wilhelm Groener, the First Quartermaster-General of the army, whereby the army commanders would retain their authority over the troops following the inevitable surrender. This was announced on 10 November, the day before the armistice. Ebert was elected president of the new Weimar Republic in February 1919 and Groener served as Minister of War from 1928 to 1932, during which time he had endeavoured to keep the Nazis and other extremists in check.

3. Anton Saefkow (1903–1944). A working-class Berliner who joined the German Communist Party (KPD) in 1924 and from 1928 to 1933 headed its regional branches in Saxony, the Ruhr and Hamburg. In 1935 he was sent to concentration camps for two years. In 1942 he took over the decimated communist resistance group in Berlin. In 1944 he made contact with non-communist resisters, was arrested in July, before the failed coup, and executed in September 1944.

4. From 1920 the Reichswehr provided the Soviet military with technical assistance in return for training facilities on Russian soil, which contravened the stipulations of the Versailles Treaty.

5. Hans Bernd Gisevius (1904–1974). Germany's wartime Vice-Consul in Zürich, Switzerland. A staunch opponent of Nazism from 1933, he contacted anti-Hitler groups within the *Abwehr*. It was Canaris, head of the *Abwehr*, who had him posted to Zürich, where he made contact with British Intelligence and with Allen Dulles, then head of America's secret service in Europe. Gisevius must be seen as Goerdeler's mouthpiece, warning Dulles to stop Stauffenberg from doing a deal with the communists.

6. Neidhardt von Gneisenau (1760–1831). Career officer instrumental in reforming the Prussian army, by introducing compulsory short-term

military service and effective training. This paid dividends when Prussia and its allies defeated Napoleon at the Battle of Leipzig in 1813.

XI. The 'German Way'

1. Leopold von Ranke (1795–1885). The greatest German historian of his age, he concentrated on the history of Prussia, France and England. He was appointed historiographer to the Prussian state in 1841.
2. Hermann Brill (1895–1959). Elected to the Reichstag as a Social Democrat in 1932. From 1933 he opposed Nazism and in 1936 co-founded the 'German People's Front'. Arrested in 1938 and sentenced to 12 years imprisonment – the years 1943–1945 in Buchenwald concentration-camp. After the war he held several government posts and was an SPD member of the Bundestag 1949–53.

Chapter 4: The Kreisau Circle and the future reorganization of Germany and Europe

1. The Kreisau Circle was named after the country estate of its leader, von Moltke. It contained Protestants and Catholics, socialists and conservatives. Though the group formally opposed a coup d'état against Hitler, many individual members supported such a move. After the failed attempt on Hitler's life on 20 July 1944, Moltke, Trott and Yorck von Wartenburg were executed.
2. A nostalgia for the Catholicism of the Holy Roman Empire, as opposed to Protestant Prussia.
3. Othmar Spann (1878–1950). His works include *Types of Economic Theory* (London, 1930).
4. The Boberhaus Circle was another name for the Work-camp Movement, a youth movement combined with adult education, which existed from 1920 to 1923.
5. Eugen Rosenstock-Huessy was a leading light in the above movement and a youthful admirer of Freya von Moltke.
6. Rosenstock-Huessy stated in 1963: 'In Moltke's mind no connection existed between the work-camp movement and the Kreisau Circle.'
7. The Schwarzwald Circle was named after a Viennese family.
8. Arthur Mahraun (1890–1950). The leader of the *Jungdeutscher Orden*, a paramilitary organization loosely modelled on the Teutonic Knights. Founded in 1923, it achieved a membership of 100,000. The 1927 Manifesto sought to replace parliament and parties with a structured corporatist order in which the concept of 'neighbourhood' would be merged with the *Führer*-principle. The movement evolved into the German State Party (DSP) which fielded candidates in the 1930 election.
9. Hans-Bernd von Haeften (1905–1944) entered the German Foreign Office in 1933 but refused to join the Nazi Party. A close friend of Trott, he was

linked to the Kreisau Circle and after the July Plot was tried and executed. His younger brother Bernd was adjutant to Stauffenberg in his post as chief-of-staff of the Reserve Army, and closely involved in the July Plot. He was shot, along with Stauffenberg and others, on 21 July at the Bendlerstrasse military headquarters.

10. Zehrer was the editor of a neo-conservative journal, *Die Tat* ('Action'), in the late Weimar period.

Chapter 5: Fritz-Dietlof von der Schulenburg and the Prussian tradition

1. He should not be confused with the older Friedrich-Werner von der Schulenburg (1875–1944) who was ambassador to the Soviet Union 1934–41, also joined the anti-Nazi opposition and was tried and executed in October 1944.

2. Kurt Daluege (1897–1946). From 1933 a member of the Reichstag and head of the uniformed police force in Prussia and later the whole of Germany. In 1942 he succeeded Heydrich as 'Protector' of Bohemia and Moravia and was hanged by the Czechs in 1946.

3. Hermann Göring (1893–1946). One of Hitler's closest associates and for a while his heir-apparent. When the Nazis seized power his first post was Minister of the Interior for the state of Prussia, where he created what soon became the Gestapo, or secret police. He was condemned to death at Nuremberg and committed suicide soon afterwards.

4. One of several rightwing, nationalist youth organizations that existed in Germany prior to 1933.

5. Gregor Strasser (1892–1934). A radical Nazi, he organized the party in the industrial Rhineland and founded a party newspaper which stressed the socialist and proletarian aspects of Nazism. He even called for an alliance with the Soviet Union against the capitalist west. He resigned from the Nazi Party in December 1932, and was killed in the Röhm Purge of June 1934.

6. Oswald Spengler (1880–1936). German historian whose *Decline of the West* (1918) claimed that Europe was returning to a new Dark Age.

7. Ernst Niekisch and Friedrich Hielscher were both rightwing revolutionary writers, associated with the conservative opposition to the Weimar republic.

8. Later, in December 1932, the newly appointed Chancellor, Kurt Schleicher, approached Strasser hoping to persuade him to join his government. He failed, and in January 1933 Hitler was appointed Chancellor in his place.

9. In fact Strasser retired to Italy for a few months. In February 1934 Hitler awarded him the Gold Medal of the Nazi Party, but had him murdered in June of that year.

10. The *Königsberger Kreis* was founded by Schulenburg's superior, Gauleiter Koch of East Prussia. Its aim was to modernize that neglected region, but it became corrupt and Schulenburg resigned.
11. Josef Wagner (1899–1945). A loyal Nazi since 1922, had an exemplary career in the party until, in November 1941, a letter from his wife to his daughter was discovered, in which she refused on religious grounds to allow the daughter to marry an SS officer. Wagner was tried by a party court, dismissed from his post and the party and was eventually murdered by the SS.
12. Arthur Moeller van den Bruck (1876–1925). A nationalist pamphleteer of the First World War and early Weimar periods. He is perhaps best known for having coined the term 'Third Reich'. His 'young nations' were the Germans and the Russians, as opposed to the 'old' – Britain and France.
13. Walter Darré (1895–1953). One of Hitler's early associates but faded into the background after 1933, despite serving as Minister of Food and Agriculture (1933–42). His ideas for protecting the peasantry as the 'life source of the Nordic race' influenced Himmler. In 1945 he was sentenced to five years imprisonment.
14. This was a conscious revival of the Bismarckian system of government by *Ämter* (offices, not ministries), which were totally subordinated to the Reich Chancellor.
15. The party leadership decided in 1937 to remove its officials from state offices except at regional level. Many of them chose to resign from their party posts but to remain in the civil service.
16. These two 'Führers' were envisaged as separate and distinct individuals.
17. E.g. those put forward by Frick and Rosenberg, which came to nothing.
18. August Winnig (1878–1956). A labour leader in the construction industry before the First World War. As a member of the SPD's right wing, he was appointed *Oberpräsident* of East Prussia in 1919. But after taking part in the rightwing Kapp Putsch of 1920 was dismissed from office and expelled from the party. He flirted with 'National Bolshevism' but then joined the *Volkskonservativen* and after 1931 aligned himself broadly with Nazi ideology. He later embraced Christianity and in 1953 gained an honorary doctorate in theology. His writings include *European Thoughts of a German* (1937) and *The Hand of God* (1938).
19. Baron Werner von Fritsch (1880–1939). Commander-in-chief of the army from 1934 to 1938. Though loyal to Hitler he questioned the planned annexation of Austria and invasion of Czechoslovakia. He was concerned about the military ambitions of the SS, and it was they who framed him on spurious charges of homosexuality. Forced to leave the army, he later rejoined as an honorary colonel and was killed in action in Poland.
20. A harking back to the confederate Holy Roman Empire of the sixteenth and seventeenth centuries.

21. Joseph Fouché (1759–1820). A former priest who, in the French Revolution, spearheaded the ruthless attempt to de-Christianise France. (As a devout Christian himself, Schulenburg was presumably unaware of this). When Napoleon removed the Directoire in 1799, Fouché became his chief of police.

Chapter 6: German anti-Hitler resistance and the ending of Europe's division into nation states

1. Fabian von Schlabrendorff (b.1907). A prominent member of the resistance, he was sent to London in 1939 to warn Churchill and others of Hitler's intention to invade Poland. During the war he was ADC to Major-General Henning von Tresckow, and together they organized an unsuccessful attempt on Hitler's life. He later recruited Stauffenberg for the 20 July Plot. When that also failed he was arrested and tortured. He escaped when the People's Court was destroyed by bombs in 1945. After the war he wrote a book published in English as *The Secret War Against Hitler* (London, 1966).
2. Memel, a Baltic seaport with a German-speaking hinterland, had been transferred from Germany to Lithuania by the Treaty of Versailles. In 1938, on the analogy of the Sudetenland, Hitler demanded its return by Lithuania, which ceded it in March 1939.
3. See Henry O. Malone, 'Between England and Germany: Adam von Trott's contacts with the British', in Francis R. Nicosia (ed.), *Germans against Nazism: Essays in Honor of Peter Hoffmann* (New York, 1990). C.f. also Klemens von Klemperer, *German Resistance against Hitler: The Search for Allies Abroad, 1938–1945* (Oxford, 1992).
4. The post-war independence of Austria was raised with the Soviet Union by the British in 1943. In the event, however, Soviet troops occupied eastern Austria, including Vienna, in 1945 and remained there until 1955, when Russia agreed to withdraw in return for Austrian demilitarisation and neutrality.
5. *Die Weisse Rose* was the name of the predominantly Catholic anti-Nazi group founded by a brother and sister, Hans and Sophie Scholl, at Munich University. From 1939 until 1943 they distributed newsletters and leaflets detailing Nazi crimes, including the mass killing of Jews. They also called for a return to democracy, social justice and a federal state in Germany. In February 1943 the Scholls and some of their associates were arrested, tried and executed.
6. Hans Robinsohn (1897–1981). From a Jewish merchant family in Hamburg, joined the liberal German Democratic Party in 1918, where he met Ernst Strassmann. Both were ardent supporters of the republic and in 1934 co-founded a resistance group, with links throughout Germany. In 1938 Robinsohn was forced to flee to Denmark, from where he made contact with Britain on behalf of the resisters. In 1958 he returned

to Germany and worked with Willy Brandt. Later headed the Centre for Research into National Socialism.

7. Ernst Strassmann (1897–1958). A jurist who, despite his anti-Nazi activities (see above), served as a district judge in Berlin until 1939. In that year he travelled to London with Robinsohn to seek financial support for the resistance movement. In 1942 he was arrested on his way to Sweden for negotiations with British representatives. He remained in prison without trial until the end of the war, when he joined the SPD and worked in the economic and labour fields.

Chapter 7: Julius Leber and the German resistance to Hitler

1. With the abolition of all political parties by the Nazis in 1933, Leber's strong anti-Nazism made him a marked man. He was imprisoned, latterly in Sachsenhausen concentration camp, from 1934 to 1937.

2. Gustav Dahrendorf (1901–1954). Elected to the Reichstag in 1932 as an SPD deputy, he was twice imprisoned in 1933. Later took part in the planned coup with Beck and Goerdeler. Arrested and imprisoned in 1944, liberated by Soviet troops in 1945. In East Germany he opposed the forcible merger of the communist and social-democratic parties into the Socialist Unity Party (SED), and fled to the west. Father of Ralf Dahrendorf (q.v.).

3. Ernst von Harnack (1888–1945). Staunch social democrat and anti-Nazi. Member of the Federation of Religious Socialists, he had family connections with the resisters Hans von Dohnanyi and the Bonhoeffer brothers. Though not involved in the July Bomb Plot, he was arrested and tried in 1944, and executed in 1945.

4. Ludwig Schwamb (1890–1945). Social-democrat lawyer and associate of Mierendorff and Leuschner, he was arrested, tried and executed after the July Plot.

5. After studying history and economics Leber volunteered for the army in 1914, became an officer and remained in the service until 1920, when he took part in suppressing the Kapp Putsch (see below).

6. Alsace and Lorraine are territories lying west of the Rhine between France and Germany, which had long been a bone of contention between the two nations. Originally part of the Holy Roman Empire, Lorraine and German-speaking Alsace were annexed by Louis XIV in 1648. Alsace and part of Lorraine were ceded to Germany in 1871, at the end of the Franco-Prussian War, but returned to France in 1918. Alsace-Lorraine was again German from 1940 to 1945, but has been part of France since that time.

7. In March 1920 a *Freikorps* brigade marched into Berlin to protest against the Treaty of Versailles. The paramilitary rebels proclaimed Wolfgang Kapp, a rightwing politician and Prussian official, Chancellor and declared the fledgling Weimar republic at an end. However, the workers mounted a general strike against the coup and it collapsed after five days.

8. In 1812 Prussia, still allied with Napoleon, contributed 180,000 men to the *Grand Armée* that invaded Russia. However, Stein, acting independently, persuaded the Prussian commander, von Yorck, to go over to the Russian side in December 1812. The Prussian king only reluctantly accepted this; and men like Scharnhorst and Gneisenau on their own initiative raised a new Prussian army of over 330,000 which helped to defeat Napoleon at Leipzig in October 1813. Thus the 'uprising' was masterminded by an elite who exploited a growing popular sense of German national identity. See James J. Sheehan, *German History, 1770–1866* (Oxford, 1989).

9. Hans Bernd Gisevius (1904–74). German Vice-Consul in Zürich during the war. An anti-Nazi lawyer, he compiled dossiers on the wrongdoings of the Gestapo, and survived by moving from post to post. His Zürich posting was as a member of the *Abwehr*, counter-intelligence. There he made contact with both the British and American intelligence services. After the July Plot, he was helped by Dulles to escape from Berlin back to Switzerland.

10. The SPD leadership had gone into exile in Prague, but when Germany invaded Czechoslovakia in 1939, the group moved to London. With the outbreak of war they were interned for some time.

11. Leber had been arrested by the Gestapo on 5 July, i.e. two weeks before the coup. Stauffenberg was anxious to mount the coup quickly enough to save Leber from execution.

Chapter 8: Wilhelm Leuschner and the resistance movement of 20 July 1944

1. Wilhelm Leuschner was one of the most influential social-democrat politicians and labour leaders of the Weimar period. As well as being an executive of the General German Federation of Labour Unions (ADGB) he held the post of Minister of the Interior for the state of Hessen (1928–1933). He was arrested in August 1944, sentenced to death by the People's Court and executed.

2. In November 1931, a disaffected Nazi party deputy in the provincial parliament of Hessen handed over to the police a record of a meeting of local Nazi leaders, which clearly revealed plans to abolish state and local government institutions, introduce the death-penalty for resistance to any party decrees and generally suspend the rule of law. This was seen by many as high treason, yet the pro-Nazi attorney-general in the Weimar government, Karl Werner, chose to exonerate the Nazis on a technicality.

3. The *Reichsbanner* was founded in 1924 and became the largest organization aimed at defending the Weimar republic and constitution against all undemocratic forces, including the Nazis. Its membership reached 3 million in the late 1920s, mainly social democrats and labour unionists.

Though not armed, units were formed to provide physical protection for public meetings. In 1932 when Chancellor von Papen effectively ended Prussia's autonomy, the Reichsbanner staged protests. Though dissolved by the Nazis in 1933, a small illegal core continued to operate, distributing anti-Nazi leaflets. Many of its members were imprisoned.

4. From 1930, the failure of German democracy to stem the tide of political violence led to the introduction of rule by presidential decree.

5. Gregor Strasser (1892–1934). Head of the Nazi Party organization and leader of its left wing until December 1932. Schleicher tried to woo the Nazis but was rejected by Hitler, though for a time Strasser showed interest in joining the government.

6. This suggestion had come from Aufhäuser, a leading leftwing unionist who, unlike Leuschner, refused to make any accommodation with Nazism.

7. *Treuhänder der Arbeit*, regional officials within the Ministry of Economics, whose task was to monitor wage agreements, thus bypassing the DAF.

8. Leuschner's predecessor as head of the ADGB, arrested for being an SPD member.

9. Fraenkel was an author (*The Dual State*, 1938) and labour lawyer working for the Free Labour Unions. He stayed in the USA and after the war taught law at Columbia University.

10. Max Habermann (1885–1944). Until 1933 leader of the rightwing, white-collar union of commercial employees (DHV). Made contact with Leuschner in 1935 and helped plan the unitary labour union. Associated with the July Plot, he was arrested by the Gestapo and committed suicide while in prison.

11. Baron Kurt von Hammerstein-Equord (1878–1943). Commander-in-chief of the Germany army 1930–34, he had expressed doubts as to Hitler's suitability as Chancellor and was removed from his post. In retirement he maintained contact with Goerdeler, Beck and the others plotting to oust Hitler in 1938. He also had some involvement in the July 1944 plot but died before it was carried out.

12. This refers to Chancellor von Schleicher's attempt to win the support of the labour unions for his government in December 1932.

13. Leuschner wanted all contacts with the SPD to go through him. He was unhappy about Goerdeler dealing with them directly.

14. These were the so-called 'yellow' unions, workplace-based and financed by the employers, as a means of combating industry-wide wage-bargaining.

15. Christian Solidarism was a Catholic movement of the 1920s. It supported Rome's desire to dissolve the Catholic Centre Party in Germany, and wanted to use direct, non-parliamentary methods to obtain social and industrial peace.

16. Schärf was the Austrian SPD leader, who in 1943 held out for post-war independence for Austria. He became President of Austria in the 1950s.

17. Adam Stegerwald (1874–1945). A Centre Party politician and Minister

of Labour in the Weimar republic. In his speech to the Congress of Christian Trade Unions in Essen in 1920, he proposed a broad Christian-socialist movement that would largely replace existing party alignments.

Chapter 9: Carlo Mierendorff's 'Socialist Action' programme

1. Carlo Mierendorff (1897–1943). After voluntary army service in the First World War, studied philosophy and economics, graduating from Heidelberg in 1923. He had joined the SPD in 1920 and in 1929 became press officer and a close associate of Wilhelm Leuschner in the government of Hessen. Elected to the Reichstag in 1930. After his protests over the 'Boxheim Documents' affair, he was on the Nazis' 'wanted' list. Despite warnings from friends he returned from Switzerland in 1933 and was arrested, tortured and held in concentration camps until 1938. On his release he joined forces with Theodor Haubach and, through him, came to the Kreisau Circle, where he contrived to bridge the gap between Catholics and socialists. He was killed in an Allied air raid on Leipzig in 1943.
2. An SPD politician and adviser to Mierendorff.
3. A rightwing liberal party of the Bismarck era. Supported by big business, it strongly advocated Germany's industrial and geographic expansion. Under Weimar it became the *Deutsche Volkspartei* (DVP).
4. After the first secret meeting, a second was planned, but all concerned were arrested before it could take place. In contrast to the version usually related, that the second meeting with the communists had been betrayed by an informer, Theodor Steltzer has told the author he is convinced that it was a tapped telephone conversation that exposed them.

Chapter 10: Adolf Reichwein's road to resistance and the Kreisau Circle

1. Adolf Reichwein (1898–1944). Teacher and educational theorist. In 1930 he was appointed professor of history and citizenship at the newly opened Pedagogical Academy in Halle. He was dismissed from the post on political grounds soon after the Nazis came to power. As a member of the resistance group around Leuschner and Leber, he initiated contact with the outlawed communist party, leading to his arrest early in July 1944. He was tried and executed in October of that year.
2. The *Reichnährstand* was a Nazi farmers' organization founded by Walther Darré, the minister of agriculture.
3. A movement comparable to William Morris's Socialist League in Britain.
4. The *Arbeitschule* was intended as an institution in which industrial skills were taught in conjunction with general education, in order to ease the transition from school to job.
5. Ironically, Moltke was arrested because the Gestapo had a 'mole' in the

Solf Circle in Berlin; Moltke had been in contact with that group. He remained in prison and after the July Plot was exposed, was tried for treason and hanged in January 1945.

6. As explained in Chapter 7, Stauffenberg hoped to stage the coup quickly enough to have Leber released before his trial and inevitable execution.

Chapter 11: The position of the military opposition to Hitler in the German resistance movement

1. In the German invasion of Russia in 1941, Army Group Centre was the force that advanced through Byelorussia with the objective of capturing Moscow.

2. Kurt von Schleicher was both an army general and Chancellor (December 1932–January 1933).

3. The 'Commissar Decree' stated that all communist political commissars, who were present in every unit of the Red Army, should be liquidated.

4. *Feldmarschall* Günther von Kluge (1882–1944). Replaced von Bock as commander-in-chief of Army Group Centre in December 1941. In July 1944 he replaced Rommel as commander in France, but was quickly relieved of his post by Hitler, for failing to uncover the July Bomb Plot. Though he had refused to join the plotters, he had promised help after Hitler's removal. When ordered back to Germany, he committed suicide.

5. Otto Braun (1872–1955). Prime Minister of Prussia in the Weimar republic, who pursued a notably independent line until forcibly removed from office by Chancellor Papen in 1932.

6. Erich von Manstein (1887–1973). One of Hitler's most brilliant army commanders. In 1940 he masterminded the invasion of France. In the Russian campaign he commanded the 11th Army on the southern flank and then the Army Group Don. He was promoted to field marshal in July 1942. However, he had frequent strategic disagreements with Hitler and was relieved of his command in March 1944. Having some Jewish blood (his real name was Lewinski), Manstein may have felt insecure and therefore anxious not to show any sympathy towards the Jews.

7. The *Einsatzgruppen* ('action squads') were irregular units commanded by SS officers, which assiduously performed the task of murdering hundreds of thousands of Jews, Soviet officials and other Russians behind the lines and sometimes with the active assistance of the regular Wehrmacht.

8. Arthur Nebe (1894–1945). An enigmatic figure, he secretly joined the Nazi Party before 1933. However, as head of the Criminal Police he refused to have Hitler's rival, Gregor Strasser, liquidated, and later leaked information about the Gestapo to the resistance, through Gisevius (q.v.). On the other hand, as a senior SS officer he commanded an *Einsatzgruppe* in Russia in 1941, was seen as a possible successor to Heydrich in 1942 and, in 1944, was sufficiently trusted by Himmler to be put in charge of

investigating the July Bomb Plot. In the end his links to the resistance were uncovered and he was himself executed.

9. This was the message of a series of events in January–February 1998 put on by the press office of the City of Frankfurt for the opening of the Resistance Exhibition mounted by the Office of Research into Military History.

Chapter 12: Anti-Hitler resistance and the Nazi persecution of the Jews

1. The group organized by Herbert and Marianne Baum brought together young Jewish communists and, in 1938 when the Jewish Youth Movement was banned, other young Jews. Its anti-Nazi leafleting led to the arrest and imprisonment or death of several hundred members, including the Baums, in 1942.

2. The general party programme of the conservatives, named after the Berlin meeting-hall where it was launched.

3. These treaties permitted the inhabitants of former Prussian territories ceded to Poland to opt either for Polish or German citizenship. Due to the level of anti-Semitism in Catholic Poland, many Jews opted for Germany.

4. In 1917 the German Ministry of War arranged a census of Jews in the armed forces.

5. The *Räterepublik* was set up in Munich amid riots and demonstrations led by Kurt Eisner, a charismatic intellectual of independent views, who declared himself opposed both to Bolshevism and to violence. Bavaria's Wittlesbach monarchy was deposed and a cabinet formed with Eisner as premier. In elections in January 1919, Eisner was defeated. He was about to resign when he was murdered by a rightwing aristocrat on 12 February, only to be replaced by a Bolshevist faction which survived until April 1919.

6. Rabbi Leo Baeck, Chairman of the Jewish Council in Germany.

7. Walther Rathenau (1867–1922). Appointed Germany's Foreign Minister in January 1922. Because he was Jewish and an internationalist, he immediately became a target of the extreme right. While being driven to work on 23 June 1922, he was shot by three members of 'Organization Consul', a nationalist group dedicated to killing senior Weimar politicians.

8. Theophil Wurm (1868–1953). A politician (representing the *Bürgerpartei* in the Württemberg state parliament until 1920) then an evangelical cleric, he was appointed to a bishopric in 1933. In 1934 he left the Nazi-backed 'German Christians' and joined the Confessing Church. Because of his anti-Nazi protests he was banned in 1944 from public speaking and writing. At the end of the war he was elected chairman of the Evangelical Church Council.

9. The now notorious conference of senior civil service, Nazi Party and SS

personnel, held in a lakeside villa outside Berlin on 20 January 1942. Chaired by Reinhard Heydrich, the meeting discussed in coded language the arrangements for the 'Final Solution' – the mass deportation and extermination of Europe's Jewish population.

10. There were 7,200 Jews in Denmark, who until 1943 had been left alone by the occupying Germans for diplomatic reasons. When the deportations were announced, all but 500 Jews were spirited away to neutral Sweden in Danish fishing boats.

11. Heinrich Himmler (1900–1945). From 1929 the *Reichsführer* ('national leader') and principal architect of the SS and later head of the entire police and Gestapo. The SS had the task of building and running the concentration camps and death camps.

12. A non-political reporter of the Holocaust.

13. Baron Axel von dem Busche was an army officer who twice attempted, in 1943 and 1944, to kill Hitler with suicide bombs. He survived the war and died in 1992.

14. 'U-7' was the codename for an operation mounted by Hans Oster within the *Abwehr* to smuggle Jews to safety in Switzerland. However, it was discovered and stopped at an early stage.

Bibliography

Balfour, Michael, *Withstanding Hitler in Germany, 1933–45* (London and New York: Routledge, 1988)

Balfour, Michael, and Julian Frisby, *Helmuth James von Moltke: A Leader against Hitler* (London, 1972)

Benz, Wolfgang, and Walter H. Pehle (eds), *Lexikon des Deutschen Widerstandes* (Frankfurt am Main: S. Fischer, 1994)

Bethge, Eberhard, *Dietrich Bonhoeffer: Theologian, Christian, Contemporary* (London: Collins, 1970)

Bull, Hedley (ed.), *The Challenge of the Third Reich* (Oxford: Clarendon Press, 1986)

Deutsch, Harold C., *The Conspiracy against Hitler in the Twilight War* (Minneapolis: University of Minneapolis Press, 1968)

Fest, Joachim, *Plotting Hitler's Death: The Story of the German Resistance* (New York: Henry Holt, 1996)

Geyer, Michael, and John W. Boyer (eds), *Resistance against the Third Reich, 1933–1990* (Chicago and London: University of Chicago Press, 1994)

Gisevius, Hans-Bernd, *Bis zum bitteren Ende: Vom 30 Juni 1934 zum 20 Juli 1944* (West Berlin: Ullstein, 1964)

Graml, Hermann, et al, *The German Resistance to Hitler* (London: Batsford, 1970)

Hamerow, Theodore S., *On the Road to the Wolf's Lair: German Resistance to Hitler* (Cambridge Mass. & London: Harvard University Press, 1997)

von Hassell, Ulrich, *The von Hassell Diaries, 1938–1944* (London: Hamish Hamilton, 1948)

Hoffmann, Peter, *The History of the German Resistance, 1933–1945*, 3rd. edition (Montreal & Kingston, London, Buffalo: McGill-Queen's University Press, 1996)

Hoffmann, Peter, *Stauffenberg: A Family History, 1905–1944* (Cambridge: Cambridge University Press 1995)

Holmes, Blair R., and Alan F. Keele (eds), *When Truth was Treason: German Youth against Hitler: The Story of the Helmuth Hübener Group* (Urbana and Chicago: University of Illinois Press, 1995)

Jacobsen, Hans-Adolf (ed.), *Opposition gegen Hitler und der Staatsstreich vom 20 Juli 1944 in der SD-Berichterstattung*, 2 vols (Stuttgart: Mundus Verlag, 1989)

von Klemperer, Klemens, *German Resistance to Hitler: The Search for Allies Abroad, 1938–1945* (Oxford: Clarendon Press, 1992)

Merson, Alan, *Communist Resistance in Nazi Germany* (London: Lawrence and Wishart, 1985)

Müller, Klaus-Jürgen, *General Ludwig Beck: Studien und Dokumente zur politisch-militärischen Vorstellungswelt und Tätigkeit des Generalstabschefs des deutschen Heeres, 1933–1938* (Boppard am Rhein: Harald Boldt Verlag, 1980)

Nicosia, Francis R., and Lawrence D. Stokes, *Germans Against Nazism: Nonconformity, Opposition and Resistance in the Third Reich. Essays in Honour of Peter Hoffmann* (New York, Oxford: Berg, 1990)

von Oppen, Beate (ed.), *Helmuth James von Moltke: Briefe an Freya, 1939– 1945* (Munich: Deutsche Taschenbuch Verlag, 1995)

Ritter, Gerhard, *The German Resistance: Carl Goerdeler's Struggle against Tyranny* (New York: 1958)

van Roon, Gerd, *Neuordnung im Widerstand: Der Kreisauer Kreis innerhalb der deutschen Widerstandsbewegung* (Munich: 1967)

Rothfels, Hans, *The German Opposition to Hitler. An Appraisal* (Chicago: Regnery, 1962)

Schmädecke, Jürgen, and Peter Steinbach (eds), *Der Widerstand gegen den Nationalsozialismus: Die deutsche Gesellschaft und der Widerstand gegen Hitler* (Munich: R. Piper Verlag, 1985)

Siefken, Hinrich (ed.), *Die Weisse Rose: Student Resistance to National Socialism, 1942/1943: Forschungsergebnisse und Erfahrungsberichte* – A Nottingham Symposium (Nottingham: University of Nottingham, 1991)

Schöllgen, Gregor, *A Conservative against Hitler: Ulrich von Hassell: Diplomat in Imperial Germany, the Weimar Republic and the Third Reich, 1881– 1944* (Basingstoke: Macmillan, 1991)

Sykes, Christopher, *Troubled Loyalty: A Biography of Adam von Trott* (London: Collins, 1968)

Steinbach, Peter, and Johannes Tuchel (eds), *Widerstand in Deutschland, 1933– 1945: Ein historisches Lesebuch* (Munich: Verlag C.H. Beck, 1994)

Index